SCREAM LOUDER

Through Hell And Healing
With An Incest Survivor And Her Therapist

Marsha Utain, M.S.
and
Barbara Oliver

Foreword by John Bradshaw

Health Communications, Inc.
Deerfield Beach, Florida

Marsha Utain, M.S.
Barbara Oliver
Chino, California 91710

Library of Congress Cataloging-in-Publication Data

Oliver, Barbara.
   Scream Louder / Barbara Oliver and Marsha Utain.
       p.   cm.
   ISBN 1-55874-019-8
    1. Adult child sexual abuse victims.   2. Incest victims.
3. Psychotherapy.   I. Utain, Marsha.   II. Title.
RC569.5.A28043   1989   89-1895
616.85'83—dc19   CIP

Published by: Health Communications, Inc.
               3201 S.W. 15th Street
               Deerfield Beach, Florida 33442

Cover design by Reta Thomas

Dedication

From Barbara

To John Oliver, beloved husband and friend, who freely gave of his love and encouragement during the writing of this book, as well as through the long healing process, for caring, for understanding, and most of all, for believing in me.

From Marsha

To Arthur, my wonderful husband and best friend whose continual love, encouragement and brilliant insights have supported me throughout our marriage and especially this project.

Contents

Acknowledgments

The authors acknowledge the support of many people during the writing of this book.

To John Bradshaw, our friend, our support, our greatest cheerleader, with deep appreciation for his brilliance and the healing place he creates for those around him.

To Candice Fuhrman, our agent, for believing in us and our work.

To Brad Leathers for unselfishly sharing his process with our radio audience and for supporting our efforts in this book.

To Marie Stilkind for her wonderful editorial support.

To our friends: Lolita Domingue for her clever graphics, for "getting" what we were communicating and translating that into pictures, for her friendship, her humor and her loving support. Patrick Philbin for his "friend" and his friendship. Pat Lauer for her support in the early stages that got us off to a wonderful start.

Lisa Ortiz for her belief in and encouragement of this project. And Monday Night Class for a continual healing process.

From Barbara

To Arthur Melville in grateful acknowledgment of his invaluable support, for patiently reading many pieces of the material in rough form, for honest and useful feedback, for support as I worked my way through the maze of wanting to look good, and for encouraging me to stay focused on what I wanted to achieve.

To Jason and Andrea for encouragement, love and allowing me to make mistakes and to grow as a mother and a person.

To "Shawn" and to "Carol," my brother and sister, for being there when I needed you, and for your love.

To Marsha, with profound gratitude for your faith in me, for unwavering support of my process and for teaching me the tools that supported the release of a victim and the birth of who I am.

From Marsha

To Barbara for her incredible courage and persistence in the healing process, her wonderful ability to tell her story with honesty and vivid detail and her delightful company that made this book a joyful project.

To Dr. Carol Hunter for her continuing faith in me which began during my days as a graduate student.

Foreword

By John Bradshaw

Scream Louder is a pioneering work in what Riane Eisler has termed "partnership mind."

Barbara Oliver and Marsha Utain have joined together and allowed us to share in their joint venture of spiritual healing. They have gone beyond the simple breaking of the "no talk" rule that surrounds incest. They have allowed us to enter the heart and soul of Barbara's secret. With courage and insight they offer us the privilege of witnessing and understanding the "original pain" work that is essential for the healing of sexual violation.

The original pain work is gripping. I was into my own residual grief from the first chapter on. I know of no place where a better view of the healing power of legitimate suffering has been offered. We can almost re-experience the pain surrounding Barbara's abuse. Marsha Utain's clarifying analysis offers all victims of violation a cognitive life raft, i.e., a way to grasp that the original pain work, although difficult, leads to a fresh new life.

This book offers hope for all incest survivors. As far as I'm concerned, it is a must for anyone carrying the wounds of sexual abuse. It is also relevant for anyone who suffered any form of violation as a child. I recommend it to any adult child from a dysfunctional family.

Finally, I have the privilege of having a growing friendship with Barbara and Marsha. Barbara has a sensitivity and courage that is a part of her real life personality. Marsha is one of the most intuitively skilled therapists I know. Her deep commitment to the integrity of her client is inspiring. I congratulate you for buying this book. It is really a gift of love.

Introduction

Marsha

When Barbara approached me several years after she had completed her therapy with me, she said she wanted to use her story to demonstrate that the healing process works in therapy. She asked me if I would be willing to write the clinical material. I saw an opportunity to participate in a book that was not only a story of incest, alcoholism and a dysfunctional family, but would give an illustration of the actual process of recovery from trauma. I also saw an opportunity to demonstrate viable process tools for both survivors and therapists alike.

Another important reason for writing this book is to answer the question: Does incest ever happen in a functional family? My own clinical experience tells me that incest does not occur in functional families. Since I agree with John Bradshaw's figures that 96% of all families are to some degree dysfunctional, it would not be out of line to say that dysfunction has shown up earlier in the incest family before the actual perpetration of the sexual abuse. Such was the case with Barbara's family.

Being a survivor of physical abuse myself, I know from experience that there are certain tools Adult Survivors must have in order for continuing recovery to occur with or without formal therapy. This book was written to demystify recovery by presenting specific examples of processing to demonstrate how these tools are used for healing. This book is for those of you who have suffered through a horrifying shame-filled childhood as a Child of Incest or Alcoholism or any Dysfunctional Family. It is to let you know that there is a way through the pain and devastation of the past.

In recent years therapists have begun to acknowledge the tendency of Adult Survivors to somatize their pain and turn it into physical symptoms. Because I have found that, in actuality, everyone who has emotional incompletions will somatize those emotions to some degree, I wanted an opportunity to show how this works and how to use process work for a better understanding of the storage of trauma. The book demonstrates how Barbara was able to learn to use her physical symptoms and illnesses to find out more about herself, to reduce her stress and to promote her healing process.

Anne Wilson Schaef said in an interview on our radio show, *Mental Health Magazine,* that nobody ever healed from understanding alone and that while people needed to be working a 12-Step program in order to confront their addictive processes, the program "really doesn't have a place in it to work deep intense feelings." She is accurate. Deep emotional work beyond the 12-Step program is also necessary.

This book was designed to show you how to approach your healing at a deeper level. It not only gives you the opportunity to confront your dysfunctional family background, it provides a look at various types of deep process work and the way insights are gained as a result of the process work. Through Barbara's growth, you will see how a person can reorganize her entire contextual frame of reference and learn how to love and accept herself.

Barbara

The story of my childhood is not unlike many others. I was the child victim of incest perpetrated by an alcoholic stepparent. Perhaps you have read other books on the trauma of incest and books that have given you insight into the private hell of being raised in an alcoholic home. What makes my story different from some of the others, is that it does not end with the telling.

Ten years ago I embarked on a therapeutic recovery process under Marsha's guidance. With her support I began an intense two-and-a-half-year journey into the painful memories of my childhood. Week after week we confronted not only the secret of incest, but also family dysfunction, parental alcoholism and my need to try to be in control of every aspect of my life. Most important we disentombed all the feelings I had virtually buried along the way. Screams I had never screamed were finally released, and with them childhood sadness, anger, pain and terror, feelings that had plagued all of my adult life.

Marsha gave me tools that served me not only during therapeutic sessions, but also as a part of my ongoing everyday recovery process. I have traveled far beyond the early needs to reach out through the darkness of my denial and secrets to shed light on my deepest fears and pain, light years past the mere understanding of the problem which many of us seek in the beginning.

Marsha taught me that "secrets breed sickness," and John Bradshaw has said that "a family is as sick as their secrets." From personal experience I concur with their conclusions. Telling our secrets is crucial to our recovery. If you have disclosed your secrets, you are already on your way. This book will give you steps to continue your process. While talking about the past is an important beginning, true recovery requires more work.

I recognize that each of the other people mentioned in this book may have recollections and memories that differ from mine, since each of us views the events in our lives from a unique perspective — our own. I leave their interpretations, their process and their recovery to them. I have changed names, geographic locations and other minor details that did not detract from the point of each story because it is not my purpose to cause anyone else undue public scrutiny. This is my story, after all, not theirs. My stepfather has given his blessing to this book, telling me that it is a "story that needs to be told." I acknowledge the courage it took for him to do that. My brother and his family have also given their support. As this book went to press, Mother was angry, confused and terrified at my willingness to "go public," and has voiced her preference for keeping the secret within the family.

When my healing work first began, I thought that recovery meant personal acceptance of the belief that childhood problems were the result of inherent defectiveness. If I could just accept that, I thought, I would be fine. Little did I know that I would not only shed that shaming belief, but ultimately uncover who I am: whole, healthy, loving, nurturing and powerful.

PART I

Barbara,
Life And Therapy

1

First Scars

The front door opened. The boards of the hardwood floor creaked and groaned under heavy footsteps. Daddy was home. Sitting on the floor in my room, I stopped playing and tilted my head to one side, listening. He was talking to Rose, my baby-sitter, telling her that Mother wouldn't be home for about an hour and that it was okay for her to go home. Rose said that there was a meatloaf in the oven, and that my older brother, Shawn, would be eating dinner and spending the night with a friend. A few moments later the front door opened and closed again as she left.

I heard him walk down the hall towards my room. My body tightened. In the few seconds it took for him to reach my door my mind raced quickly over the day. I tried to remember if there was anything I had done to make him mad. Had I forgotten anything? Were there any toys left in the living room? Was my scooter put away in the garage? I couldn't think of anything, but that didn't mean I was safe. I never seemed to know everything that could make Daddy mad.

His footsteps stopped outside my room. I took a deep breath and held it. The doorknob started turning. I froze. Would he be mean or nice? The door began to open. I looked up to see what I was in for. "What are you doing, Kitten?" he asked with a smile.

I relaxed and started breathing again. Everything seemed to be okay.

"Nothin', Daddy," I answered, "just playing paper dolls."

"Well, it's time to clean up your toys," he said. "I'm going to take my shower and then we'll have our dinner." His head disappeared but before he closed the door I heard him say, "Take off those clothes and put on something warmer. Don't you know how chilly it is outside?"

It was the middle of autumn, 1953, and I was six years old. An unseasonably warm day had turned sharply cold in late afternoon when rain clouds that had threatened on the horizon all afternoon finally moved into our little valley. I was still dressed in the pink shorts and white peasant blouse I had changed into after school.

I should have stopped playing and put on warmer clothes right then, but I didn't. I wanted to finish cutting out one last dress. Besides, I knew that I had a little more time.

Daddy had a nightly ritual. He always showered and shaved when he came home, and then put on a clean, starched and freshly ironed white shirt and black slacks. He said that being clean was important. He must have been really serious about that because sometimes he showered two or three times a day, each time changing into clean clothes.

When I heard the sound of the shower a few minutes later, I realized I didn't have much more time. "Better get moving, Barbara," I said out loud. I stood up and started to clean up the mess and put my things away.

As I put paper dolls into the toy box, I discovered that my favorite doll was not in her usual place. I looked in the toy chest, under the bed, and in the closet. She wasn't in my room. I remembered with dismay that I had taken her to Kathy Elliot's house that afternoon.

"Oh, no! I forgot to bring her home!" I said to myself. Daddy became enraged whenever I accidentally left my toys at someone else's house.

"If you don't care enough about your toys to keep track of them," he would say, "you don't deserve to have them." Then he would take the toy away and hit me.

Without stopping to think about what I was doing, I ran out of the house and over to Kathy's house.

I knocked on the door. Mrs. Elliot answered.

Before she could say anything I blurted out, "I left my doll here this afternoon, Mrs. Elliot, and I have to find it before Daddy finds out!"

"Calm down, Barbara, it's all right," she said. "Come on in. Kathy's in her room."

I ran down the hall to Kathy's room. She was sitting on the bed reading a book.

"Kathy, I left my doll here, I have to find her right away and go back home before Daddy finishes his shower!"

Kathy knew how mean my father could be. She had once watched him rip up every single one of my paper dolls when she came over to return one I had forgotten at her house. She stood up right away and helped me look.

"Are you sure?" she asked. "I don't remember seeing her here after you left."

"I must have," I cried, "she's not anywhere in my room."

We searched for several minutes without luck. My doll didn't seem to be anywhere. I was almost in tears and about to give up when I looked under the bed. She had been there all along! I pulled her out, hugged her to my chest and heaved a sigh of relief.

Knowing I didn't have much time, I told Kathy I'd see her the next day and left. As I came up the walk, I saw Daddy staring at me through the living room window. His arms were crossed, his eyes and mouth set in a frown. I stopped dead in my tracks. I knew with dreadful certainty that I was in trouble. I wanted to turn and run. But it was no use. He was bigger and faster than me. There was no escape.

I walked slowly up to the front door and reached for the knob. Before I could push the door all the way open, he was at the other side yanking it with such force that I was thrown off balance. I stumbled into the room, cried out, tripped over the rug and fell down. I looked up to see him looming above me. He slammed the door so hard that the windows rattled and a picture fell off the wall. He barely missed my legs.

"Where have you been?" his voice boomed out at me.

Still reeling from the fall and paralyzed by the intensity of his anger, I couldn't speak.

"I asked you, where have you been?" he shouted again, seething with rage. "Answer me this instant!"

"I - I - I just went to Kathy's house," I stammered, "to - uh - to get my doll. I'm sorry, Daddy, I left her there by accident . . ."

Before I could finish trying to explain and apologize, he grabbed the doll out of my hands. Holding her by one leg he smashed her against the wall and her head exploded into a thousand pieces. Wide-eyed with shock I watched the pieces fall to the floor. I couldn't even cry.

"Not only are you careless, you are disobedient," he hissed. Pointing at me he shouted, "I told you to change your clothes!"

I looked down and my heart sank as I realized that he was right. In my rush to get the doll I had forgotten to carry out his orders. I took a deep breath and forced myself not to cry. He hated it when I cried.

"I - I - forgot, Daddy, please don't be mad! I won't do it again, I promise!"

But it was too late for apologies, and besides, he wasn't listening anyway. Horrified, I watched him slowly unbuckle his belt and remove it from the pant loops.

"I'll teach you to disobey me," he yelled.

I lay shivering as I watched him slowly coil the buckle end of the belt around his hand.

"Stand up and take off your clothes!" he shouted. "If you won't wear what I tell you, then you won't wear anything!"

I started to cry.

"Stop sniveling and do as I say," he bellowed.

"Okay, Daddy, okay!" I cried. I took off the blouse. He grabbed it from my hands and with one mighty tug, ripped it in two. I took off my shorts and he threw them across the room then pointed at my underpants. I took them off and dropped them on the floor. I stood naked and shivering in front of him.

"Go stand over the heater and put your hands on the wall!" he ordered, pointing to the wall by the floor furnace vent. I could barely move.

"Now!" he shouted.

I ran to the wall, faced it, straddled the floor vent with my legs, and put my hands on the wall. Filled with dread, I couldn't stop shaking.

I heard the belt whistle through the air just before it hit my buttocks. I screamed as the first blow connected, and then reached back to protect myself. The next swing of the belt hit squarely on the palm of my hand.

"Ow!" I wailed.

"Put your hands back on the wall!" he bellowed.

I did as I was told.

He hit me again. And again. I screamed and sobbed, begging him to stop. He didn't stop until I was covered from waist to ankles with stinging red welts. Finally I heard him collapse in the chair behind him.

Even though my whole body convulsed with uncontrolled sobs, I kept my hands on the wall. I could hear him behind me but fear kept me from turning around to look. He was breathing heavily. I didn't dare move, knowing that he might start hitting me again if I did. After several minutes, when his breathing returned to normal and my sobs had subsided into pitiful shuddering whimpers, I heard his voice behind me.

"Did you learn your lesson, young lady?"

"Yes, Daddy," I mumbled.

"Next time do as you're told and I won't have to punish you," he said. "Now go to bed."

I turned without looking at him, and walked out of the room and down the hall into my bedroom. The back of my knees hurt so much that I could barely bend my legs. Without even stopping to put on my pajamas I climbed into bed. Stuffing my face into the pillow, I sobbed myself into a fitful sleep.

I awoke with a start from a nightmare some time during the night. In my dream Daddy had been looming over my bed about to hit me again. I imagined that lurking somewhere in the darkness of my room, he was watching me, waiting for me to do something wrong. I curled up in a little ball in the far corner of my bed and lay awake the rest of the night.

In the morning my legs were stiff and sore and I could barely stand the feel of my bathrobe against my skin. I winced with each step. When I walked into the dining room, Mother was already sitting at the table. I watched her out of the corner of my eye for some sign that would tell me if she knew what had happened. She acted as if nothing was wrong! Pouring milk over the cereal already in my bowl, and in a voice that sounded almost cheerful, I heard her say, "Hurry up and eat your breakfast, it's almost time for school."

"Maybe she doesn't know!" I thought. "But can't she tell how much I hurt? Maybe she's mad at me for disobeying Daddy!" I decided that it was better not to say anything.

No one ever mentioned what had happened to me. No one asked me how I felt. I would have thought that maybe it was all a nightmare, except that I had these welts on my legs. It wasn't the first time he had hit me and it wouldn't be the last. No matter how hard I tried to figure out what would make him mad, there was always something I messed up. What I didn't know was that Mother had noticed and was getting upset.

One day, less than a year later, without any warning, she pulled me aside and told me that Daddy was going to be moving away. She had a sad look on her face. I started to cry. She turned away from me and left the room before I could ask her why he was leaving or where he was going to stay.

Part of me thought that he must be leaving because I was really bad. The rest of me was relieved. Even though he stayed in the house for a few more weeks, that night he moved all his clothes to the hall closet and started sleeping on the couch.

On the night before Daddy moved away, I was sitting on the living room floor, reading a book and he was sitting in his chair. "Come sit on my lap, Kitten," he said. He hardly ever asked me to do that, and suddenly I felt special. I stood up and walked over to his chair and he lifted me up and sat me on his knee.

"You know that Daddy loves you, don't you, Kitten?" he asked in a solemn voice.

"Uh-huh," I answered. Daddies were supposed to love their little girls so I guessed that he probably loved me.

He gave me a hug and then, holding my face in his hands, he asked, "You don't want me to leave, do you, Kitten?"

Surprised that he would ask me such a question, I saw that he had tears in his eyes. I had never seen him cry and I didn't know what to do. I started to cry, too.

"Well, Barbara," he insisted, "do you want me to leave?"

"No," I cried, not because I didn't want him to leave, but because I didn't want him to cry. Had I told the truth, I would have said that I wanted him to stop being so mean. I didn't need him to leave, I wanted him to change. I wanted him to stop being mean to me, to Shawn and especially to Mother. I felt so helpless when he hit Mother. But I didn't say anything. If I had, maybe he wouldn't have hurt her again. But I didn't, and he did, that very same night.

Shawn and I were already in bed sound asleep. Daddy was sleeping on the couch and Mother was alone in her bed. As Mother tells the story, she was rudely wakened when Daddy jerked the blankets off the bed, grabbed her and violently lifted her off the bed.

Holding her chest high, he announced, "If I can't sleep in this bed, no one will!"

With that he dropped her onto the hardwood floor. He left the room, leaving her lying in a heap. He never went back to see if she was conscious or even alive.

Most but not all of the mean things stopped after he moved out of the house. There were some exceptions. Many nights I would see Mother crying as she sat and stared out the window to the street. I hated it when she cried because I didn't know how to help her. Daddy would be outside in his parked car watching the house. Night after night — just watching.

One night she was so upset that she called the police for help. They said they could do nothing because he wasn't doing anything illegal. She called our neighbors and they took turns watching the street to make sure he didn't try to come into our house. He didn't stop this strange ritual until after the divorce.

The first year and a half were difficult for me. I didn't know if I was still acceptable to my friends. I didn't like being part of *the divorced family*. None of my friends' parents were divorced and even though no one ever said anything, I was pretty sure they all thought that something was wrong with me. I wondered if they were right. I fretted constantly wondering if there was something I could do to make everything better. Mother was also worried that the neighbors might be talking about us. She warned me to never repeat anything about the family to any of my friends. She said that people wouldn't talk about us if we didn't give them anything to say.

People must have been talking about us anyway, especially the first Christmas after Mother and Daddy divorced. Daddy wasn't giving Mother any money and Mother was trying to support us on her small salary.

"We might be poor," she said, "but it's important that we don't act poor. There will be few gifts under the tree, but don't be sad, because Christmas isn't just about how many presents you receive, it's about who you are with."

We set up our little cardboard Nativity, lit from behind with a small yellow light, one of our important traditions. We hung our favorite ornaments on the tiny tree that we picked out at the neighborhood lot, added tinsel and garlands, doing our best to make the house as festive as possible.

One of Mother's favorite Christmas customs was joining the ladies of our church as they solicited donations of toys and food to give to the less fortunate or needy families in our community. Mother was always active in these collection drives and each year contributed something from our household as well. The ladies would then put together packages and deliver them to the indigent families.

A few days before Christmas, we came home and found, sitting on the floor in our living room, several boxes filled with food, toys and games. Shawn and I both screeched with delight. Pulling everything out of the boxes I found a beautiful doll. I examined her, feeling her silky blond hair, and looking into her blue eyes that closed when I laid her down. She was dressed in a white lace-trimmed blue gingham dress with a white slip and panties underneath. She even had real socks and white shoes that buckled! I had never owned such a beautiful doll.

I looked at Shawn and saw that he had a baseball bat and mitt, which he had told me secretly that he hoped Santa would bring him. In his box there were also games that both of us could play. In the other boxes were bags of sugar and flour, a turkey, bread and even some cookies which were a rare treat.

"Oh, Mother, look," I cried holding up the doll. "Isn't she beautiful?"

The smile froze on my face as I saw that, instead of sharing my joy, Mother looked very angry.

"There's been some mistake," she said through pursed lips, turning and stomping into the hall.

I didn't know what was wrong so I looked at Shawn to see if he knew. The shrug of his shoulders told me that he didn't. I heard Mother pick up the phone and start dialing. She asked about the boxes sitting in our living room. She no sooner hung up the phone when she made another call. I heard her say that a mistake had been made, we were not needy and to have the boxes picked up immediately. Bang! She slammed the phone in its cradle.

Mother stormed around the house for several minutes while Shawn and I watched. She shouted, "Who told them we were one of those families?" I was silent. I didn't know what I had done wrong.

"Everyone at the church must be laughing at us." She stared at us and pleaded, "How will I ever face any of them again? I can just imagine what they are thinking. Don't they think I can take care of my own children? This makes me look terrible." I didn't know what she was talking about, but knew better than to ask.

Suddenly she stopped pacing and turned to look first at Shawn and then at me. I was shivering. Her face changed from angry to sad. Staring at the doll in my arms she took a deep breath, slowly shook her head and said, "Barbara, put the doll back in the box. Those toys don't belong to you. They were supposed to go to a poor family. Someone made a mistake. I'm sorry, we have to give them back."

"But, Mommy, they must have meant them for us. Look, there's even a baseball mitt for Shawn, just like he wanted," I protested.

"Barbara, you don't understand. Now do as I say." She turned to Shawn and said, "You, too, Shawn. Put the mitt and bat back. They don't belong to you."

I gave up. She wasn't going to change her mind. Unable to suppress my tears, I walked to the box and gently laid the beautiful doll on top of the other toys and games.

I knew I shouldn't feel so sad and that I was wrong to be so selfish, but I couldn't help feeling resentful that some little girl from a poor family was going to have a better doll than I'd ever had. Mother was still so upset she didn't even notice that I was crying.

A few hours later there was a knock at the door. It was the man from our church come to pick up the packages. Mother answered the door and, after a few muffled words, let him in. I was sitting on the couch watching television. He smiled at me. I didn't smile back. I was too sad.

"You all ready for Christmas, little one?" he said in a happy voice. "Bet you can hardly wait for all those toys Santa will be bringing you."

"What a stupid man," I thought, wanting to tell him that Santa was just a child's game. No one was going to come to our house and bring us presents. Besides even if they did, Mother would just send the presents back. I wanted to lash out at someone. But I knew that would just make Mother upset with me. I looked up at her and saw the "Don't-say-anything!" look on her face.

Gritting my teeth, I turned back to the television. The man stacked the boxes on top of each other, carried them out to his car and left without saying another word. Mother, Shawn and I never spoke of it again.

We didn't have much money. What we had mostly went for rent and food. We didn't even have a car. I felt so sorry for Mother. Every day she walked a mile and a half each way to work. I felt sorry for myself. New clothes didn't come my way very often. I wore mostly hand-me-downs from cousins, or second hand clothes that Mother bought at church bazaars and rummage sales. Mother said, "Having used clothes is nothing to be ashamed of. As long as you look clean and neat, no one will look down on you." I tried my best not to show that I was envious of friends who had nicer or prettier clothes. I wanted Mother to be proud of me. But deep down inside I hated having clothes that were second-hand.

After she divorced Daddy, Mother struggled to stretch the money she earned from payday to payday. We ate hamburger instead of steaks but we never went hungry, and we always had clothes to wear. Mother wasn't going to let us act poor. I took dance lessons from a woman on our street, and Shawn was active in Cub Scouts. Mother belonged to a women's civic club, was a member of our church choir and did volunteer work for the local civil defense organization. She said that it was important to "give back to the community."

She also started dating other men. One after the other they came and went without much fanfare until she met Jim. I didn't hear the names of most of the other men, but suddenly I was hearing Jim's name often. She seemed to like him a lot. She was smiling more and yelling less. I liked that.

When she was ready for Jim to meet Shawn and me, Mother invited him to have dinner with us. That Saturday morning she woke me early, washed my hair and set it in pincurls, and then she cleaned the house until everything sparkled. She spent the afternoon in the kitchen, cutting up vegetables, roasting a chicken and baking a lemon meringue pie.

I sat in the corner of the kitchen eating an apple, watching. I knew that this one must be pretty special for her to go to that much trouble, especially after that first time he had asked her for a date.

On a Saturday evening several months earlier Mother was preparing to go out on her first date with Jim. Rose, our baby-sitter, came over at six o'clock in the evening. Jim was supposed to pick Mother up at seven o'clock and take her out to dinner at a Chinese restaurant. While Mother dressed, Rose made us dinner, had me take a bath and saw to us both putting on our pajamas. At about seven o'clock Rose set up the ironing board in the dining room, and Shawn and I went into the living room to watch television.

Mother, all dressed up in her prettiest blouse and skirt, walked into the living room and sat down on the sofa, looking at her watch. She gave Rose some last-minute instructions, explained where they were going for dinner, and pointed out that our bedtime was eight-thirty. Then she picked up the book she had been reading. I went back to watching television.

Several minutes later I heard a car in the driveway and saw the lights reflected in the dining room window. Mother stood up and looked out of the window. The car backed out of the driveway and left. Mother walked back to the sofa and sat down, looked at her watch, frowned and picked up her book.

"Isn't Jim supposed to be here already, Mommy?" I asked.

"I'm sure he's on his way, Honey. Watch television and never mind," she answered.

A little while later, just as the next program was starting, Mother stood up again and went into the kitchen. I heard her take a glass from the cupboard and fill it with water from the tap. In a few moments she walked back into the living room and looked out of the window. She looked at her watch again, shook her wrist, held the watch up to her ear, looked at the watch again, stared out of the window, and shook her head. Then she walked back over to the sofa, set down her glass of water, picked up her book and started to read again.

"Is something wrong, Mommy?" I asked, beginning to feel nervous.

"Barbara, leave me alone. Watch television, for goodness sake, and mind your own business."

Something was wrong all right, but her tone of voice told me not to ask any more questions. I turned around, making myself watch the television and mind my own business.

The phone rang. Mother jumped up to answer it.

"Hello?" I heard her say. Silence. Then, "Oh, hello, Carol." It was her best friend. She chatted for a few minutes, then hung up the phone and came back in the living room and sat down. One more look at her watch, one more frown, and one more attempt at reading the book. Even though I wanted her to reassure me, I knew better than to speak.

When the next program was over, I looked at Mother again. She was staring at the door, her forehead creased in a frown. She stood up and walked down the hall to her room and slammed the door. I looked up at Rose. She put her finger to her lips and shook her head. Mother's door opened again and she came back into the living room. Her eyes were all red like she had been crying.

"Rose," she said. Her voice was trembling like she was sad but she had a smile on her face. "I guess I'm not going out after all. You can go on home now and finish the ironing on Monday when you come to baby-sit. I'll put the children to bed."

Rose left and Mother sent us right to bed. She didn't even make me brush my teeth. I didn't hear anything more about Jim until a few weeks later. Again it was a Saturday night. Mother wasn't going out, we were all going to be home together. Around seven-thirty she told me that if the phone rang, we shouldn't answer it. She didn't want anyone to know we were home, and something about "standing him up." At eight o'clock the phone rang five times, then stopped. And again at eight-fifteen, eight-thirty, eight-forty-five and the last time at nine o'clock. All the while Mother sat on the sofa in the living room reading a book. Each time it rang I saw a little smile on her face. I was pretty sure that I would never hear Jim's name again.

But a few weeks later Mother told me that he had called to apologize. She was going to give him one more chance. I was finally going to meet him.

At four o'clock she sent me to change my clothes and then she combed my hair. Shawn took a bath and put on clean clothes. Mother went into her room to change. When she came out she was wearing her new soft pink blouse and her pretty black skirt with the slit up the back. Her brunette hair fell in soft waves on her shoulder. She was wearing pink lipstick and the faintest hint of blush on her cheeks.

"Mommy, you look so pretty!" I exclaimed.

She gave me one of those special smiles that made me feel warm and safe. Nothing could be really wrong in my world when my mother smiled.

Bending down to kiss me on the cheek she said, "You look pretty, too!" I loved her so much.

After a last-minute check on dinner, a final inspection of Shawn and me, a look around the house to make sure everything was perfect, she sat down in the living room, picked up a book and told Shawn and me to sit on the sofa and keep still. He was supposed to come over about six o'clock. I looked at the clock. Five more minutes. I looked at Shawn. He was picking at his fingernails. I pressed my hands on the sofa to try to look out the window without standing up.

"Barbara, sit still! Shawn, quit picking!" Mother demanded. She started reading again.

I looked at the clock. Six on the dot. I heard a car pull in the driveway. I jumped up to look out the window.

"Sit down, Barbara. We mustn't look anxious," Mother said with a frown.

I sat down and held my breath, wanting him to hurry up. Did he think I could sit there forever? Besides I had to go to the bathroom. I jumped up when the doorbell rang. Mother slowly stood up, pointed at me to sit back down, then casually walked to the door. She opened the door and said, "Oh! Hello, Jim," like this was nothing special. "Come on in."

She stepped back and Jim walked into our living room and into our lives. He was almost six feet tall, with neatly trimmed brown hair and the most captivating blue eyes that crinkled at the corners when he laughed. He kissed her on the cheek, and said, "Hello, Maureen."

"Jim," Mother said, "I'd like you to meet my son, Shawn."

"What a fine looking young man you are, Shawn. It's a real pleasure to meet you," he said walking over to Shawn with his hand extended.

Shawn stood up as tall as he could stretch himself, shook Jim's hand and said, "How do you do, Sir?", just like Mother had told him.

Jim turned to me. I sat up straight and smiled. "And you must be Barbara," he said. "Your mother didn't tell me how pretty you are. You have the most beautiful blond hair I have ever seen." He stole my heart from that very moment. I was in love.

That night at dinner Jim kept us entertained telling one funny story after another. I giggled and laughed until my sides ached. When bedtime came, I begged to stay up just a little while longer. I didn't want to leave him and didn't want him to go.

When Mother insisted that it was bedtime, I began to pout. Jim noticed my look, picked me up in his arms and carried me to my bedroom. "Don't worry, little Sweetheart," he said, "I'll come back again." I put my arms around his neck and kissed him.

"I like you," I whispered, my head nestled on his shoulder. "I hope you do come back."

After that night, Jim came over two or three times each week for dinner. He treated me like a princess. Whenever he came to our house, he picked me up in his arms and kissed me on the cheek, and called me his little blue-eyed sweetheart. Unless they were going out after dinner, he usually played games with Shawn and me, sitting right down on the floor with us. At times he even went outside with us to play games of tag or hide-and-seek. Sometimes he would grab my hands in his and swing me high in the air, spinning around and around while I laughed and squealed, stopping only when we were both out of breath. When we watched television, I always sat on his lap. When I fell asleep, he would carry me in his arms and put me to bed, tucking my blankets around me.

As Jim became more a part of our lives, we started doing some things that we had never done before. One of my favorites was digging for clams at the beach. We would wake up just before dawn, dress in warm clothes and load Jim's car with a picnic lunch and clamming paraphernalia. I felt warm and cozy as we would drive into the dense coastal mist that wrapped everything in an eerie blanket of half-light.

On our first clamming trip, the air was damp and cold. Carrying our buckets, shovels, burlap sacks, picnic basket, thermos, blankets and towels, we walked across the wet sand, trudging up and down, over and around a maze of sand dunes towards the sound of the waves crashing upon the shore.

Barefoot with my pants rolled up to my knees, my feet were soon so cold that my teeth chattered. Mother was walking right in front of me. I started to whimper.

"Mommy, my feet are freezing!" I cried.

She turned around and looked at me with her "I-don't-approve" frown and in an irritated voice she said, "If you can't stand the cold, you can just go sit in the car. We're not going to spend the whole day listening to you complain, Barbara. We're here to have fun!" With that she turned her back on me and walked away.

I looked down at the sand. I was so ashamed for having upset her. I knew I should have just gritted my teeth and kept my mouth shut. No one else was complaining. I was just a big crybaby! After that I didn't say anything no matter how cold it was. Believing that the only reason I was in pain was because there was something wrong with me that ought to be controlled, it never occurred to me that it would be okay to put something on my feet to keep them warm.

Early the following spring, just as Mother's flower garden began to sprout buds that promised a riot of color along the front of our house, she told me that Jim had asked her to marry him and that she had accepted. They would be married two months later. I was elated. All our happy times seemed to have started with Jim. I loved him so much and I could hardly wait until he would be my "daddy."

A few weeks before they were married, Mother announced that I was going to have new clothes for the wedding and that we were going shopping at the J.C. Penney store downtown. I almost cried with joy.

The following Saturday afternoon, we took the bus into town together. We walked around the store admiring dozens of racks of beautiful clothes. Mother picked out several dresses she thought would be appropriate, and I went into the dressing room to try them on. I pranced up and down the hallway and back and forth in front of the mirror in a ruffled yellow dress, turning first one way then the other, hands on my hips, making faces at myself in the mirror. Looking at myself, I fantasized that I was very rich and could buy all the pretty dresses in the whole store. I would buy one in every color! I posed with my left hand on my hip and the index finger of my right hand placed daintily in the dimple on my chin.

Delighted with my game I was starting to giggle when out of the corner of my eye, I noticed that the sales clerk was watching me, her lips pursed to one side, her eyebrows raised. She looked like she was about to laugh at me.

I was sure that she knew that I was poor and that she thought I was being ridiculous. Dropping my hands to my side and slumping my shoulders, I looked away.

I turned and walked back in the dressing cubicle and took that dress off without showing it to Mother as I had done with the others. I tried on two other outfits and finally we settled on a dress with a coat because Mother thought it was the most appropriate outfit.

With Jim as my daddy I believed that all the unhappiness of the past would be forgotten. Jim loved me, wanted to be my daddy, and thought I was pretty. Now everyone would be happy. That is, except for my grandparents, my father's parents. They were pretty upset with Mother. She told me that Grandma called to say that she was worried because Jim had a bad reputation for drinking too much. I wasn't sure what that meant, but it sounded pretty bad.

Mother told me that the real reason they were upset was because they wanted her to still be married to Daddy. She said that they would disapprove of anyone else, that any talk about Jim drinking too much was "just vicious gossip." She wanted to be happy and that was all there was to it. I agreed. I wanted to be happy, too. Jim made me laugh and I wanted him to be my daddy, no matter what my grandparents said.

It seemed like Mother was usually mad at Grandma for something, like being too picky about her house being clean. I heard Mother tell friends that Grandma was "neurotic" about cleanliness and that it was a shame that Shawn and I had to be so careful all the time in Grandma's house. Grandma was so afraid we would break or soil something. I thought that Mother meant she thought that Grandma was being silly.

Grandma didn't come over to our house very often after Daddy left, but when she did, I would see Mother running around the house cleaning every corner, polishing the faucets, cleaning the windows, washing and waxing the floors, vacuuming the carpets and shaking out the rugs. She would even look in my closet and under my bed to make sure they were clean. If they weren't she would yell at me, "Barbara Jeanne, clean up this pigsty. Your grandmother is coming over!" I couldn't understand all the fuss, because Grandma never looked in my closet or under my bed.

Then there was that stuff about "thank you" notes. Grandma usually sent me a card with a check for five dollars for my birthday. Mother always had me sit down that very same day and write a flowery thank you to Grandma, telling her how much I liked her gift and how thoughtful and wonderful she was to have remembered my birthday. Mother told her friends that she thought Grandma was "tacky" for sending money, because it wasn't a proper gift. "When you care about someone," Mother would say, "you should take the time to shop for a special gift." She said that sending money was thoughtless and lazy.

I decided not to let what Grandma thought interfere with how I felt about Jim. "Besides," I thought, "she's never even met him and I have!" The only thing that was really important was that I loved Jim, he loved me and he was going to be my daddy.

Origins Of Personal And Family Dysfunction

What makes a person dysfunctional? What makes a family dysfunctional? How does the structure of the family affect the individual? What does Barbara's story reveal that would allow us to understand how incest could occur in a "nice middle-class home?"

Taking the material that Barbara has already presented and integrating it with information about human development, awareness and family dysfunction, we can begin to identify the emergence of Barbara's, Maureen's and Shawn's individual problems. We can also evaluate the family's dysfunction and the interaction between the individuals and the family that set up the conditions for the incest.

The physical abuse that you saw in the beginning of the story would obviously have taken its toll on Barbara. However, it may not be clear yet that Maureen's behavior and overt and covert communications were just as detrimental to Barbara's development of a healthy self-image as her natural father's physical and emotional abuse.

We human beings are a mind/body/spirit complex. As with the rest of us, Barbara formed intricate patterns of thoughts, emotions, physical sensations, decisions, beliefs, judgments and attitudes which she used to function throughout her life. Then she interacted with her environment as a result of those previously accepted patterns. That interaction became a type of habit.

In order to function at a greater level of awareness, Barbara would have had to be able to go beyond the habit state and make honest contact with herself and her environment. She would have needed to separate herself from her programming. That means she would have had to be able to recognize and designate her "I" boundaries, distinguish between what was "Barbara" and "not Barbara," and then decide what part of "not Barbara" to integrate into "Barbara."

For Barbara, distinguishing between what was Barbara and not Barbara would have been extremely difficult because children raised in dysfunctional homes do not have this ability to distinguish their boundaries nor create positive integrated self-images. Children define who they are as human beings by their contact with other humans. When their early contact is with dysfunctional parents in a dysfunctional system, the children are not given realistic reflections of who they are nor are they given viable tools for finding out. They are not taught to make healthy distinctions between "me" and "not me" because their *dysfunctional parents, who are also operating with faulty tools and self-deception, cannot make those distinctions.*

Dysfunctional parents, like Maureen, lack the appropriate tools for integrating new information into a healthy non-conflicted internal system. They also have boundaries between themselves and their children so blurred, they cannot tell where they end and where their children begin. As a result the children develop blurred boundaries, becoming so enmeshed with their parents that they become repositories for their parents' unresolved issues, pains and conflicts. This is what happened to Barbara.

Several years ago, during a therapy session with a mother and son, I asked the child where he would like to go after the session. Although I made it very clear that I was addressing the child, the mother answered, saying, "We would like to go get something to eat."

I pointed out to her that I had clearly asked the question to the person sitting on my left and not to her. She seemed confused. Her boundaries were so blurred that she did not even realize that she was an entity who was separate from her child. She saw herself and the child as one being called "we." This example may seem trivial, but it was indicative of their ongoing relationship. Living in that environment, the child had difficulty separating himself from his mother and took on many of her problems.

If we consider that children not only learn to define themselves by feedback from their parents but must also function as an integrated part of a larger structure called the family, then we will recognize that some greater forces are at work. A family is a system which operates as a single entity and follows certain definite system principles.

1. The whole is greater than the sum of the parts.
2. Any change in any part of the system affects *the system as a whole as well as each and every* part of the system.
3. All systems attempt to maintain their original structure and balance (homeostasis).

Keeping these principles in mind, we may now understand how much we are actually affected by these systems.

It would also help to remember that the individual is a system within the system, and must internally abide by the same principles that govern the larger system. When the individual child reacts to the movement within the larger family system, his internal system also responds to maintain internal balance. The child, who takes on the role and activities of the "little father" in his family after his own father disappears, may develop illnesses or new behaviors, like bed-wetting, in response to the new family system role he has taken.

Barbara's Personal And Family Dysfunction

If we now turn to Barbara's story, we can explore what the already existing personal and familial dysfunctions were and how they could become fertile ground for the Alcoholic Family Syndrome and the incest.

1. Barbara's natural father was a brutal, sadistic, violent, rigid, controlling, compulsive man who had to wear three clean shirts a day and demanded that everyone abide by his rules or be abused.

   Barbara's mother made his behaviors and beliefs right by never communicating their unacceptability to her children and by never requesting any input or courting any protests from Barbara. Whether she realized it or not, Maureen was implying that the world outside of Barbara had a basic *rightness* to it while Barbara had a basic *wrongness* to her. This is precisely what Barbara came to believe.

   Her mother also implied in the same way that horrendous emotional and physical abuse was an acceptable consequence for disobedience or disagreement. The belief in her own wrongness, the abuse and its tacit acceptance all caused shame and trauma in Barbara which left emotional scars neither Barbara nor her mother had tools to heal.

2. The divorce came at least in part as a result of the violent abusive behavior Barbara's father acted out on the family, but Barbara never knew that. Barbara's mother never spoke about the divorce nor the reasons for it. Barbara sensed her mother's upset about the divorce and the failure of the marriage and decided that the divorce was definitely not okay. Barbara's father implied, when he asked Barbara if she wanted him to leave, that he was against the divorce.

   Without communication about the negativity surrounding the failure of the marriage, children will often believe that they are the cause of that negativity. This is especially true if there was violence toward the children who will reason, "I have been bad. My parents don't want this divorce, but they have to get it because of me. If only I had been better, this divorce would never have happened." Barbara already mentioned that she felt that somehow she was to blame for the divorce.

3. Barbara came from a Divorced Family. In an era when divorce was infrequent and frowned upon, Barbara not only was different from her friends, she was, in her own self-judgment, inferior, not good enough.

4. Control issues helped crystallize the family dysfunction. Both Barbara's natural parents were rigid and placed a heavy emphasis on rules, cleanliness and perfectionism. Her mother's need to have everything spotless and perfect along with her fear of looking bad, her fear of all feelings, her fear of dealing with those feelings and her fear of dealing with her children's needs, made control for Maureen an absolute necessity. To hide from feelings and anything else that she was uncomfortable with, she had to emphasize control and make rules right. *Emphasis on rules and the rigidity of rules are ways to control feelings.*

   There are two types of rules a family develops. There are *spoken rules,* such as, "Never leave clothes or toys lying around," and there are *unspoken rules,* such as, "Emotions are bad so don't have them." Rules may also be general or specific in nature.

   Maureen's inability to deal with emotions, as well as her need to look good, to control other people's perceptions of her, contributed to the development of what we will later explore as a closed family system. These factors were the driving forces in the development of both the general and specific unspoken family rules which emerged for Barbara as . . .
   - Emotions are bad so don't have them.
   - Protect Mother at all costs.

- Do not make Mother uncomfortable (i.e., do not make Mother deal with emotions.)
- Do not raise concerns (i.e., being cold) so Mother will never appear in error, you will not draw attention to yourself or her and she will not have to deal with your emotions or hers.
- What other people think or feel is more important than what you think or feel, even if you do not like them. You are not important. Put on a good act.
- Do not talk about your feelings or problems inside the family (to protect Mom) or outside the family (to protect the image).
- Children must always obey parents absolutely.
- Parents are always right.
- Never disagree with Mother, even if she contradicts herself. (There is something wrong with you if you cannot figure out which contradictory statement to agree with at any given time.)
- Do not discuss any of these unspoken family rules.
- Keep the family secrets.
- Deny everything that does not fit the rules or the disturbed thinking that results from the rules. (This will lead to not trusting your own experience, intuitions or reality.)

Concern For Appearances And Distortions Of Reality

Through Barbara's eyes, we see Maureen's concern with what the community might think of her as a mother and citizen. How she appeared to others (or rather how she believed she appeared to others) was more important to Maureen than what her children felt or needed. In fact, her appearance was so important to her that she failed to see that some of her children's needs were never met that first Christmas of the divorce.

This self-centeredness is fairly typical in the dysfunctional thinking which is an integral part of co-dependency. Co-dependents like to think of themselves as saviors of the world, but they are so concerned with looking good, looking like they are doing the "right" thing, they miss the real needs of those closest to them.

Maureen's self-centeredness also prevented her from seeing the mixed messages she was sending her children. She thought it perfectly natural to donate to the church Christmas collections for the needy, while obviously making it wrong to be one of those needy. Telling Barbara that they were poor but should not act poor gave her daughter the real message that poverty was bad, and things that are bad should be hidden. Therefore, all the people that the church collections went to help were in some way bad.

She also told Barbara that not having money was nothing to be ashamed of and that as long as they looked clean and neat, no one would look down on them. Underneath all of this, the most important message was, "Try to figure out what others think and then try to manipulate it." Although children tend to believe their parents' actions more than their words, this conglomeration of beliefs, actions and attitudes would have been enough to bewilder anyone. Barbara was no exception. She was constantly trying to determine how to be good, and when she was unable to make any sense out of this chaos, she blamed herself.

In addition to that confusion, Maureen was torn by her own conflicting concerns about the opinions her ex-husband's mother held of her and her own disapproval and paradoxical emulation of her mother-in-law. She ended up completely swallowing beliefs, opinions, rules and judgments from others without breaking them down and integrating them into a healthy internal system. Instead of combining the external material with her own internal material into a healthy, honest whole, she became a patchwork of confused and conflicting beliefs, double-bind situations and double messages to her children.

Because there was no room for honest discussion in the family, the children could not sort out the conflicting messages and were left in a confused damned-if-you-do-damned-if-you-don't position that is the basis for many dysfunctional mechanisms, such as disassociation from reality, confused thinking or denial.

When Maureen was faced with Jim's reputation around town, she chose to deny it, to ignore input from outside sources without ever checking out the experience. This is very typical of the co-alcoholic/co-dependent. While she was extremely concerned with what she feared people were thinking about her, her need to be involved with Jim allowed her to justify as "vicious gossip" what was being said about him and his drinking. Although Maureen was usually concerned about the opinions of her ex-husband's parents, she chose to believe that their disapproval was based on the fact that she was no longer married to their son.

This continual twisting and distorting of reality through denial and justification marks the onslaught of the convoluted type of thinking that the co-alcoholic/co-dependent must perpetuate to keep the dysfunctional system in place. Co-alcoholics/co-dependents do very little reality testing. Although they want the approval of the outside world, they cannot take in any information that would contradict what they already believe about themselves or their needs. They cannot allow information in that would break up their pseudo-image.

Maureen was actually very well thought of and loved as a person in her own right in the community, but she could not allow that into her awareness because of her own belief that she was not worthy. This unworthiness arose out of her own dysfunctional upbringing.

During some information gathering in therapy, Barbara told a story about her mother and her mother's grandfather, who was a righteous rigid minister.

Barbara's mother was attending college and her grandfather was helping her out financially by paying some of her living expenses. One day she received a phone call from her mother telling her that her father had suffered a heart attack. Terrified and upset, Maureen left school and drove a four-hour drive home to be at her father's side for many days and nights. Only when he was past the critical period did she think of returning to school. She hesitated leaving, believing that it was her duty to stay with her mother, but her mother insisted that she return to college.

When she arrived back at her boarding house, she found that her grandfather had moved all of her belongings over to his house. He had wanted Maureen to leave school and stay with her parents during the time of crisis. Maureen's mother insisted that Maureen stay in school. Her grandfather reluctantly agreed but insisted that Maureen live with him from then on. He claimed that he found a partially empty flask of alcohol in her room at the boarding house and accused her of being on the road to sin and ruin. He disapproved of any use of alcohol. If Maureen wanted to finish school, she had to live with her grandfather and adhere to his unshakable rules and his stern unwavering sense of right and wrong. Maureen escaped living with her grandfather by marrying Barbara's natural father.

It is fairly easy to see that having grown up in a stern religious environment, where she was seen by her grandfather's righteous perceptions as bad, selfish and a sinner, Maureen would have had to continue to attempt to prove to herself and others that she was worthy. However, because she already believed she was unworthy, nothing she did could ever be taken as proof of her worth.

In addition, her grandfather's all-or-nothing attitude toward drinking left her vulnerable to an alcoholic. Maureen appears to have tried alcohol in college. She probably found that she liked some of its effects, and that it was not the absolute "evil" her grandfather proclaimed. She could have easily made the mistake of deciding that there was nothing wrong with alcohol. She would not have been able to see that she did not have enough information on alcohol to make that decision. She would also not have been able to see that her thinking was conditioned to follow an all-or-nothing mentality, and that this thinking would throw her into accepting even the extreme drinking of her alcoholic first husband. She had no frame of reference to look for some graduated measure for alcohol consumption and behavior.

It is possible that Maureen did not realize when she initially married her first husband that he drank too much and was an alcoholic. She probably had not made the connection yet, as she had been very protected, very naive and very gullible. It appears that even after the divorce, she did not make the connection between at least some of the behavior of her first husband and alcohol.

No one knows what Maureen actually thought to convince herself to marry Jim. He appeared to be pleasant and fun-loving. The fact that he had stood her up for something else on their first date did not make any impact on her. She merely played the game back. She did not realize that this foretold how he would treat her in the future.

Maureen also probably believed that Jim was solvent. Although it appeared that she needed him financially (because she was struggling to make ends meet when they first met), in actuality she was quite capable of financially supporting herself and her children. After the marriage Jim was frequently out of work while she held down a very responsible position for a number of years. She may have believed, as Barbara had believed about herself, that she was incomplete and needed a man to provide for her in order to be normal.

Before Jim married into the family, it was already ripe for another alcoholic. Barbara's natural father resembled Barbara's maternal great-grandfather in his sternness, his control, his coldness, his inaccessibility. Since we seek out that which is familiar, even if it's painful, it is understandable that Maureen would first marry a man with whom she would have to relate as she did with her own grandfather. What she did not realize was that she would continue that pattern again with her second husband, who, at first, appeared superficially to be very different from her grandfather and her first husband. Later when his behaviors became as rigid and controlling as her former husband's and grandfather's, she was so accustomed to that treatment from the past and so enmeshed in her denial, that she simply slipped further and further into her co-dependence and the Alcoholic Family Syndrome.

The Wedding

It was a spring day of 1957. I yawned, rubbed the sleep from my eyes and discovered a clear blue sky beckoning me through curtains fluttering in the early morning breeze. Extending my arms over my head I began a slow luxurious stretch, flexing each muscle and joint from my fingers to my toes. Sitting up, I bent over, grabbed my ankles and touched my head to my knees. Laying back down on the pillow, I put my hands under my head and smiled. I wasn't in any hurry to get up. This day was going to be the most perfect of my nine and a half years and I didn't want to rush one single moment.

I listened to the sounds of morning. In the back yard my duck, the one I had won at the Penny Toss at last summer's County Fair, was quacking for his breakfast. A neighbor was mowing his lawn, and down the street a car engine started. My brother, Shawn, was already in the living room watching television. Mother was humming a happy song as she moved about the kitchen. I heard cupboard doors opening and closing, pots clanging, the tinkling of dishes and silver being placed on the table. The smell of fried bacon and fresh-brewed coffee signaled that breakfast would be ready soon and then I would have to get up.

I sat up and looked across the room and saw my wonderful new clothes on wooden hangers hooked over the door frame of my closet. I could hardly wait until I would put them on, and everyone, especially Jim, would tell me how beautiful I was.

Everything else in the room was the same as usual. At the foot of my bed, Smokey, my beloved long-haired grey and white cat, lay curled up and sleeping. In one corner was the toy chest filled with favorite games, dolls and paper doll families. Sitting on top was my most favorite doll wearing a bright yellow dress. Beside her, smiling at me with his red felt mouth and black button eyes, was my well-hugged ragged old teddy bear. Next to the toy chest was a faded blue table and on top of it was my most prized possession, a second-hand doll house, a gift from Mother the Christmas before.

Everything may look the same, I thought, but after today, everything would be different, changed for the better! I looked once again at the new dress, new coat, new shoes, new socks, new slip, the new changes that were happening in my life, and felt shivers in my body. That night Mother would get a new husband, and more important I would get a new Daddy! After so many years of wishing and waiting, life would be perfect. My mother, my new daddy, my brother and me. A real and perfect family, just like on television.

I heard the sound of Mother's footsteps, and I looked towards the doorway to watch her walk down the hall with a bounce in her step that hadn't been there in a long time. It made me feel warm and safe.

"Time to get out of bed, sleepy head," she said with a smile. "Breakfast is ready and you don't want to be late for school."

School! Darn! I had forgotten it was Friday.

"Do I really have to go to school? Today? Mommy, can't we pretend it's a holiday and then I can stay home? Please?" I begged.

"Barbara Jeanne," she said and I knew when she used both my names, she was getting angry, "you know better than that. I've told you a hundred times how important school is. You're not sick! This isn't a holiday! And besides, I don't want you underfoot all day."

"I could help you," I offered.

"Come on now, you're going to school!" She sounded impatient. "Quit stalling and get out of bed!"

I jumped up still knowing this had to be a happy day. I didn't want to do anything to make her mad. Not today! I ran to her and gave her a hug. "I love you, Mommy," I said.

"That's my good girl," she said, patting my hair. "Now run along and brush your teeth. Breakfast is already on the table."

"Okay, Mommy!" I said with a smile.

I ran down the hall and into the bathroom. After I brushed my teeth, I examined my reflection in the mirror. I saw the same shoulder-length stringy blond hair, which I hated because it would never hold a curl, the same pale skin, which only seemed to burn and never tan, the silly looking turned-up nose, and the beanpole of a skinny body. The only thing I liked was the color of my eyes, a brilliant blue. I wondered if I'd look different after the wedding. Maybe my face would change, or I'd get taller, or rounder, or prettier or something like that. At least people would know that we were a real family! Feeling the chills in my body again, I made a silly face in the mirror, brushed the tangles out of my hair, quickly washed my face and ran to the kitchen.

Mother and Shawn were already eating. I was amazed to see that there was crisp bacon, scrambled eggs, toast with strawberry jam, and a big pitcher of ice-cold milk. One thing was clear, since Jim had asked Mother to marry him, we were eating much better. Shawn's plate was already half empty. Mother was drinking her coffee. Looking up from the newspaper she said, "You better hurry up, Barbara. You still have to get dressed and you don't want to miss the bus."

I filled my plate and ate as fast as I could. Everything looked so good that I wanted to eat it all. I looked across the table at Shawn. He was gobbling down his food like he hadn't eaten in a week. "Shawn," I whispered, "this is the day we get a new daddy." I expected that he would be as happy as I was.

"Yeah, I know," he said. "That's all you've been talking about for over a week: 'Four more days, three more days, two more days, one more day,' like you think I don't know!" He frowned, shook his head, rolled his eyes towards the ceiling and went back to eating his breakfast.

"But, Shawn," I protested, "aren't you happy . . .?" I started to say when Mother interrupted.

"Children, no fighting. Barbara, be quiet and eat your breakfast. I don't have time for this!"

I looked down at my plate and felt tears stinging my eyes. I wanted everyone, especially Shawn, to feel the same way I did. I wondered what was wrong with him, but wasn't going to let him get the best of me! I wiped my eyes not knowing if he was having a mood or not feeling good. Either way, I wasn't about to let him spoil the day for me.

I rushed to my room, made my bed, got dressed, and hurried to the bus stop behind Shawn. Amanda, my best friend, was already there waiting for me.

"Today's the wedding day!" I announced as I greeted her, feeling important and special and wanting to share it with her. Shawn frowned and turned away.

"Oh, yeah, that's right. And did you do your math problems last night?" she asked. The smile left my face, but she went on, "I didn't understand the fractions, did you?"

What was wrong? She seemed to be more interested in some stupid homework than the most important day of my life. Was I the only one who felt excited? What was happening? Was I wrong to be happy? Was I supposed to act like this was some ordinary day?

"Yes, Amanda, I did the math problems," I answered trying not to show my disappointment and anger just in case maybe I was wrong. "You can copy my homework on the bus," I finished.

In the classroom I ran to my teacher, Mrs. Graham. "Today's the day my mother's getting married," I exclaimed.

"I know, Barbara, and it's such a pretty day for a wedding, isn't it?" she said with a warm smile that told me that finally here was someone who noticed my excitement. "I bet you can hardly wait for tonight."

Finally, someone understood. I hugged her and then ran to my desk, put my books away and waited for the bell. I was much too excited to pay attention. While the rest of the class listened to Mrs. Graham explain a math problem, I rehearsed a little speech I planned to deliver to Jim after the wedding. Actually it was a question. I knew he would answer the way I imagined, if I asked it just right. And that would mean that he really loved me.

When I came home from school, Mother was still at the beauty parlor getting her hair fixed. Rose was already there. Mother had left her a note that I was to take a bath and wash my hair right away. I used the bubble bath. Rose set my hair in pincurls. Amanda came over to play. I led her to my room, wondering how to play marriage. We started with my favorite game, paper dolls. I quickly pulled out my "grownup" boy and girl dolls and the set of paper wedding clothes. We played pretend wedding until Amanda got bored with it and insisted we play "house" with my real dolls and doll house. As usual, we made up perfect families, just like Amanda's family.

Amanda's parents were not divorced. Her mother didn't have to work. She baked cookies and taught several of us girls ballet and tap dancing in her garage. Amanda's father was a police officer and her sister had been the queen of our local rodeo. They were "the perfect family." Ours was "the divorced family." I thought Amanda was better than me, that is, until the wedding.

At four-thirty, Rose announced that it was time for Amanda to go home, and for me to start getting ready. She wanted to make sure my hair looked perfect for "the pictures," she said.

My hair never curled easily. Even when it did curl, the curl wouldn't last. Grandmother Louella thought the problem could be solved by a permanent wave, so Mother had let her take me to the beauty parlor. But I thought it looked even worse because now it was frizzy.

Rose brushed out the pincurls, and separated them in three sections, one on each side of my face, and one in the back. After carefully braiding each side section, she pulled them together at the back and secured them with a rubber band, tied them with a red ribbon and finally brushed the back into a soft "pageboy." Even I had to admit that my hair looked very pretty. Everything was working perfectly for the wedding.

Mother got back from the beauty parlor at five o'clock. She looked so beautiful. She hugged and kissed me, and said, "Your hair looks perfect, sweetheart." I beamed. "Come with me now, it's time to get dressed," she said taking my hand.

We went into my room where Mother helped me put on my wedding clothes, adjusting each piece carefully. Rose supervised Shawn. He finished before me. When I was finally dressed, we both stood in the middle of the living room for Mother's final inspection and approval.

"You both look wonderful," she proclaimed, as she re-tied the ribbon in my hair. "I'm so proud of you both." Mother was happy with me and that was all that mattered to me at that moment.

Rose took Shawn and me in her car to Loretta's house where the wedding would take place. Mother would finish dressing and then drive herself in Jim's car. Working for the county, he was provided with a car so was able to let Mother borrow his.

The house was already a buzz of activity with last-minute preparations in full swing. Several of Mother's friends from her civic club were helping. Rose ushered Shawn and me to an out-of-the-way corner in the living room, telling us to stay put until Mother arrived, then she went off to help in the kitchen.

Vases filled with spring flowers of every color decorated the house. The fireplace mantle was trimmed with paper wedding bells, and crepe paper streamers swung everywhere, even from the clock on the wall. It was six-thirty and the wedding would start at seven-thirty. The dining room table was laden with casseroles and salads prepared by the ladies of our church. In one corner was the beautiful three-tiered wedding cake. Loretta's best dishes, fine crystal glasses and polished silver were set on a table in another corner.

I cautiously peered over a lamp to look at the clock on the mantle over the fireplace. The hands had hardly moved. I forgot to bring a doll to play with or even a book to read, so I had nothing to do but watch the clock and the people. I began to feel bored and unimportant and started to sulk. No one seemed to notice that I was even there. Nobody said hello or told me how pretty I looked.

This was my most wonderful day and nobody seemed to care. They seemed to have enough time to talk to each other, but no one talked to me.

"Maureen seems so happy these days, but I sure hope she knows what she's doing. Do you think this marriage is really for the best?" Loretta asked quietly.

I wanted to ask her what she meant by that. I knew what we were doing and I knew it was for the best, at least for me.

Ever loyal to my mother, Rose answered, "He's a good man, Loretta. Good to Maureen, good to the children. I'm sure he'll make her happy."

I was glad somebody knew the right answer. I looked at the clock. The hands still hadn't moved. I stood up and looked out of the window in time to see Mother getting out of Jim's car. Hurrah! I thought, it must be close to the time for the wedding. I ran to greet her, opening the door just as she stepped up on the porch.

"Mommy!" I shouted. "Wait 'til you see how beautiful everything is." I reached out to hug her and let her know how much I loved her but before I could touch her, she had her hands on my arms, holding me away.

"Barbara, be careful. You're going to wrinkle my dress. Now go back inside."

I didn't understand why Mother was so cross or what was happening to my perfect day. I was about to ask her what was wrong, when Loretta quickly whisked her into another room and told me to go back to the corner and sit.

I sat down but immediately began to squirm again. I couldn't seem to sit still. I looked over at Shawn. He was playing with his army knife and not paying any attention to me or anything else. I had to go to the bathroom but I didn't know if I should say anything. I crossed my legs and tried to sit still.

The wedding guests began to arrive, and within a short time Loretta's house was filled with people. Several waved to Shawn and me or said "Hi!" but no one came over to talk with me or to ask me how I was. Maybe they didn't know how important this day was to me. I got up and went to the bathroom. There were a few women waiting outside the door. They were chatting and didn't seem to notice me. I stood against the wall, arms folded across my chest, frowning, and waited my turn. I wasn't important anymore. I wanted someone to pay attention to me, but this was Mother's celebration, not mine.

Shortly after Reverend Russell and his wife arrived, the wedding began. Mrs. Russell played the piano softly as everyone took their places in front of the fireplace. Jim and Mother in the middle, Loretta standing next to Mother and Jim's friend, Carl, standing next to him. Shawn and I stood behind, trying to peek around the tall bodies.

Reverend Russell gave his speech about the importance of marriage. Blah! Blah! Blah! I wanted him to hurry up and make them man and wife. Even though I had a smile pasted on my face, I thought I might be getting sick. It was a warm evening, but I began to feel a chill. My teeth started chattering and I felt weak. I began to sweat and the room felt smothering and hot. My stomach started to hurt and I knew I was getting sick. Still Reverend Russell went on. Just when I thought I couldn't stand it any longer, I heard Reverend Russell saying congratulations. I looked up and Jim was kissing Mother on the mouth.

It was over. They were married. I had a daddy. I didn't feel perfect. I felt sick. I started to cry. I couldn't tell Mother because she usually said my upset stomachs were to get attention. I took some deep breaths and tried to get control of myself.

Suddenly, everyone was talking and hugging. Mother turned to me and Shawn. She had tears in her eyes, too, and when she saw that I was crying she bent down to hug me. "I'm so happy, sweetheart," she gushed, "and I know you are, too." I bit my lower lip and tried not to let on that I was crying because my stomach hurt.

Before I could sit down and get my strength back, Loretta got the photographer and started lining us up for pictures. I tried to look happy. One of the pictures he took shows Mother and Jim, Loretta and Carl, Reverend Russell and Shawn with broad smiles, while I am standing with arms folded in front of me, a serious frown on my face.

I thought maybe my stomach hurt because I was hungry, so I loaded up my plate and proceeded to stuff myself. Then I really did get sick. I wasn't doing a very good job of hiding it, because one of the ladies asked me what was wrong. I started to cry, and told her my stomach hurt. She took me into the bathroom, gave me a drink of water and washed my face telling me I didn't look pretty when I cried.

When it was time for Rose to take Shawn and me home, Mother kissed us. As she scooted us out of the door, she said she would say good-night when they came to get her suitcase before leaving on the honeymoon.

I eagerly climbed into bed, so exhausted from this long and emotional day that I could barely keep my eyes open. But I willed myself to stay awake. The day wasn't finished for me. I still had my speech and question to deliver to Jim. He had married Mother, told me that he loved me and wanted to be my daddy. I needed to cement the contract. I had to be sure.

I lay in bed, my thin body shaking, rehearsing each line, each word. I had to say it just right.

After what seemed like hours, the front door opened and I heard their voices whispering as they walked down the hall and into what was now "their" bedroom. I waited a few minutes, hoping they would come to see me. When they didn't, I climbed out of bed and walked quietly to their door. They were kissing. I didn't know what to do. I stood waiting. After several moments, Mother noticed me.

"What's the matter, Barbara?" she asked softly as she took her arms from Jim.

I didn't answer. I had forgotten the words to my speech. I stood and to my embarrassment began to cry. This wasn't at all like it was supposed to be. I was doing it all wrong.

Jim turned to me with a frown on his face. He put down the shirt he was about to place in the suitcase. "What is it, little sweetheart? What's wrong?" he asked gently.

I stood in frozen silence as tears drizzled down my cheeks. They gave each other puzzled looks.

Wiping my nose on the sleeve of my nightie, I looked Jim directly in the eye. Taking a deep breath and with every bit of courage I could summon, I mumbled, "I . . . I . . . I just wanted . . . to ask you something."

"Yes?" said Jim, coming closer.

I couldn't go on. I was afraid he might say no to my question. I thought I'd die if it didn't turn out like I'd planned. I took another deep breath and blurted out the question.

"Can I call you 'Daddy' now?"

I looked down at the floor, waiting for his answer. He was silent and I thought my worst fears had come true. I felt my knees begin to tremble. Maybe he didn't really want to be my daddy. I had to know, so I made myself look up at him.

He had tears in his eyes. And he was smiling. He came to me, picked me up in his arms and hugged me to his chest.

"Yes," he answered, patting my back gently, "you can call me Daddy."

I began to sob as I relaxed my head on his shoulder. I was right. Everything would be perfect now.

Interactions Between Symptoms
Of Personal And Family Dysfunction

If we were to isolate the many small incidents in Barbara's life, such as the scene before the wedding when Maureen pushed Barbara away so that her dress wouldn't get wrinkled, we might say that they were normal everyday events. We might conclude that Barbara's natural father was the only problem, and he had already been eliminated. Nothing could be further from the truth. The fact that most of the everyday incidents in Barbara's life appear normal, does not mean that they were healthy for Barbara.

Yes, it is true that Maureen was nervous on her wedding day. Yes, it is also true that she was nervous waiting for Jim to show up on their first date. And yes, it is true that she was uncomfortable when her children complained, but none 'of that excuses Maureen, the adult, from her responsibilities of dealing with her children in a healthy nonabusive manner.

In order for young children to grow healthy, they need their parents to model and acknowledge emotions, to nurture their developmental needs, to give them quality time and attention, to communicate openly and without secrecy. Barbara's background had none of those things.

Instead, Barbara's upbringing created an environment of ongoing stress. Fear of doing wrong, fear of feeling or expressing feelings or having the wrong feeling, emphasis on rules and a "rightness" outside of herself all led Barbara to distrust her own experience. This distrust of herself, her negative judgments about herself and her trained acceptance of emotional and physical abuse as a normal standard established her in her role in the Alcoholic Family Syndrome and set her up for the later ongoing incestuous relationship with her stepfather.

Because of the nature of the family dysfunction and the existing dysfunctions of Barbara and the other members of the family, her Alcoholic stepfather had fertile soil to continue his own disease process:

1. Denial was rife.
2. Maureen's self-esteem was poor.
3. Her need to look good and also to please others was firmly in place.
4. Her connection to the outside world was via her "act;" that is, who she thought she should be, rather than who she was.
5. Her coping skills were rigid and governed by her need to keep her image and avoid pain at all costs.
6. Real communication between herself and her children was non-existent.
7. She needed to keep everything under control, or believe that everything was under control, so that she would not have to deal with her own emotions or with situations for which she had no tools.

There was no safe place in Barbara's relationship with her mother to talk about her experience or tell the truth. If the truth did not support Maureen's distortion of reality, she did not want to hear it. If what Barbara felt did not match what Maureen said she should feel, then Barbara had either to lie to herself about what she was feeling or as was the case later on, not even examine what she felt and simply "stuff it." Barbara was learning to relate to the world via her "act," that is, who she was *told* she should be rather than who she was. The lack of communication between mother and daughter, the assumption of the shame and wrongness of who Barbara was and what she felt and perceived, and the development of her act would make it almost impossible for Barbara to seek help to stop the incest after the initial rape.

Barbara's mother did not have to be raised in an alcoholic home in order to develop co-dependent traits. If either or both parents demonstrate emotional or physical inaccessibility, compulsivity, rigidity, compulsive religiosity, secrecy, inability to communicate, constant unresolved fighting or long periods of verbal withdrawal (the "silent treatment"), scapegoating, authoritarian parenting or image control, the children growing up in that environment are likely to have low self-esteem, be outside-of-themselves oriented, have poor emotional skills, and become co-dependent and more dysfunctional as they grow up. Virginia Satir has said that if the rules are unrealistic, inflexible and permanent, if communications are vague, dishonest and indirect, and if the ties outside the family are suspicious, blaming and placating, then the family is unhealthy.[1] As you have seen, Barbara's family fit that description exactly.

In the unhealthy family the children develop no sense of self or personal power. Raising children in such a family where their feelings and perceptions are denied, ignored or made to appear wrong, causes the children to lose touch with who they are as physical, emotional/ psychological and spiritual beings. The children suffer from boundary disorders, not knowing where they end and their parents begin so that they become part of an undifferentiated family ego-mass. They cannot make contact with the Self or with their Higher Power.

Polster and Polster defined several important human contact boundaries: the "I" boundary, the body boundary, the value boundary, the expressive boundary, the exposure boundary and the familiarity boundary. The child's "I" boundary, which is the boundary of "permissible contactfulness"[2], includes the ability to see the Self, to make truthful and honest contact with Who we are and how we-are-in-the-world.

Growing up with Maureen, Barbara was having difficulty creating any personal "I" boundary. Her mother expected Barbara's frame of reference to the world to be the same as Maureen's and Barbara was complying. As she did so, she was surrendering her own identity and taking on most of Maureen's co-dependent traits, such as people-pleasing.

For the first six years of Barbara's life, as with most children, the significant power figures were her natural parents. These were the people with whom she made her initial contacts. It was from her experience of their boundaries that Barbara began creating her own. Sadly, from her first conscious experiences and contacts with her early environment, Barbara was developing, for the most part, a sense of self that was seen by her as unacceptable. At the same time, she was also trying to do the almost impossible task, given Maureen's blurred boundaries, of learning to distinguish her boundaries between *Self* and *Not-self*.

In Dysfunctional Families, the sense of self that the child develops often is not the actual Self but rather a false-self. When this happens, as was the case with Barbara, the child winds up at odds with herself. Instead of accepting *who Barbara was,* she accepted *who others,* especially Maureen, *told her she was,* and instead of accepting the *way she was,* she attempted to be the *way she was not.* She "bought into" beliefs, attitudes and ideas that invalidated and made wrong the emotions, feelings, needs and perceptions that she brought with her to this world.

Once a child invalidates herself, as Barbara did, she will either project those now unacceptable aspects of self onto others or throw them back onto herself in a destructive manner. Take, for example, the belief that Barbara got from her parents that all her emotions were bad. She desperately tried to deny, disown or to somehow rid herself of the emotions that she felt. Since part of being human and alive is feeling emotions, and since it is impossible to stop the flow, Barbara's attempts often failed, so she would then turn them back against herself in the form of a negative self-judgment. Instead of allowing herself to feel hurt and angry because her mother did not respond to her feet getting cold while clamming, Barbara called herself a cry-baby and gritted her teeth. As you will see later, Barbara would take all her stored emotion from situations where emotion was not allowed and over-react in situations where any emotion might be allowable. She would then be made to feel wrong for over-reacting and find herself in a never-ending Gordian knot of emotional upheaval. As a consequence, she would lose her ability to stay present and function in the world.

Remember, Barbara's inability to be in the world directly related to her original environment in which she developed her distorted perception of herself and the world.

Barbara's original family was severely dysfunctional. Each of her parents' rigid rules and strict judgments about right and wrong, which had nothing to do with who Barbara really was as a person, set Barbara up for her later attention addiction.

By the time Jim came into the family, Barbara was well on the way to developing severe problems. She had already clearly decided that her emotions were not acceptable, that she was not good enough, that other people were more important than she and that any confusion that she experienced had to be her fault and not due to the poor communications and double messages from her parents. Barbara believed she was "wrong, bad and awful," but more than that, she had learned that outside of herself was "right" and that she had to look outside of herself for the answers to life. This she did almost continuously and in doing so, she would set herself up for constant stress and confusion since she lacked the tools to discriminate between all of the different "rightnesses" outside of her own very blurred boundaries.

2

Death Of A Dream

Two months after the wedding we moved to a suburb of Los Angeles and lived in the left half of a duplex. In the fall I entered the fourth grade and near the end of that winter my life began to fall apart. Mother became very sick. Her doctor performed several tests and the results indicated that she needed kidney surgery.

The morning she was admitted to the hospital, I was dazed and scared, not even coming out to say goodbye. All day long I kept asking myself what would happen if she died. I couldn't take my mind off that idea no matter how much I tried. As if lost in a bad dream, I imagined Jim walking into my room with tears in his eyes to tell me Mother was dead. With real tears in my eyes I imagined throwing myself into his arms and the two of us crying and holding each other. But the bad dream turned into a nightmare as I saw Jim sadly telling me that I would have to go to live with my natural father, to tormented memories of beatings and impossible rules and cruel punishments. Snapping out of the dream, I shivered with the realization that my wonderful new life could be snatched from me at any moment and be replaced by the terror of the past. That night, unable to sleep, I lay quivering in the darkness of my bedroom. I made a vow to myself that if Mother were to die in the hospital, I would do everything I could to make sure that Jim always loved me so I never had to live with my father again.

Jim wasn't like my real father in any way, I thought, trying to distract myself from Mother's sickness. Even though Jim punished me whenever I broke the rules or misbehaved, he was never cruel. Lying in bed I thought back to the first time Jim punished me, right after he and Mother came back from their honeymoon.

It was early evening, about an hour before dinner. Shawn and I were playing in Shawn's room. Jim was in the living room watching television and Mother was in the kitchen cooking. Shawn and I started to wrestle and play-fight. He pushed me on his bed. I bounced up giggling and tried to push him back. But being a year older, he had the advantage. He pushed me back down, ran to the other side of the bed and pulled one of my braids. I squealed in pain and tried but missed again.

"You'll never reach me," he laughed. "I'm bigger, faster and stronger than you'll ever be!"

"You're mean!" I cried as I rolled over and scrambled to the side of the bed trying once more to grab him. Again he moved to the side and one more time I missed. He pushed me and I fell real hard, hitting my temple on the headboard. He laughed and pointed his finger close to my face. My eyes filled with hot angry tears. I wanted to punch him. I wasn't playing anymore. I hated it when he pulled my hair, even more when he pushed me and, worst of all, when he teased me.

I lay still for a moment, rubbing my head, waiting for a moment to catch him off guard. Then I'd really show him! Just then the phone in the hall rang and he looked towards the door. Seizing the moment, I jumped up and lunged, hoping to grab his shirt or pants and pull him onto the bed. But he moved out of the way just in time.

"You're just a stupid sissy girl! You can't hurt me!" he taunted as he backed me into the corner next to the bed and began slapping me in the face with his open hand.

Frustrated and cornered, I reached down to the bedside table and fumbled for something, anything, to hit him with. The first thing my hand touched was a pencil. In a fit of rage I grabbed it and struck out at him. This time he didn't move out of the way.

Neither of us moved for a few seconds. Both of us stared at his arm as the wound began to bleed. I could see that the lead had broken off and was in his arm. Shawn looked up at me as if he didn't believe what I had done. He started to cry. Then he screamed. My eyes wide with terror, I wanted to scream, too. Seconds later Jim was in the doorway with a questioning frown of disapproval on his face and a bottle of beer in his hand.

"What happened?" he asked, stepping into the room.

"Nothing," I answered, trying to hide how guilty and wrong I felt.

Holding his wounded arm up for Jim's inspection, Shawn cried, "She stabbed me with a pencil, and look, the lead is still stuck under the skin." The blood was dripping onto the floor. Jim quickly put his beer on the bureau, pulled a handkerchief from his pocket and pressed it on the wound.

"My God, Barbara, is that true?" Jim demanded.

"I didn't do anything," I mumbled, wishing I was invisible.

"You did, too!" Shawn protested. "She's lying to you, Jim!"

Jim stared at me and demanded, "Barbara, tell me the truth!"

I took a deep breath and held it. Jim kept looking at me, waiting. I looked away. I knew I should be telling the truth, but I was too scared. I was certain that if he knew that I had lied, he wouldn't love me anymore. I backed slowly into the corner, looking at the blood streaming from the wound and realized that I had to tell the truth.

Through my tears I looked at the handkerchief soaking with blood and whispered, "I did it. I had to. He was beating me."

Jim called for Mother. When she came into the room, he told her what had happened. She looked at me, disappointed. I felt ashamed. She took Shawn's arm and escorted him into the bathroom. Jim took me firmly by the hand and walked me down the hall to my bedroom. He closed the door and had me sit on the bed.

Sitting down next to me he said in a solemn voice, "I have to punish you, Barbara, because you hurt Shawn and because you lied. If you had told me the truth, I wouldn't be as hard on you but since you lied, your punishment will be double."

I watched in horror as he stood up and took off his belt. I was flooded with memories of my real father's belt, the beatings, the welts, the pain, the humiliation. I began to tremble.

He folded the belt in half and took a swing at the bed next to me. I jumped. He told me to lie on my stomach. Shivering and sobbing in bitter disappointment, I did as I was told, and waited for the blow that would end my fantasy of a perfect life. Devastated, I realized that nothing had really changed after all, that life wasn't going to be any better than with my natural father.

He hit me with the belt. I waited for the pain but felt none. He hit again. Still no pain. The belt barely made a sound, much less hurt. I knew I was supposed to be crying. I didn't want to risk him hitting me harder, so I pretended to cry. After hitting me about five times, he said in a very serious voice, "I hope you've learned your lesson, young lady," and left the room.

I was astounded. The fantasy wasn't over! If this was an example of double punishment, then life had changed for the better. I was convinced at that moment that Jim loved me so much that he would never really hurt me. I was nine years old and I was in love. My daddy was perfect. And it was important that I constantly think of ways to please him so he would know how much I loved him and to make sure that he always loved me.

He continued to treat me like a princess and to shower me with affection. So a year later, when he gave me extra attention while Mother was in the hospital, I accepted it as another example of how much he loved me.

The first night that Mother was gone, Jim came into my room and invited me to cuddle with him in their bed. I was grateful that he knew how scared I was. He told me not to tell Shawn because Shawn might be jealous. This would be our secret. I felt important. He was so good to me. He held me, caressed and comforted me, soothing my fears, helping me to feel less alone. Lying in his arms, I felt warm, safe and loved. He gently rubbed my back, my shoulders, my chest and my stomach until I fell asleep. We did that each night. Jim was really comforting me.

It was the fourth evening since Mother had gone. As usual Jim came home from work about six o'clock. I hugged and kissed him. He walked to his favorite chair, took off his shoes, leaned back, took a pack of cigarettes from his shirt pocket and lit one. I sat down on the floor in front of him waiting for the question. He looked at me, smiled and asked. "Why don't you bring me a beer, sweetheart?"

Every night he had the same ritual, asking whomever he saw first to fetch him a beer, then sitting in his chair drinking and smoking. I felt very special when I was the one asked, especially while Mother was in the hospital. I jumped up and ran to the kitchen. I brought back his can of beer, sat down on the arm of his chair and asked, "How was your day today, Daddy?" It was just like Mother would have done.

"Okay, little sweetheart," he answered, "but I'm really tired. How was your day?"

Feeling very important and grownup, I told him about school. He had me fetch him another beer, sipped it for a while, then went to his room to change from his work clothes.

Our neighbors Cheryl and Carl had invited us to dinner that night. When Jim was ready, the three of us went next door. After dinner Jim went to the hospital to see Mother. While he was gone, I helped Cheryl clean up the kitchen. Shawn and I played until Jim came back at eight-thirty, then we went home.

"How's Mommy?" I asked as we walked to the house.

"She's doing a little better," he answered, "but she's still in a lot of pain."

Following him into the kitchen where he took a beer out of the refrigerator I asked, "Are you sure she's all right?" I was feeling scared about her pain.

"Yes, sweetheart, she's going to be fine. Now stop worrying!" he said, sounding annoyed with me.

"Okay, Daddy, I'll try."

"Good girl," he said with a little smile. "Now give me a kiss good night, it's way past your bedtime."

I kissed him good night, went to bed and fell asleep almost immediately. I awoke to a hand gently shaking my shoulder. The house was dark and very quiet and for a moment I felt confused. With his face very close to mine, Jim whispered, "Why don't you come sleep in my bed again tonight, Baby? I know how sad you feel about Mommy."

I wrinkled my nose at the smell of stale beer and cigarettes. I didn't really want to wake up but then thought that maybe he was lonely, too. Without saying a word, I left my bed and followed him across the hall, climbed up into his bed and curled up ready to go back to sleep. I glanced at the alarm clock on the night stand. It was ten forty-five.

The now familiar caresses began at once. For several minutes, I lay motion-less and relaxed, letting his gentle fondling lull me to sleep. But then his hands began to move across my body with more intensity. My body tightened as I became very aware of his movements. I held my breath.

His hand slid between my legs, and he began tickling me roughly with his fingers. My body stiffened. This was very different!

He told me to relax and that he loved me as his hands and fingers became more insistent, more intense, more demanding, with none of the gentleness of the other times. Then he pulled me over so that I was facing him. I trembled. He kissed me, not the normal peck but something very different. This time he kept his lips on mine and tried to bite my lips and even tried to put his tongue in my mouth. I didn't know what to do. I was petrified and thought I would throw up from the smell of beer and stale tobacco.

Just as I was sure I would vomit, he rolled his body on top of mine. He was so heavy that I could just barely breathe. This was not like the other nights or anything I had ever imagined. I didn't like this at all. I wanted him to stop but I wasn't sure if telling him to stop would be okay. I started to struggle.

He tightened his hold on me and whispered, "Sh-h-h-h! It's okay." I knew I should believe him, but it didn't feel okay. It felt like I was dying and I couldn't do anything about it.

I stopped struggling and lay still, holding my breath. Suddenly his hand was back between my legs massaging my privates, then as suddenly, he was pulling my legs apart as he continued to kiss me and tell me to be quiet. There was something sticking into my privates. His body shifted abruptly and I felt a hideous stabbing pain between my legs. I gulped for air and the pain sharpened. In the darkness my eyes bulged with fear. I almost fainted. I held my breath for an instant then opened my mouth to scream. I managed barely a muffled cry against his body when he slapped his hand over my mouth.

"Shut up!" he hissed, "Lay still!" He was angry with me.

I thought he was going to kill me. I began to cry.

He wouldn't stop hurting me. He was bouncing his body on me. I didn't know what was happening. Everything had gone crazy. I didn't know what he was doing or why he was hurting me or what I had done wrong.

This was my new Daddy! He took care of me and loved me! My mind whirled with confusion.

I was not strong enough to fight him or to push him off. I surrendered in confusion and pain. An eternity seemed to pass before he collapsed on top of me. I thought I was going to die under his weight. After a few moments he rolled off. I turned to the wall and stuffed my fist in my mouth to stifle my sobs. Silent tears coursed down my face and onto the pillow. My whole body trembled.

"That wasn't so bad, was it?" he whispered to me in the darkness. My body stiffened again. I said nothing. I couldn't speak or move. I could barely breathe. Slurring each word he said, "I love you, sweetheart."

I wanted to shout back that I hated him! He had made me trust him and then he had hurt me. But I couldn't force myself to speak. Every muscle in my body was a solid mass of tension. I lay silent and painfully still, hating him and knowing I must be a terrible person to deserve so much punishment.

Before long his deep breathing let me know he was asleep. Controlling every movement so as not to awaken him, I crept out of the bed, turning once to make sure he was still asleep. I tiptoed out of his room, across the hall to my room and climbed back into bed. In the darkness of my room I retreated deep within my blankets, curled up as tight as I could and buried my face in my pillow.

I sobbed as silently as possible, fearing that even the smallest sound might awaken him and bring him into my room. My legs, my mouth, my back, my insides, every part of my body felt hurt and assaulted. Terror reached out of the night and taunted me. I could not huddle deep enough under my blankets to make myself feel safe.

Unanswered questions bombarded me in the darkness as I wept. Why had he done that? Had I done something wrong? What was the matter with me? Why did he want to hurt me?

Deep disappointment replaced my dream of having a perfect life with a loving daddy. Nothing had changed, I thought bitterly. It was even worse. I'd never be okay. I'd never have what I wanted. No one cared about me and no one really loved me. I felt so alone.

The next thought filled me with alarm. What if he wanted to do that again? What would I do?

There might be some chance that he still loved me, but if I didn't let him, for sure he wouldn't like me anymore. What would I do then?

I wished Mother was home. I wanted someone to cling to, someone to talk to. The pain, both physical and emotional was terrible. Still I thought maybe he didn't mean to hurt me.

I tossed and turned for hours and finally drifted into a fitful sleep. Sometime during that night I opened my eyes with a start and saw him standing next to my bed. I pulled the blankets tight thinking he was going to do it again. A chill swept through me as he bent down and whispered, "This is our little secret. We won't ever tell anyone, will we, sweetheart?" I quickly shook my head. He nodded and left the room. My body ached. I could not sleep again that night.

First Breakthrough

When Barbara first came to see me, her presenting problem was her inability and yet urgent desire "just to be able to cope from day to day." She believed that the reason for that inability to cope was the rape by her stepfather and the subsequent incestuous relationship that continued for five years until she finally put a stop to it.

To the outside world Barbara may have appeared to be coping. We might even say that she *was* coping if coping means *making do* with feeling miserable. Now in a second marriage with a kind, gentle young man who had started his own construction business, she lived in a quiet suburb near Los Angeles. Her son and daughter, who were at that time living with their father, her first husband, came to visit bimonthly.

Barbara had all the appearances of stability. She worked as a secretary for another construction company where her boss respected her. She was sociable and well-liked. But she had a weight problem and internally she was a volcano waiting to erupt.

The first day Barbara came in, I asked her if she had done any therapy or counselling prior to that session. She said she had been in a 12-Step program, had seen a therapist for a year between 1972 and 1973, before her divorce and that she was now "seeing" her best friend, Lorna.

Lorna, as it turned out, was unlicensed. She had a bachelor's degree and a Parent Effectiveness Trainers' Certificate. Barbara intentionally did not tell me at the time that her friend had actually referred her to me after one of their quarrels, so I assumed that Lorna did not know. I told Barbara that if Lorna had been licensed, I could not have worked with her until she had told her therapist that she was leaving her. I pointed out that although Lorna was not a licensed therapist, it would still be a good idea for Barbara to be responsible for telling her friend what she was doing and make a clean break with her friend in the therapeutic aspect of their relationship.

As Barbara sat reeling off a capsule version of her life and therapy, I could see clearly that her previous psychological work had barely reached the tip of the iceberg. Neither her friend nor her therapist had dealt with her addictive process nor the family dysfunction. What Barbara had achieved in her previous therapy and in a 12-Step program was the ability to talk about the incest. She had taken a first step that was vital. Had she not, our work would have had to start with that.

"Secrets breed sickness" is a phrase that I have been using since I began working as a therapist. An important part of the healing process is the communication of *our* secrets. The reasons for this are numerous. First, secrets keep the dysfunctional system, whether it is the personal or the family system, a closed system. Second, when we need to keep something a secret, we have already assumed that it is wrong and that we are bad. Third, without talking about the secret, there is no way to find help and to learn how to heal the emotional pain.

Since Barbara had achieved the first stage of letting out the secret and reaching out for help, what remained was the long process of learning to heal the emotional pain. The question was how. Observing Barbara's recitation, I realized she was very good at explaining things and that she was also trying very hard to look as if she were "together," as if she didn't need therapy. I decided that Barbara was already too cognitive and out of touch with her emotions. She needed to do as much deep experiential process work as quickly as she could possibly allow herself. Gauging from the strength that I saw in her, I estimated that she could manage very deep work rapidly.

The therapy that I did with Barbara was my own technique of combining self-generated sensory imagery with Gestalt and Psychodrama processes. To supplement Barbara's experiential work and her subsequent insights, I integrated information about and involvement with family systems ideas, Virginia Satir's material on communication and the Drama Triangle. Later, with the appearance of Adult Children of Alcoholics (ACoA) literature at the end of Barbara's therapy, we were able to take a closer look at the specific dysfunctions of her Alcoholic Family.

After taking a brief history, I asked Barbara if she would be willing to try an experiment with me. When she agreed, I asked her if she would close her eyes, return to that period of time of the initial rape and describe her house as it had looked back then. Having her describe the house gave Barbara an opportunity to approach that time period safely with somewhat objective material. It would give her the chance to pace herself while moving her into, what I call, a right-brain process. This type of process would enable her to experience the events as if they were happening in the present and would also allow her to begin contacting and releasing the stored emotional trauma.

Barbara started by describing the exterior of the house. She approached the front of the house, opened the door, and walked in. She said that she found the house dark and quiet. Suddenly she stopped talking and started to shake.

"Where are you?" I asked.

She replied, "I'm in a corner of my room. It's very dark. I'm all curled up in a ball — a fetal position."

As she spoke, Barbara began to draw her knees up onto the chair, her head moving from side to side, tears streaming down her face. Taking my cue from her head movement, I asked her if she could verbalize the action by saying, "No." Softly and haltingly, she started saying "No."

Deciding to give her verbal permission to let out the pain, I said, "Louder, Barbara, say it louder."

The "No" picked up speed and volume. She was speaking louder. I encouraged her again saying, "Scream it, Barbara."

She did. The "No" eventually turned into blood-curdling screams. The hair on my arms stood up.

Barbara continued screaming until she collapsed into coughing choking sobs.

I had a sense that this was a symbolic scene for Barbara, that she needed to experience and express a general sense of fear and pain before she could manage to deal with the terror of the actual rape.

After the first onset had subsided and Barbara had calmed down a bit, we talked about the nature of the first scene. As I suspected, her perception of what had just happened was that the scene represented how she felt in life, backed into a corner and terrified. More important than that, Barbara noted that she had never felt able nor *allowed* to express her terror nor her objection to the way she was treated. This process gave her the opportunity for the first time in her life to experience and voice both her fear and her protest to the treatment that she had received. This was the beginning of self-support and a return to a sense of self and personal power. Or as Barbara calls it, "The First Breakthrough."

Following our brief exchange about her perceptions, I asked Barbara if she was willing to handle more trauma in this first session. She said she was so we began that night to work on the initial rape. I invited Barbara to go back and be the ten-year-old child and describe the events leading up to the attack. Barbara closed her eyes and in a small frightened voice said that her mother had gone in the hospital four days earlier for emergency kidney surgery.

Every night while her mother was gone, Barbara's stepfather had called her to his bed. Children often believe in the omniscience of parents, and ten-year-old Barbara thought that her stepfather understood her terror about the possibility of losing her mother and having to go live with her natural father.

It was easy to see that she had adored her stepfather and was desperate to please him. Given her prior family background, she was already set up to take care of the emotional needs of the adults in her life. In addition she was frightened of the consequences of disobeying him and thus incurring both his and her mother's disapproval. So Barbara went each night at the summons. What she received at first was pleasant. He fondled her, told her that she was pretty, told her that he loved her. He also told her not to tell her brother. This cuddling was their "little secret."

To a ten-year-old, who was desperate to keep the kindness and attention of her new daddy, this fondling seemed an answer to her untold fears and unspoken requests for the continuing love from her new parent. The fact that he wanted her to keep the cuddling a secret only reinforced her desire to feel and be special.

The fourth night when Barbara was called to his room, he raped her. Remember we are talking about the assault on a slender ten-year-old child by a large man (who also happened to be one of the important authority figures in her life). If we acknowledge that rape by a stranger is an extraordinary trauma for an adult woman, think how much worse it is for a small sexually naive child who had put all her faith and love in her new daddy.

In her book, *Father-Daughter Rape*, Elizabeth Ward notes that:

> Psychological, sociological and theological concerns about the blood or kindred relationship between the victim and the offender, which are contained within the usage of the word "incest," also blur reality, by focusing attention upon who is involved, rather than what is happening. What is happening is that a child is being victimized and that she and the offender usually belong to, and live in, the same family. The particularities of this rape dynamic mean that the offender has almost unlimited access to the victim, in space, and over a long time, as well as the access of parent/adult/male over a girl-child.[1]

What we are talking about is something that most people squeamishly avoid dealing with and that is a form of familial "enslavement." John Bradshaw addressed the issue, in *Bradshaw On: The Family,* when he said,

> The poisonous pedagogy plays a major role in the tragedy of incest and sexual abuse in general. I believe it implicitly gives permission for sexual abuse by promoting a kind of ownership principle that justifies the inequality. If children must obey and honor their parents at any cost, then the parents implicitly have the right over their children's bodies.[2]

When we declare the family sacred and inviolate, we are participating in creating the type of closed system that breeds amazing kinds of dysfunction. When we adhere to the tenets of the poisonous pedagogy which exalts obedience above all else, we are laying the foundation for not only child abuse and incest, but all human abuse and injustice.

If we return to look at Barbara's initial description of the night of the rape in that light, we see that Barbara noted her own distaste of the stale smell of alcohol and cigarettes but put up no protest to that or Jim's awakening her from a deep sleep. Conditioned to obey and to think of others' needs first, her only thought was, "Maybe he's lonely, too."

As Barbara sat with her eyes closed talking about the events on the night of the rape as if they were happening right then, the scene came alive for both of us. She described the preliminary caresses as gentle and soothing, just as they had been for four previous nights. She continued speaking slowly when suddenly she began thrashing again in her chair, tossing her head sideways. She began whimpering, and then a moment later, she started choking and sobbing as she attempted to continue describing the episode. She was having trouble staying with the scene. Her eyes flew open; they were glazed. She was obviously terrified. I asked her if she felt that she could close her eyes again and go on; she nodded and closed them.

Then abruptly she brought her hand up to her mouth. I asked her what was happening. She said that he was placing his hand over her mouth to keep her from screaming out and that he was hurting her. She was sobbing with her hand still tightly clasped over her mouth.

This hand-to-mouth motion, although originating with her stepfather, was to show up frequently in the therapy. It had become symbolic of Barbara's need to "keep her mouth shut" and remain secretive about her feelings and the events in her life. It became indicative of her powerlessness.

I asked her if she could remove her hand. She did. Then I supported her in her next step in that long journey towards personal power and healing. As in the first piece of work, I asked her if she could tell him, "No." At the time of the attack, she could do little more than struggle and whimper with his hand over her mouth. Released from the inability to open her mouth, and having practiced earlier in the symbolic scene, Barbara started softly, hesitantly, to say "No."

Repeating the process of the symbolic scene, I encouraged her once again, "Can you scream, Barbara? Can you really let it out?"

Taking the support, Barbara started to shout and built to a crescendo of the same type of blood-curdling screams that she had expressed before. Then she choked, coughed, and collapsed again into sobs.

After giving Barbara the next few moments to calm down, I asked her if she felt like talking. She said that she did and proceeded to say only one phrase. "I've never done any therapeutic work like that before!"

She then stopped talking and appeared to be watching me for some cue. I asked if she needed something from me? She said she had been waiting for me to tell her that what she had done was unacceptable. Because it was the end of the session, I filed away a mental note to deal later with the issues that were the basis of her fear that she had done something wrong. Instead of opening up another deep painful area, I simply gave her the acceptance she so desperately needed. I told her that there was nothing wrong with what she had done. She would probably be doing it a lot more. I explained to her that most of us have traumatic experiences that we store because we do not know how to complete them, and that judging just from her initial description of her family, she would have many more sessions like this one.

As it turned out, Barbara was to deal directly with the rape scene in the four subsequent sessions and then many more times throughout the therapy. Much later in therapy, Barbara would work on other incest scenes and issues. She would often tell her stepfather how much she hated him and scream out her outrage over the betrayal. Sometimes she would simply shiver and cry. At other times she would pound violently on the futons. Other times she twisted towels into knots. Almost always she would end with choking sobs and coughing. As therapy progressed, she told me she recognized that no matter what she did from that initial session on, she knew that she had begun taking some personal power back in her life and that she was healing. She continued to build on that in each successive session.

I was not surprised that Barbara spent the first five sessions almost entirely on the initial rape. The terror, shock and betrayal, the degree of abandonment that she experienced and the overwhelming sense of shame and self-degradation were to be ongoing issues for Barbara in her recovery process.

Furthermore, the first attack had apparently become a focal point and held symbolic meaning for Barbara. It represented *to her* the beginnings of her adult problems and solidified her belief that something was terribly wrong with her. She did not realize when she first started her process that the difficulties began long before the first assault.

The original rape and the subsequent shock were, as Barbara was to find out, only the first pieces to emerge of the larger picture of both her and her family's dysfunction. With no human to comfort her and driven by a desperate need to avoid the pain and bury the terror, Barbara immediately took to eating both as an avoidance mechanism and in an attempt to soothe herself. As the incest and Jim's already apparent alcoholism both continued to progress, the Alcoholic Family Syndrome began to intensify, and Barbara's early negative programming exploded into full-blown emotional, psychological and behavioral dysfunctions.

The Day After

As the first light of day filtered through my curtains I heard Jim's alarm clock and my body tightened again. Quickly closing my eyes I pretended to be asleep so maybe he would leave me alone. I listened intently for footsteps that would tell me where he went in the house. I heard him walk past my bedroom, through the living room and into the kitchen to make coffee. I had to go to the bathroom really bad, but I was afraid to move. Curling up under my blankets, I lay very still, barely breathing. I heard Jim walk back across the living room, through the hall, into the bathroom. Hearing the door close, I opened my eyes just a bit to make sure he was out of sight. Seeing no one, I relaxed a little, breathed deeply and waited. When I heard the door knob turn, I quickly closed my eyes, held my breath for a moment and listened. The sounds of drawers opening and closet doors banging told me he was putting on his clothes for work.

At last hearing his footsteps take him back to the kitchen, the clink of his cup as he poured coffee, the front door open and close as he left for work, I could finally go to the bathroom. But first I had to make sure he was really gone. I opened the drapes just a crack and watched as he backed his car out of the driveway and drove down the street. I was safe.

Jumping out of bed, I ran to the bathroom and closed the door and sat down on the toilet. I felt a burning sensation as I started to pee. My body tensed. Is something wrong with me? I felt scared. I had no one to ask. I hoped the pain would just go away by itself so I wouldn't have to tell anyone. So I hadn't made it all up, it had really happened. I shivered involuntarily as I remembered the hideous nightmare. I didn't want to remember, I didn't want to think about it. Do something else quick, I screamed in my mind.

I stood up, flushed, looked into the mirror and saw a haunted face staring back at me. I started to cry, then looked away. If I looked any longer, I would lose control. I had to stay in control. I couldn't let on what had happened. I had promised to keep the secret. If I cried, Cheryl would want to know what was wrong. Then I might really be in trouble.

Without stopping to brush my teeth or comb my hair I stumbled out of the bathroom, stopped for a moment to regain my composure and looked to the right. Their bedroom loomed in front of me like a dark and scary cavern. I shivered again and turned as fast as I could. I took a deep breath and tried to calm myself. "Just don't think about it," I muttered to myself.

I walked back across the living room, through the dining area and into the kitchen. After taking a glass from the cupboard, I walked over to the refrigerator, took a carton of milk and sat down at the kitchen table. I filled the glass, gulped down the milk, and refilled the glass.

I started to think again. I wanted my mommy! Desolate tears streamed down my face. I wanted her to hold me, to make all the bad thoughts go away. But Mother was still in the hospital and I had vowed not to tell her. Burying my head in my arms I sobbed. Up until the night before I thought I could go to Jim when I was upset. I had no one, nowhere to turn.

Taking a deep breath to help me control myself, I wiped my tears with a napkin, blew my nose and then tried to figure it all out. Maybe I did something to make him do that, I thought guiltily. I stood up and walked back over to the refrigerator. I opened it and looked in. I pulled out a half-eaten lemon meringue pie.

What had I done? Had it been something I said? Maybe I shouldn't have been so scared about Mommy. After all, she was going to be okay! Perhaps I shouldn't have needed him!

Closing the refrigerator door, I opened the drawer next to it and pulled out a fork.

Maybe if I just acted like nothing happened, he wouldn't want to do it again. I sat down at the table. I would have to act like nothing happened.

I drank the glass of milk and poured another. What about Jim, I wondered. How was he going to act? Maybe if I watched him, I would know what I was supposed to do.

I picked up the fork. I could act more grown-up, like I didn't need anyone to take care of me. If I just stopped worrying, it wouldn't happen again. Gritting my teeth, I made a fist and pounded the table. Act grown-up and stop worrying. That was it, I thought with a burst of determination.

Finally, the bad feelings began to fade and I stopped crying, took a deep breath and stared out of the window.

"Hey!" Shawn shouted at me and I nearly jumped out of my skin. I didn't hear him come into the kitchen. "What are you doing?" he yelled pointing to the table in front of me. "I'm going to tell Jim!"

I looked down at the table. The pie pan was empty. I had eaten half a pie! I had never done that before. I didn't want Shawn to know how bad I felt, so I tried to think of something to say.

"I was hungry!" I whined. "Besides I didn't eat as much dinner as you did last night and you always eat the biggest pieces of pie anyway, so I'm just paying you back!" I countered.

"You're crazy!" he shouted back and stomped out of the kitchen. I knew I was right that he always ate the bigger pieces. I stood up and carried the plate to the sink, washed it and put it away, trying to get rid of the evidence. I convinced myself that Shawn was just being selfish, that he had wanted all the pie to himself.

After he took a shower, he came back in the kitchen, glared at me and took a bowl, spoon, box of cereal and carton of milk to the table. Trying to ignore his anger, I took out my own bowl and spoon and sat down at the table with him. I felt angry, too. He was always putting me in the wrong no matter what I did. I glared right back while I filled my bowl with cereal, sprinkled four spoonfuls of sugar on top and poured in the milk. I was just about to tell him how awful he was when the back door opened and Cheryl, our neighbor, walked in carrying a cup of coffee and a newspaper. Cheryl was helping Jim while Mother was gone by making sure we ate breakfast and left for school on time.

Giving me a little hug and a pat on the head, she said, "Hurry up and finish your breakfast; you still have to get dressed." She walked around the table, kissed Shawn on the cheek, then sat down and started reading the paper. I gobbled up the rest of my cereal, carried my bowl and spoon to the sink and left the kitchen. I didn't think much about anything until later, when Mr. Parker gave the geography lesson.

I couldn't concentrate on the lesson. I felt hungry. I looked at the clock to see how long it was until lunch. The clock read ten forty-five. Suddenly bits of memory from the night before flashed into my thoughts. I shivered, shook my head and ordered myself not to think about it. I wanted something to eat. It wouldn't be lunch time for over an hour, but I didn't know if I could wait. I wished that I had stuck a few cookies in my pocket. My stomach started growling. By eleven-thirty I had a stomachache. Fifteen minutes before the bell rang, I put my head down on the desk and closed my eyes, hoping that the pain would go away. The minute I closed my eyes I saw Jim's face as it had loomed above me the night before. My eyes snapped open and I sat up straight and tried to listen to Mr. Parker.

Finally the bell rang and I ran to the cafeteria. Normally, I was so anxious to join my friends on the playground that I didn't eat all my lunch. But that day I ate every bit of my lunch and even went back for seconds before the hungry feeling started to go away.

At home that afternoon after school, I did my chores. I vacuumed the living room, swept the kitchen floor, shook out the rugs, cleaned the bathroom. The same as every other day. Afterwards I tried to do my homework but I couldn't concentrate. Shawn was still angry about the pie and wasn't speaking to me. I felt guilty and decided to do something to make it up to him. I went next door to Cheryl's house and asked her if I could bake some cookies. She said okay and came over to our house to help me. We made a double batch of chocolate chip cookies, Shawn's favorites. I ate six of the cookies as they came out of the oven. When they were cooled, I put six more cookies on a plate and took them with a glass of milk to Shawn.

"See, I made these just for you!" I offered. Then as an afterthought, "Please don't tell Jim I ate the pie."

"Okay, I won't . . . this time. But you better not do it again, or I will tell him," he warned. I was safe.

Two days later Mother came home from the hospital, looking pale and thin. Dressed in a bathrobe and slippers, her steps were small and stiff as she leaned heavily on Jim and walked the 20 feet from the carport to the front door. I walked next to her, wanting to help, too, but afraid that touching her might hurt her, wanting her to take care of me and feeling guilty for needing attention when she was so sick.

"Open the front door for Mommy," Jim instructed. I ran ahead and held the door open as they walked past me into the house. Jim helped her into their bedroom. I followed and stood in the doorway and watched as he helped her take off her robe and climb into bed. I felt scared when I saw her wince as she sat on the bed. I wanted her to feel better but I didn't know what to do. Jim pulled the blankets over her, tucked her in, and handed her a book to read. He was being tender and caring. A sudden wave of jealousy swept over me as I realized that he loved her more than he loved me.

"We're going to take good care of Mommy while she recovers, aren't we, sweetheart?" Jim said to me.

I nodded my head, but on the inside I was wondering sadly if anyone was ever going to take care of me again.

Turning back to Mother, he said, "Barbara and I are going to make your dinner. You just rest and read. We'll take care of everything." Mother smiled at me and I felt a little safer. She leaned back on her pillows, sighed and closed her eyes.

I followed Jim into the kitchen, glad to have him to myself. Together we prepared tomato soup and tuna sandwiches for dinner. Following his directions, I toasted the bread and stirred soup, and set the table. When everything was perfect and had passed Jim's inspection, he helped Mother to the table. They chatted with each other during most of the meal while I ate both my sandwich and half of hers, two bowls of soup and two big glasses of milk. Before I went to bed, I ate a banana, six cookies and two more glasses of milk. Lying in my bed I felt a little sick and wondered if I was getting the flu.

I was wrong about Jim. Even though I learned to act like nothing was happening, his attacks didn't stop. When Mother was well enough to go back to work and back to her frequent activities with her women's club, he came at me again. He was usually drunk, and Mother was usually gone. And I didn't tell anyone.

A few years later, I started to gain weight.

Origin Of An Eating Disorder

Considering Barbara's vivid description of the "day after," you would think that her understanding of the origin of her eating disorder was an easy and immediate accomplishment. It was not. Barbara had spent months in a 12-Step program exploring the issues of overeating. She intellectually understood that the weight was a barrier she had put up, the only boundary she had between herself and "them." It took her many more months of painful processing to piece together the experiences of the "day after" and begin to acknowledge and break down the barrier to her own emotions that the eating had become. That work came only after she was more prepared to deal with the larger implications of the family problems.

What we are presented with is the picture of an abused and abandoned ten-year-old child, a child in pain with nowhere to turn now except to food. From previous information we know some of the real reasons Barbara chose not to tell her mother. Barbara's early training subconsciously told her that her mother would not be able to deal with the problem. Although she recognized her mother's inability to fix things, Barbara assumed that it came from the fact that something "unfixable" was wrong with her. She had always been to blame for the things that went wrong. Why not this, too?

Tortured with shame, desperate to find a solution to her pain, unable to deal with the traumatic effects of the rape and misunderstanding the turmoil in her body, Barbara ate. She ate to deal with the gnawing feelings of terror and grief in her gut that she had not known how to identify, to avoid the memory of the face looming over her in the darkness and to dull the pain of her loneliness and abandonment. Barbara had found her drug of choice, food.

The Healing Goes On

Process work is rarely linear. The emotional traumas, the negative self-image and tapes and the myriad of defense mechanisms are woven into a patchwork quilt that raises issues based on the importance of associations rather than on linear time. So when Barbara came back the second time and attempted to apologize for the work of the first session, I remembered her fear of doing wrong and her strong need for acceptance that had surfaced at the end of the first session. I was not sure where Barbara would go with the second session as I let her take the lead.

She said that she was feeling very guilty for being so "dramatic." Taking into account that most people are very uncomfortable when they first do processing, I was struck by her use of the word "dramatic."

When I asked her who had told her that she was so dramatic, she blurted out, "Everyone — my mother." I asked her when this had happened. Briefly and in an obvious hurry, she mumbled, "Lots of times." When I asked for an example, she hastily described a scene in which her mother had accused her of becoming more hysterical after offering Barbara some comfort.

Guessing at her answer but figuring that I would give it a chance anyway, I asked Barbara if she wanted to work on that scene. She said, "No, I think I'd rather work on the rape." Barbara was not ready to broach the subject of Mother. She appeared to be sticking with something that she somehow now saw as safe, even though it was immensely painful. Since it was only the second session, and since she was dealing with and progressing through the initial trauma and pain, I decided not to confront her yet on other problem areas.

She needed to learn to trust her own feelings and perceptions and allow her strength to build as she completed the emotional pain of the past. She would have sufficient time in therapy to experience the basic life decisions that she had made about herself and the world and to discover the processes and defense mechanisms that she used to deal with her environment.

Actually, it didn't take Barbara long to approach the other problems. By the sixth session, the issue of Barbara's relationship with her mother surfaced in such a way that she decided that she could no longer avoid it. Coming into that session with the agenda that I often request people to have, Barbara was ready to deal with her relationship with her best friend, Lorna.

As Barbara started to describe her friend's behavior, I asked her, "Who does she remind you of?" Before Barbara could stop and think, she answered, "My mother." She paused, pursed her lips, looked up at me and said, "I knew that this was coming." She then smiled, adding, "You did, too."

During the second and third session I had explained to Barbara that numerous other scenes might surface for her when she was processing or when we were talking. I mentioned that she might wish to make a mental note about them for further sessions or for processing at home by herself. Barbara said that she realized that each time, during the five previous sessions, when I would ask her where she had got some of her rules or ideas about emotions, her answer would always come back to her mother. She told me that although she had not worked on any of the scenes with her mother that had flashed into her head as a result of my questions, she did realize that her mother, and not just her stepfather, really was an issue for her and that she had been avoiding it.

She also realized, as a result of the processing, that she had not reached out to her mother for help during the incest and had never even told her about it. She said that she was beginning to have a sense that her mother was more deeply associated with her eating problems than she had wanted to admit. Barbara decided that it was time to explore what that association was and also what had prevented her from communicating with her mother about her pain.

"You're Not To Blame, Barbara"

Two of the early topics that I broached with Barbara were Jim's alcoholism plus Maureen's and the family's severe dysfunction. Neither topic had been approached before. Even though Barbara mentioned the huge amounts of beer that Jim consumed, she obviously did not realize that she was from an alcoholic background. Frequently in alcoholic homes the denial is so all-encompassing, the family members not only do not talk about the alcoholism outside of the family, they cannot even recognize it as alcoholism. Barbara's family was no exception.

The first time I asked Barbara if Jim was an alcoholic, she looked puzzled and replied, "No, he only drinks beer." Realizing that telling her he could be alcoholic even if he only drank beer might simply result in denial, I decided to ask her if he and the family demonstrated any of a number of behaviors that we, in the helping professions, have come to identify as associated with alcoholism and dysfunctional families. When Barbara asked me how I knew so much about her family, I simply told her that the things I had enumerated were either recognized alcoholic or dysfunctional behavior. At the time that Barbara and I began this work, there was no Adult Children of Alcoholics literature, but there was sufficient information on dysfunctional families to give Barbara an understanding of her disease process.

I began by asking Barbara, "Did your mother or Jim ever make you feel that you were to blame for his drinking? Do you feel that Mother is a hard-working saint and that you're the only thing wrong with the family? And if they could have fixed you, everything would have been perfect?"

When I finished the list, Barbara sat quietly for a moment before she burst into tears, saying, "I can't believe I'm not to blame."

As in many alcoholic or severely dysfunctional homes, Barbara's parents chose to ignore the real problems and looked for a scapegoat to blame for the family ills. Actually Maureen had already been blaming Barbara for her emotional responses long before Jim came on the scene. So given that dynamic in the family and given the enormous shame and guilt that Jim would have felt and denied after the rape, it was not so unusual for him to begin to use Barbara as a scapegoat in order to mask his reprehensible behavior. As the incest continued, along with Jim's escalating alcoholism, it became more and more important for Jim to make Barbara wrong in order to justify to himself the ongoing incest and to assuage his own growing shame. Although none of Jim's actual emotional process has come to light yet even in his recovery, what we do know about all types of perpetrators (alcoholics, abusers, co-dependents alike) is that they are desperate to place the blame elsewhere to avoid facing their own growing subconscious shame.

The continuation of Barbara's eating disorder was inter-related with numerous other issues. Enveloped in the growing shame of the ongoing incest, programmed to look outside for approval, and having been designated as the family scapegoat, Barbara's life was to become a downward spiral of self-blame, shame and dysfunctional behavior. Later on, she would try anything she could think of to feel normal and be accepted.

She would try a name change at age thirteen to Bobbi. She would try diets, pills, other drugs, promiscuity, marriage, a child and she would find that nothing worked. With the eventual help of a 12-Step support group, she would lose weight. She would even go into what she now calls talk therapy, only to find that the pain and suffering would not diminish.

Barbara was later to discover that the suffering did not diminish because she needed to deal with these types of problems from a broad approach which included not only confronting the addiction, but also dealing with the family system and doing the kind of deep process therapy that allows a person to reclaim selfhood.

Without a broad-based approach to the healing process people will, more often than not, simply switch addictions or develop other psychological or emotional symptoms. Barbara was a good example of that. She was multiple addicted when she came to me . . . addicted to cigarettes, addicted to the up-and-down diet-binge cycle and for a short time she had been addicted to diet pills.

She was also, as she once so aptly put it, an acceptance junkie. In fact, in addition to her addiction to food, her other main addiction was to attention and acceptance. This need for acceptance and attention and her eating disorder all became tangled up in the other issues of her self-image, powerlessness, emotional dysfunction, defense mechanisms, boundary issues and, of course, the incest.

The beginning of her healing process came when Barbara found out at a 12-Step meeting that she was not the only woman in the world who had been molested by a parent or stepparent. This realization was a vital piece in her healing process and the fact that someone was able to stand up in front of an entire group of mixed company and share it, did a lot for Barbara's self-debasing judgments.

The pitfall in her talk therapy, especially where there was no acknowledgment of the addictive process, was that the cognitive information and understanding that Barbara had about herself had not stopped the pain nor supported her in implementing any new viable tools with which to deal with the world. It had also reinforced the idea that someone was to blame for her pain.

In process work, Barbara was to learn that she was responsible for learning to complete her own pain, no matter who had caused the circumstances in which that pain had occurred. She was also to learn that true understanding occurs as a part of the experiential insights, not cognitive intellectualization. This type of insight comes from the inside out, not the outside in. In time as a result of her process work, Barbara's internal insights integrated into a working whole, and supported her in developing new tools to function within the world. As the work progressed, Barbara began to experience, little by little, the unfolding of her true Self.

3

"Stop It,
Barbara Jeanne!"

Several months after my birth in suburban Los Angeles, we moved north to a sleepy town on a main highway near the ocean and lived in a dilapidated trailer. When I was two, we moved north again, this time to the outskirts of San Luis Obispo where we rented a small two-bedroom house on the edge of a run-down housing development.

One warm evening after putting me in my crib, Mother opened the window above me, and pinned the curtains back with a thumbtack to let the evening breeze cool the room and lull me to sleep. She adjusted a light blanket, smiled and lovingly patted my head.

"Sleep time, sweetheart. See you in the morning," she said bending down to kiss me, then turning on the night-light before leaving.

I wasn't interested in sleeping and began exploring my crib and the dresser beside it. Seeing one of the curtains dancing in a sudden gust of wind, I reached to grab it, but missed. I stood up and then succeeded in grabbing it and began to pull. As I tugged one way and then the other, the curtain came loose and something fell into my crib with a soft "plop."

I began to search for whatever it was. I found it, picked it up and examined it. One end was flat, round, smooth, and painted red. The other end was sharp. Ow! It stuck my finger. I put my finger in my mouth and sucked on it, and then put the tack in my mouth and stood up again while rolling the tack around with my tongue. Suddenly the tack was in the back of my mouth. I started to gag, became scared and then it was gone!

I felt a burning pain, grasped at my throat and fell backwards as my whole body stiffened. I stopped breathing for a moment. My eyes widened and then momentarily glazed. I did not cry or scream for several moments, but lay rigid and unmoving, hearing Mommy's voice inside my head.

". . . Bad girl . . . . Spit it out, Barbara! . . ."

I tried but couldn't spit it out. It was too far in my throat. I swallowed and a red hot pain ripped through my throat. I screamed.

I screamed again. And again. Finally, I looked up and Mother was standing at the door.

"Mommy, Mommy," I cried, and started to stand up reaching out to her.

Then, to my astonishment, she suddenly turned and ran from the room.

"Mommy! Mommy! Mommy!" I shrieked, reaching out my arms to the silent empty doorway.

Pain ripped through my neck. It felt like I was being torn open from the inside. There was an awful taste in my mouth and each time I screamed I sprayed blood.

Suddenly she was back scooping me up in her arms, and running through the house, out the front door, down the walk and into a car. Holding me against her chest, she shouted at the driver and the car started to move.

"Sh-h-h-h-h, Barbara, stop crying. It's okay."

After a short ride, the car suddenly stopped and Mother got out with her arms tightly around me. She ran into the building, talking excitedly to a lady, then handed me to another woman wearing a black veil over her head, who carried me to a hard, cold table and held me down. The table started moving as Mother turned away from me and walked in the opposite direction.

"Mommy! Mommy!" I begged, needing her to come with me. I was terrified, but she didn't even turn around when I called. What terrible thing had I done?

They moved me down a hallway and into a brightly lit room where I lay shivering. Along with the lady in the black veil, several people dressed in white gathered around the table, looking down at me. I didn't recognize any of them and didn't want them near me. Two of them had white masks and white hats. I had never seen anyone dressed like them. I closed my eyes so I wouldn't have to look at them. One of the masked men said something to the lady in black and she moved to hold my arms as somebody else held my legs. My eyes flew open and I began to struggle.

One of the men tried to force something hard and cold down my throat. I jerked my head to the side to make him stop. It worked! He left me alone.

But then there was a sharp stabbing pain in my left arm. I screamed and turned in time to see the woman sticking my arm with a pin.

Almost immediately everything became blurry.

I woke up as Mother was carrying me into the house. I was no longer crying. She sat me down in my eating-chair and soon was feeding me sweet creamy cereal. The warmth felt good but each swallow caused pain. Even so, back in the safety of home, I finally began to relax. Finished, Mother picked me up and carried me to my room. As she put me in my bed, I kept my arms around her neck. I was frightened and didn't want her to leave. Instead of hugging me back, she firmly took my arms from her neck. I started to cry.

Shaking her head, she frowned and said, "You're okay now, Barbara. Now be a good girl and stop crying. Just close your eyes and go to sleep."

I started to whimper as she turned and left the room. Thinking that I must have done something wrong, I cried myself to sleep.

At age three we moved to a tiny rented two-bedroom apartment. It was at the end of a dilapidated row of buildings on a dirt road near the main highway in the middle of a farming valley.

One warm sunny afternoon, I toddled over to a barn across the dirt road. The barn was being painted bright blue. Discarded paint cans lying in a heap were much too tempting for me to ignore. Within minutes I was poking around in the middle of the pile. Dipping my hands in, I finger-painted a piece of scrap plywood, then painted my dress, arms and legs. I was delighted to discover that mixing paint with dirt made wonderfully colored mud pies. I added the paint/mud mixture to my clothes and body, giggling and laughing at how funny it looked.

After nearly a half-hour, I heard Mother's voice calling, "Barbara? Barbara, come home now!"

Looking down at myself, I frowned at my mess. "Oh, oh!" I said, eyes widening. "Dirty dress!" Sometimes Mother got angry when I got dirty.

"Barbara? . . . Barbara!" she called again, "Hurry up, it's time for dinner."

I ran around the barn and across the dirt road to where Mother was standing on the porch. She had her hands on her hips, head raised and her eyebrows knitted in a frown. She glared down at me. I stopped, turned my head to the side and down, not wanting to look at her. I hated it when Mother was angry with me.

"Barbara Jeanne! What did you do?" she shouted. "Shame on you! Bad girl! Come here this instant."

I didn't move, unsure about going to her "this instant," especially after she had said "bad girl."

"Barbara?" she said in a threatening voice.

Tears forming in my eyes, I slowly walked to the porch. She bent down, grabbed my arm so tight that it hurt and dragged me into the house. "Mommy . . . !" I started to protest.

"Don't you 'Mommy' me, Barbara Jeanne," she interrupted. "Just look what you've done to your pretty dress!" she shouted. Roughly undoing the buttons of my pinafore, she yanked it over my head, then grabbing my arm again, hauled me into the bathroom. She sat me down on the toilet with a thump, then reached over to the sink and turned on the hot water full blast. I flinched as the scalding water splashed my face. Grabbing a wash cloth she rubbed it with soap under the steaming faucet.

"Stand up!" she ordered, without even looking at me.

I stood up, shivering in spite of the warm air, and Mother began scrubbing the paint. Face, hands, arms, legs and feet, hurting me with her roughness and with the hot cloth.

"Mommy! You're hurting me! Stop!" I screamed over and over, trying to pull away.

"You just hold still, young lady, and hush!" she shouted angrily, "If you hadn't made such a mess I wouldn't have to do this!" I bit my lips trying to keep from crying out. On she went until finally the paint was gone and my skin was red and raw.

Then she pulled me to my room, dressed me in pajamas and put me to bed, even though it was still light outside. I must never do anything like that again, I kept thinking, then cried myself to sleep.

Our next home when I was six was a small three-bedroom house across the street from a drive-in theater. On warm nights, Shawn and I would sit on the front porch watching movies, trying to figure out what the actors were saying or making up dialogue of our own.

One Saturday afternoon during the summer, Shawn, Amanda and I set up an obstacle race on the sidewalk using pots and pans from our mothers' kitchens. When Amanda and I raced with our scooters, I was barely in the lead with Amanda closing fast. Dashing past the last gate and sprinting for the finish line, I suddenly caught my foot in a crack in the walk, lost my balance and fell down hard. I must have slid for several feet, scraping knees and elbows. Adding insult to injury, Amanda flew past in a blaze of brown hair and red scooter, shouting "I won! I won!"

I sat up slowly, looked down at my knees and saw that one was starting to bleed. I screamed. Amanda turned around with a surprised look, stopped yelling about how she'd won and ran back to me.

"Barbara, are you all right?" she asked looking concerned.

"No," I cried, then pointed to the blood with a gasp.

Taking a deep breath I yelled, "Mommy!" I looked around and couldn't see her, then remembered that she was at the side of the house tending her small flower garden. Helping me to my feet, Amanda let me lean on her as I limped toward the driveway. As we rounded the corner I saw Mother bent over her snapdragons, a small shears in her gloved hands. Breaking away from Amanda I hobbled with an exaggerated limp, hoping Mother would feel sorry for me and help me.

"Mommy!" I cried when I realized she wasn't looking, "I fell and hurt my leg. Look! My knee's bleeding and . . ."

"Sh-h-h-h-h! Barbara, be quiet and let me see what you've done to yourself." She spent a few moments examining the knee while I sniveled and snuffled. She touched a spot that was starting to bruise and I cried out in pain.

"Come on, Barbara! It's not that bad," she ordered, sounding cranky.

What did she mean? Couldn't she see how bad it was bleeding?

"Mommy!" I protested. "It hurts — a lot!" I shouted, wanting to convince her. Her face registered surprise then anger as she grabbed my shoulders and shook me.

"You're getting hysterical. I told you it's not that bad!" she shouted. But by then I was sobbing uncontrollably and I couldn't make myself stop. The next thing I knew she slapped my face, shocking me into silence.

"Stop it!" she yelled, her eyes bulging with anger. "Stop it this instant! You're hysterical and you're embarrassing me!"

Looking over my shoulders, her face turned crimson as she seemed to notice Amanda for the first time. She frowned, stood up abruptly, and said in a harsh voice, "Come with me, Barbara" and didn't even turn around to see if I needed help. She doesn't care, I thought, and she's probably disappointed with me for having lost control and getting "hysterical!" If I could just remember not to cry so loud, she would approve of me and then maybe she would take care of me. Amanda didn't seem to make a big fuss when she hurt herself, and her mother always took care of her. I was obviously doing something wrong, I thought, as I lowered my head in shame and followed Mother into the house.

Mother washed my knee, which had stopped bleeding, announced that it didn't need a Band-Aid and sent me back out to play with my friends, saying, "See, I told you it wasn't that bad. You should be ashamed of yourself, making all that noise for just one skinned knee. Next time, try to control yourself."

I nodded my head in agreement, even though inside I felt confused. "How do people know when something is bad and when it's not?" I wondered, trying not to cry. I didn't want Mother to be angry anymore.

But no matter how much I tried to avoid it, it seemed I was always making Mother angry for some reason or another. Even when things happened that weren't my fault, she got mad at me. Like the time when Amanda and I were helping Mark, a neighbor, weed his front yard.

Mark's family had moved to our neighborhood a few months before summer vacation began. Shawn, Amanda, Mark, Louise from down the street, and I had planned an "explorer" picnic for a Saturday morning, one of our favorite pastimes. Taking sack lunches we would head off towards the pastures at the edge of town, and spend the afternoon pretending to be explorers charting new territories and forging trails in the wilderness.

Mark's dad had other plans. The front yard of their house had not been well kept by the previous owners and he wanted to start landscaping. Clearing the weeds and crabgrass was the first step and Mark had been recruited to help. We all decided to pitch in and pull weeds, hoping that his dad would let him go earlier.

A giant pine stood in the middle of the front lawn, surrounded by a foot high mass of tangled weeds. I was assigned to pull out as many as I could. Amanda and Shawn were given hoes to help break up the crabgrass. Louise and Mark were clearing weeds next to the house.

Grabbing a huge handful of stubborn weeds, I put one foot behind for better leverage. With every ounce of energy I had I strained to pull them from the earth. Just as they were beginning to loosen, there was a burning stab in my left ankle. Screaming in agony, I fell to my knees, rolled over and grabbed my ankle and found a small deep wound gushing blood. I saw a speck of white and bent closer to see what it was. When I realized that it was bone, I screamed again, this time more in fear than pain.

Amanda was yelling. I looked up and saw a horrified expression on her face and tears streaming down her face. "It's my fault. I'm sorry, I'm sorry!" she shrieked.

She held the hoe in her hands. Amanda had been laughing with Shawn and not paying attention. I stepped back to gain a better foothold as her hoe came down on the same spot.

Mrs. Small, Amanda's mother, heard our screams and ran across the lawn, first to Amanda who stood sobbing, "It's my fault, it's my fault."

"It's okay, Amanda," I cried, even though it wasn't. "But get my mother. Please get my mother," I begged.

Mrs. Small bent down to look at my ankle and said, "Looks like you'll need stitches in this one, Barbara."

I wasn't sure exactly what stitches were but knew they were painful.

"You lay here and I'll go get your mother," she ordered.

As she returned with Mother, I started crying loudly again. Mother knelt down and lifted my foot. When she touched my ankle, I squealed and tried to pull away.

"Barbara Jeanne! Hold still!" she ordered in a firm voice. "How am I going to see what you've done unless you let me look at it? Now just be quiet a minute!"

Turning to Mrs. Small, she said, "I think you're right, she needs stitches. Can you drive us to the hospital?"

The hospital? All I knew about hospitals was that people hurt you there. But as scared as I was, I didn't say anything. Part of me needed the attention.

Mother and Shawn helped me to Mrs. Small's car. On the drive to the hospital, my foot wrapped in a towel, and my body cradled safely in Mother's arms, I calmed down a little. But when we arrived at the hospital, Mother left me with a nurse and went off with another lady to "fill out some papers."

"Mommy!" I shouted holding out my arms to her. "Don't leave me alone," I begged.

"I have to leave you. Now calm down, you'll be fine!" she said in an angry voice.

Whimpering all the way I allowed the nurse to help me limp to the examining room where she helped me up on a table. "I'm going to wash the blood off your ankle so the doctor can examine it. I'll be careful and try not to hurt you," she promised. Gently she sponged my wound with a soapy solution as I whined and sniffled. When she finished, a doctor began to examine me.

"Well, what have we here?" he said, looking at me.

"I hurt my ankle," I explained.

As he looked at the wound I told him what had happened. When he was finished, he announced, "Well, my dear, you're going to need some stitching on this one." I shivered, wishing Mother was with me.

The doctor picked up a syringe. I started to cry.

"Where's my mother?" I choked. "I want my mother."

"It's all right, Barbara," the nurse answered. "Your mother's right outside. You can see her as soon as the doctor's finished. Now lay real still and it won't be so bad." I held my breath, my body tensed and my eyes bulged.

"This won't hurt very much," the doctor said right before a hideous burning pain ripped through my ankle.

"Ow!" I shrieked, trying to pull my leg from the iron grip of the nurse.

"Stop struggling. You're making it worse than it is!" the doctor said sternly. Another spasm of pain assaulted me.

"You're hurting me. Please stop!" I begged.

"If you stop screaming, it won't be so bad, I told you!" the nurse said harshly.

By this time I was sobbing and choking hysterically as wave after wave of pain raged through my ankle. Finally the torment stopped and my screaming sobs melted into pitiful whimpers. I turned my head to the side and stuck my fist in my mouth. The doctor continued to work on my foot for several more minutes. I lay on the cold table thinking about what I wanted to tell my mother.

The nurse wrapped my ankle in soft gauze, taped it in place, then she left to fetch Mother, telling me to lie still until she returned.

As soon as I saw Mother, I was about to tell her how mean the doctor had been, when I noticed that she was frowning like she was angry with me. I kept my mouth shut. What did I do? I wondered. Without asking me how I was, she said, "Climb down, Barbara, it's time to go home," sounding upset.

While she watched without saying another word, I helped myself down from the table. She grabbed my hand and we left the hospital. I wondered what I had done to make her so cross.

As we waited at the curb for Mrs. Small to bring the car around, Mother looked down at me. Through lips pursed in anger she hissed, "You were screaming, screaming so loud we could hear you all the way down the hallway and around the corner. You embarrassed me so much I wanted to die! Why do you always have to be so goddamn dramatic?"

I could not answer. My throat was tight and my stomach felt sick. I was • always messing up. I shouldn't have screamed so loud. I had to learn not to be so dramatic. Then maybe Mother wouldn't get angry.

Traumas Of Childhood

Barbara's Growing Awareness

At the time of her first therapy session with me, Barbara had large gaps in her memories of early childhood. As with many Adult Children of Alcoholic or Dysfunctional Families, she was able to remember a few of the more traumatic events, but many of the particulars of her childhood and even her adolescence were shrouded in a haze of vague uneasiness. Even though the initial rape and subsequent incest had been events that Barbara could "talk about" prior to the process work with me, she had skirted around the actual details with great aplomb. While Barbara could not consciously bring up the material from her childhood, she did, however, have nightmares about that period of time. She also startled easily, could not let anyone touch her right side near her waist, was hypervigilant and often reacted to emotional situations by either going numb or, just the opposite, over-reacting. Without any training or help in resolving her physical, emotional and psychological traumas, she found herself suffering from something professionals call Post-Traumatic Stress Disorder, known also as Chronic Shock.[1]

Often Adult Children of Incest, Torture or Emotional Abuse do not even remember that the horrors of their childhood occurred until they have spent a year or more in therapy gaining strength and courage to face the traumas. With the painful events buried in huge blank spots, Adult Children are frequently left with only a very strong sense that they are bad or defective as people. In order to survive the terrifying circumstances in which they grew up, they had to use any number of defense mechanisms that nature had provided, from total denial to delusions, phobias, addictions, compulsions, emotional numbing or disassociation from their bodies. Sometimes Adult Children like Barbara have vague cognitive memories of incest and violence but the shock is too great for them to recall the details or face the emotions of the past. They must, as Barbara did, have an enormous amount of external support and a great deal of courage, patience and commitment to gently pull down the defenses that the mind has so carefully built up.

The narratives that Barbara has told so far were only a few of the somewhat lesser traumatic events in her life that occurred prior to the rape and that had come out as a result of her processing. They actually began to surface only after the first six sessions in which she had put in some hard work on the rape and incest and had reached the point of facing her mother's part in her painful childhood.

It has been my clinical experience that trauma cases, like Barbara, subconsciously spend a great deal of their energy suppressing the details of childhood. It is as if they unconsciously know that if they were to allow any of the lesser events of the past to surface, they would run the risk of having to face the worst of the horrors that might arise and for which they are totally unprepared.

The other risk that Barbara had to face was that of having to deal with the dysfunction of the previously worshipped parent. I call this the "pedestal effect." When children grow up with one severely acting-out offender parent, the other parent (the co-dependent) will often be placed on a pedestal. It is for survival purposes that the child does this. The children need to believe that someone in the family must care about them and must know what they are doing. The child, and later the Adult Child, will do almost anything to keep that parent up on the pedestal and keep the myth of childhood. Rather than see her mother's co-dependence and dysfunction, Barbara carried with her into her adulthood the belief that she, not her mother, was responsible for the family not working.

In order to avoid contact with the pain of the past, Barbara continued to use her childhood defenses of suppression/over-reaction, going numb, disassociating, people-pleasing for acceptance and addictive eating. When those defense mechanisms failed, she later launched into full blown co-dependence. When all those defenses, which were ultimately only stopgaps, began to cause problems of their own, Barbara was faced with a decision about what to do to truly make her life work. Barbara opted for psychological and emotional health. To do that she had to begin slowly facing the pain of her greatest violations so that she could delve into the remainder of the traumatic particulars of her childhood.

When Barbara was hiding the worst of her secrets, she had a continuing need for her greatest defense mechanisms. As she began to uncover her deepest secrets and worked through the pain, the desperate need for the mechanisms subsided and she could begin the process of confronting and releasing them.

When the early scenes from Barbara's childhood (prior to Jim's arrival) finally surfaced, what struck me most was the invalidation of Barbara's emotions, Maureen's inability to be intimate with and supportive of Barbara and the damage that was done to Barbara as a result of Maureen's inabilities.

Barbara spent hours processing before she had a sense of how damaging to her self-image it had been to have tiny Barbara's skin scrubbed raw for getting dirty or how damaging it was to be slapped for supposedly being hysterical when she skinned her knee falling in the scooter race. The more Barbara processed the suppressed pain, the more she realized that the negative tapes inside her head that told her how bad she was were in her mother's voice. Working through the emotional pain she had been avoiding enabled her to begin to separate from the negative voices that had helped form her negative self-image.

One of the reasons Barbara had been unable to work through her childhood emotional and physical traumas was the lack of viable tools. She had spent countless nights, both as a child and an adult, crying herself to sleep and wondering why the pain would not go away. There were two reasons. First was the lack of support and validation; and second, and most important, was the use of ineffective emotional tools.

I explained to Barbara that when she would lie in bed at night mulling over her pain and problems, she was operating in what I call a left brain cognitive process. What she needed to learn to use was a right brain experiential process.

I gave her this exercise:

"Barbara, imagine a spool of 35mm movie film in the left side of your brain. Every time you think about your pain or an upsetting event you add more film to the spool. The more film you add to the spool, the more pain you will add, and the more you will think about it. This can go on indefinitely adding pain on top of thought on top of pain.

"Now, Barbara, imagine taking the free end of the film and pulling it through a tunnel into the right side of your brain and down through your head and out your mouth. See the film leaving the left side of your brain, going through the right side and out of your body via the mouth. This is what a right brain process will do for you."

I then explained that she needed to learn what to do to get the film to leave her brain and stop filling the spool. I taught her a very simple (although not necessarily easy) right brain tool that would help her experientially complete the stored pain. I told her to stop herself each time she *thought about* an unpleasant event with her stepfather or mother and switch from *thinking about* them and the event to *talking to* them. I had her practice extensively in the office and at home, saying the things she had thought and felt but had never said out loud. She told me that she felt some relief immediately. I warned her not to expect drastic long-lasting results right away because she had much stored pain from the actual episodes and had already added more pain from years of thinking about the events.

As Barbara used her new experiential right brain tools and began to release some of that old emotional pain, she was able to recognize the psychological devastation she had experienced as a child. She also realized that she had probably become "hysterical" and "dramatic" because she had had so few outlets for her fear and so few opportunities for attention and comfort from Maureen. Bottled up inside for long periods of time, the stored scares and sadness would escalate quickly when given any opportunity for expression, then Barbara would explode with pain, fear and a desperate need for warmth and affection. She told me she realized that her "spool" would run over and spill out of her.

Making Physical Traumas Worse By Emotional Suppression

As we look at each story we see that Maureen's dysfunction was becoming more and more obvious with each new event until the culmination in the last episode. Instead of love and concern for her child's ankle, which had been gouged so deeply that Barbara could actually see the bone, Maureen's concern was over her own embarrassment because Barbara had screamed as she was being stitched.

Picking up on Maureen's aversion for anything she deemed distasteful, Barbara used that unspoken condemnation to blame herself for her reactions to her physical or emotional hurts. Not only was she stopped from completing the emotional trauma that coincides with physical trauma, but she had to deal with the added trauma of figuring out how to please and protect her mother. This was an impossible task.

In the beginning of therapy Barbara often talked about how bad she was for not handling pain. As a result of the treatment she received from Maureen, Barbara believed that she should have been able to stop herself from crying when she was hurt. Frequently scenes would surface in which her mother ridiculed Barbara for crying over stubbed toes and bruises or made her wrong for getting sick. It took Barbara a lot of time and hard work to recognize the irony of what was happening — that her mother made Barbara wrong for her emotional reactions to physical pain because Maureen could not face even the slightest emotional discomfort. She would avoid that discomfort at all cost, even her child's psychological well-being.

As a result of this amazing degree of co-dependent self-centeredness, Maureen blocked any awareness that the doctors may have been faulty in their handling of her child. Since she had been trained by her parents and grandfather to believe (in what Alice Miller has called the "poisonous pedagogy")[2] that children are basically bad and wrong, she also came to believe the flip side of that, which is that adults are always right, especially authority figures like doctors.

Maureen displayed her belief in a dysfunctionally rigid and righteous approach to life in scenes like the one in which *three-year-old* Barbara showed up with her dress and body covered with paint. What was important to Maureen was her apparent belief, taken from her family, that cleanliness and material things were more important than her tiny daughter's creativity, aliveness and emotional well-being. Maureen's reaction was to attempt to "shame" Barbara into the behavior that Maureen needed and expected. Maureen also covertly took out her anger on Barbara by scrubbing her skin raw. When Barbara protested the hurt, her mother's response made it clear to Barbara that this was her punishment for having enjoyed herself and having dared to get dirty. The major result of growing up with this attitude was the development of an exceptionally negative self-image. A minor result was Barbara's difficulty in having fun as an adult.

Barbara's thumbtack-swallowing episode was one of Barbara's earliest images that presented a clear picture of Maureen's inability to handle even her own emotions. Because of her age, Barbara appears to have escaped from the direct verbal ridicule by her mother in later scenes. Maureen did, however, display that cold withdrawal from her child's emotional needs that was to show up repeatedly in Barbara's childhood. While she appeared to be doing all the right things, wrapping Barbara in a blanket, getting neighbors to rush them to the hospital, giving her the oatmeal and bread, Maureen was missing the most important things for a parent to have, the awareness of and the ability to soothe her little girl's terror.

That does not mean that Maureen was a bad person. She could not comfort Barbara because she did not have the tools to handle emotions or give solace even to herself. Years later after she had entered her own recovery, she told Barbara that she had felt helpless and embarrassed by what she saw as Barbara's over-reacting. Maureen did not realize that ironically she had been over-reacting to Barbara's early displays of emotion and had attempted to stop them. She did not know that emotions build up and without healthy effective ways of completing them, both she and Barbara would be forced to deal with them dysfunctionally.

Maureen's attempt to avoid her emotions resulted in several dysfunctional mechanisms. She tried to ignore her own emotions by finding something else, like work, to focus on. She tried to rationalize them away. She tried to control Barbara in any way that she could to ensure the suppression of Barbara's emotions so that she would not have to deal with her own. None of these methods worked in the long run for her or Barbara. The pain built up and drove her later in life into her particular addictions, co-dependence and workaholism. For Barbara, it resulted in a terribly damaging negative self-image, haunting abusive self-talk inside her head and multiple addictions.

The physical traumas that Barbara suffered did not have to be made worse by the added trauma of having to deal with the suppression of her emotions or the negative judgments that her mother had heaped up on her.

I can remember when I was a small child of about three and a half, my mother went to the corner store, leaving me with my aunt and my thirteen-year-old cousin. I was trying to cut my sandwich with a very large sharp knife. My cousin attempted to take it away from me. We started to argue, and in the struggle, I cut off almost the entire tip of my finger. I screamed as the blood gushed. My aunt rushed into the kitchen in panic and started screaming at my cousin. She then tried to do something to stop the bleeding. She dragged me over to the sink, got a chair for me to stand on, wrapped my finger in a towel, and began running the water.

Fortunately for me, my mother came home at that time. She saw what had happened and listened to my aunt. She took the towel off, squeezed the tip of my finger back on, applied some pressure to slow the bleeding. During all of that she continued talking to me, soothing me, telling me she knew that I was in pain and frightened. She described each step as she went along and explained that she was going to call a cab and take me to the emergency room to have my finger sewn up. She was emotionally and verbally with me throughout the whole process. I felt cared for and loved, even though I was hurt and frightened.

I relate this story from my own past to demonstrate the differences between Barbara's early frightening experience and my own. Small children often injure themselves in exploring their new environment. If the adults around them are effective and functioning, the child will move through and release the experience without the added trauma of dealing with the parent's/adult's inability to handle emotions.

To be an effective and functioning adult, we must have the tools to deal with emotions, recognize our limitations and be honest with ourselves. Dysfunctional behaviors occur when we lack the tools to complete our emotions or to experience the truth about ourselves. We then make unhealthy decisions as a result of the incompletions and self-deceptions. The decisions produce ineffective behaviors which eventually become frozen and rigid with repetition.

Both Barbara and Maureen suffered from the inability to deal with and complete emotions. Interestingly their external reactions and behaviors were often initially on opposite ends of the spectrum. Maureen stuffed emotions, became stoic and worked hard to gain approval from others. Barbara would stuff emotions to a point and when she could hold no more, she would run them to get attention. Then when she received negative attention, she would use that to make herself wrong and strive to do things to gain approval. Both Barbara's and Maureen's approaches were dysfunctional. Once those ineffective and dysfunctional behaviors began, they became self-generating. Rather than releasing the previously stored emotions or eliminating the negative self-image, they became habituated and out of control. They caused more pain and more dysfunction as they started Barbara and Maureen on downward spirals of dysfunctional responses.

The more Maureen blamed Barbara for behaviors and emotional reactions that Maureen did not like and could not handle, the worse Barbara felt about herself and the more she would "act out" the mounting pain. Then Maureen would further resist and reject her. Dealing with the negative framework in which Maureen related to her child, everything Barbara did became wrapped up in Maureen's blame and Barbara's self-condemnation and the right-wrong approach to life that she had taken from her mother.

Breaking Up The Negative Self-Image

The thumbtack scene was an excellent example of how Barbara's self-condemnation affected her perception of herself and reality. The thumbtack scene surfaced early in therapy as a result of my pointing out to Barbara that she often choked when she was crying. Barbara had responded to my comment about her choking by lowering her head, apparently ashamed of herself. In a muffled voice, she said that she had choked and coughed while crying almost all of her life and during any of the crying that she had done in previous therapy. With obvious distress, she said that her parents had used this behavior as another indication of her being overly dramatic. Her other therapist had never commented on the choking and therefore never found out how ashamed of it Barbara was.

Here was another instance of the negative family system at work, and another example of a therapeutic model that had no effective way to surface what the coughing and choking was about and no adequate way to help Barbara stop using this type of behavior against herself.

I tapped Barbara on the knee. She looked up embarrassed.

"Barbara, did you ever have any early throat trauma?" I asked.

Her eyes lit up. Tears started to slide down her face. Later she told me that she had realized in a flash of insight that perhaps she was not to blame, perhaps she was not just being dramatic when she choked and coughed that way while crying. We had done enough process work by that time for her to experientially grasp the significance of my question. I had guessed that there had to be some physical trauma back there triggering the coughing. I had seen from Barbara's initial shameful reaction that she had condemned herself for that coughing and choking. Now supported by a noncritical experiential approach, she was very interested in and excited about finding out where the choking had originated and what this symptom could tell her about herself.

We started to delve into the choking through some body-oriented process work. The first time we worked on the choking, we found that it was associated with the thumbtack scene. I had asked her to close her eyes and focus on her throat and describe how it felt in there. She said that it was tight, and that there was a sharp burning pain. I asked her to describe the physical location of the pain. This allowed her to move once again into a right-brain process and be present with the experience of the pain instead of avoiding it. What Barbara needed to do was learn how to approach the pain and not run from it as most of us try to do when we lack training.

I guided her to focus more closely on the burning pain.

"Exactly where is the pain, Barbara?"

"In the middle of my throat."

"What is the shape and size of the space that hurts?"

"It's about three inches long — but it's narrow — like two strips."

"What kind of pain is it? Is it sharp or dull or . . ."

"It's sharp, very sharp."

Gently taking her deeper into herself and her pain, I then asked if any words or pictures came to mind. Barbara began to describe the scene in her crib when she had swallowed the thumbtack. I asked her how old she *felt*. She said that she felt two years old. I continued to guide her to describe the scene as if it were happening right now in the present. The more she described it in the present tense, the more she allowed herself to become that frightened, pained two-year-old, and the more she cried and coughed and choked and called for her mommy. When that initial response subsided, I asked her to *say out loud* to her mother *the things she had thought but had not said.*

She began a communication with her mother. "Mommy, I hurt. Mommy, why don't you help me? Mommy, why are you running away? Mommy, don't leave me. Am I bad, Mommy? I'm trying to be good. Mommy, blood. I'm scared, Mommy! Why don't you say something? Did I make you angry, Mommy? I must be bad . . ."

After she finally completed her own verbalized thoughts and stored emotions, we went on to dramatize some new options and rewrote the scene with several new interactions and outcomes.

Barbara began to complete the trauma of that scene. As she surfaced and verbalized her previously silent thoughts, she was able to begin to discover and change some very early, very important life-decisions she had made about herself as a person. She could sense that by the age of two, she had already developed the belief that she was a bad person. By doing this type of processing, she had the opportunity to perceive how much the terror associated with those events and the decisions that she had made as a result of her mother's behaviors had affected her entire approach to life. She was beginning to experience how her mother's negative attitudes and cold and distant behavior had created an environment in which Barbara had decided that she was a person who was "bad."

With the type of processes that we did, Barbara could experiment with more options to gain knowledge about herself and her mother while growing in self-support. Completing the emotions allowed her to release the old decisions about herself and other people and also enabled her to begin looking for novel responses in new situations, rather than just reacting with old responses from her former beliefs. It allowed her to expand her experiential range and therefore her experiential boundaries.

Because of the decisions made as a result of the old traumas and experiences with her mother, Barbara first came to me with an extremely negative self-image and with her boundaries rigidly defined. As a result, she had lost the ability to grow and expand. The process work allowed her to begin to redefine her boundaries. It gave her the tools, not just the data, to reevaluate and reconstruct her boundaries and her life-decisions.

Through the process work, Barbara was beginning to learn that an experience of true personal power always includes the experience of responsibility. Responsibility, as I explained to her, is not guilt, shame, duty or "make-wrong." It is also not control. Responsibility is the ability to be aware of what we did and did not do in any situation, to see that we had other options and choices that we did not take and to recognize that we were run by our past, our beliefs, our feelings, our incompletions and our defense mechanisms. Responsibility also means that we realize that we now have the option to do something about it and that we were not bad in the past. Responsibility also means acting in accordance with who we are and not who we have been told we should be. Responsibility means experiencing ourselves and our emotions and recognizing our "ego defenses," and most of all it means seeking and telling the truth no matter how much it hurts.

Because of our work Barbara was starting to recognize that in order to be responsible, she would have to complete the emotions to help her unlock the negative tapes so that she could release her negative context about herself and develop a positive one. On many occasions, she had the opportunity to watch herself take some new information about possible options then blame herself for not seeing them on her own. From this type of feedback, she could see that without creating a new positive context, she would continue her tendency to use any new information against herself.

Another aspect of doing the type of process work that allowed Barbara to recontact the original emotional material was that she could then express all the unspoken or denied feelings and add any new possibilities. By doing this, she had a chance to experience the difference between the repression of emotions and the expression of them. She also had the opportunity to experience the powerful emotions that she was so afraid of in the past, without dying or causing others to die. This allowed her to start to contact and reclaim her true self. Because emotions are a creative aspect of self, Barbara had to learn not to cut herself off from them. By labeling her emotions as bad and disowning them, along with many of her other experiences, Barbara had literally cut herself off from her Self. She developed instead a negative false self-image, based on the distorted reflection from Maureen's dysfunction.

I had spent time early in Barbara's therapy discussing and demonstrating to her what the context was that she held about herself; she was able to realize that the framework in which she operated was "I am a bad person." She was also able to see that with this governing context, she was likely to take anything positive and turn it into something negative. Rather than taking responsibility for putting into effect any new options she saw, her negative self would blame herself for not using those options. However, as a result of our work, she was starting to break up the old "I'm bad" self context she had lived in and had used to judge herself and to run her life, and to replace it with a new "I'm okay" context.

Much of Barbara's work on releasing her negative self-image centered around the thumbtack scene. Barbara told me that in previous therapy she had talked about the flashes that she had experienced of the thumbtack scene, but had been unable to understand its importance or release it emotionally. Just talking about that painful memory had not enabled her to connect it with her choking nor the many negative decisions about herself that had resulted from the incident.

However, Barbara found out during her process work that the thumbtack scene had come to symbolize many issues for her. Because of the amount of emotional and physical trauma involved, as well as the number of important life-decisions Barbara had made during that event, she often found herself in therapy back in the scene dealing with some other facet of her emotional experience or her belief system. Even when we would process her skinned knee and gouged ankle episodes, Barbara would often find herself drawn back to the thumbtack scene.

That scene was, what I call, a core scene. Usually early in life (and sometimes even in the womb) a core scene is one which holds symbolic significance for us. It is a scene which contains many of the core issues from which we have created much of our negative self-image or negative false-self.

One of the discoveries that Barbara made about the scene was that somehow the choking had come to represent for her the desire to "choke back all emotion." She also realized that there was a blurring of internal experiential boundaries between her fear, sadness and anger. Many times in process when she was yelling with anger, she would find herself crying simultaneously. Eventually, with much work, she was able to separate her anger from her sadness and could then simply give herself permission to be angry without bursting into tears.

The thumbtack processing work also showed Barbara the difference between understanding something in a purely intellectual manner and understanding something as a result of an experiential insight. There were many different occasions during the latter part of Barbara's therapy when working with that episode she had an experiential "Ah-ha!"

In one of her thumbtack sessions, after she had been crying with the pain of her abandonment, I asked Barbara to see if she could take a moment to let herself experience being her mother. This would allow Barbara an opportunity to experience the event from Maureen's perspective. When Barbara went back to the scene as Maureen, she entered baby Barbara's room, trying to find out what all the screaming was about. When she saw the blood spurting from Barbara's mouth, she became terrified. It was at that point in the process that Barbara (who was then playing Maureen) was able to experience directly that Maureen's leaving the room was not because Barbara was bad, but because Maureen had been terrified and did the only thing that she could think of to do at that time, go get some help.

Because Barbara had completed most of her own reactions pertaining to the thumbtack scene and had then taken responsibility for the decisions she had made as a result of those events, she was able to let herself experience what Maureen may have been feeling. Going through what another person felt is very different than talking about it. As baby Barbara, she experienced her mother as an omnipotent, omniscient being. As the adult, when Barbara allowed herself to become Maureen, she was able to experience Maureen as a terrified, poorly prepared mother.

In another of Barbara's thumbtack sessions, I had asked her to begin the scene as usual as baby Barbara. I then asked her to switch to being Maureen. Finally I asked Barbara to go back and observe Maureen in action from Barbara's own perspective as a woman in her thirties with two children of her own. When Barbara made the final switch, she gasped and said, "My God, she's so young." Experientially, in those two sessions Barbara was able to sense some of the issues, problems and boundaries her terrified young mother had to deal with when Barbara was a baby. Had we simply talked about these areas, Barbara would have gained some cognitive information, but she would not have been able to experience for herself that it was Maureen's terror, immaturity and lack of training and skills that controlled her reactions to Barbara's screams, rather than the blame and abandonment which Barbara originally had to work through.

While keeping those experiences in mind, I also cautioned Barbara to remember not to use her new experiences as an excuse or justification for her mother's (or her stepfather's) dysfunctional behavior. People do not heal when we ignore or justify their dysfunctional behavior; we simply enable them to continue in their disease process.

From very early on in her work, Barbara had been concerned with the idea of forgiving her parents. When she first brought the subject up, I told her to forget about forgiveness. I explained that most people used the word "forgiveness" to either justify stopping themselves from dealing with and completing their pain and anger or to make themselves wrong when they found that they were not ready yet to forgive. I said that given my own experience, both personally and clinically, there wasn't any such *thing* as forgiveness. I told Barbara that forgiveness is a context (not a thing).

We have an experience of forgiveness when all the energy around the past event (the grief, the terror and the anger) is complete. If we try to forgive others when we are not ready, we end up lying to ourselves and pretending to be forgiving because we have been told that we should be forgiving. This is the same type of external referenting that is so prevalent in co-dependency. This type of false forgiveness does not allow for any new anger to occur in relation to new events because the new anger would trigger the old suppressed, falsely forgiven anger.

Ten Going On Grown-Up

The summer that I was ten, Jim started insisting that I take on more of the household chores. As a result, I spent a good part of every morning doing my assigned housework: washing dirty dishes left from breakfast, sweeping the kitchen floor, shaking out the rug, mopping the floor if dirty, dusting the living room, cleaning my bedroom, tidying the bathroom and vacuuming whenever Mother asked. It was an awful lot of work, but it was important that I obey and please Jim. What made it most difficult was that the other children in our housing complex were outside playing every day before I was finished with my chores and could join them.

Jim and Mother often told me that I was luckier than other children because I had parents who cared enough to teach me how to cook and clean. Someday I would have to take care of a husband, children and a household and they wanted me to be prepared. That didn't make much sense to me but I wanted to believe them. Even so I wanted to tell them that I didn't want to clean the house, but I didn't want to make them angry.

I didn't particularly like cleaning, no matter how "lucky" I was, because I couldn't figure out how to do it exactly right. I tried hard to please them but Mother or Jim, especially Jim, usually found something I hadn't done well. The only thing I did that really got me approval was baking and helping to prepare meals. I seemed to have a natural flair in the kitchen. Most of my attempts were greeted with success. Besides there were those important side benefits, taste-testing and eating. I soon had ample opportunity to take care of my developing appetite.

One weekday afternoon Mother was gone and I was in the kitchen alone preparing to bake a cake. I took out Mother's favorite cookbook with the red checkered cover. While looking for a recipe with directions I could manage, I imagined following recipes and creating cakes and cookies like those in the pictures. I thought of it as a great challenge that would carry almost immediate rewards of praise from Mom and Jim and, of course, the reward of eating the finished product.

I imagined Mother's smile and Jim telling me that I was becoming a great cook. Sometimes he whispered that I was better than Mother. I smiled as I imagined them bragging to their friends about how grown-up I was becoming.

I assembled all the necessary cooking utensils — a mixing bowl, the big electric beater that had belonged to my grandmother, cake pans, a sifter, spoons and a rubber spatula. Following the directions exactly, I rubbed shortening on the cake pans and dusted them with flour. Then I went to the refrigerator and took eggs, butter and milk. From the canisters on the kitchen counter, I carefully measured flour, sugar, salt, baking powder and vanilla according to the recipe and after mixing everything thoroughly, poured the batter into the pans.

Looking once again at the directions to see how long the batter was supposed to bake, I realized that I had forgotten to preheat the oven. "Darn!" I shouted at myself. "Stupid, stupid, stupid!" I knew I should have been more thorough. Mother always said there was no use doing a job if I wasn't going to do it right. I was so disappointed in myself. I knew Mother and Jim would be, too. Couldn't I just once do something one hundred percent right? I had probably ruined the cake. But I decided to put it in the oven right away hoping they never found out that I forgot to preheat.

The pilot light in our old gas stove didn't work very well, which meant the oven had to be lit manually. The oven burner was most easily reached through the broiler unit directly below. I turned the knob to the temperature specified in the recipe, opened the door and reached for the box of wooden matches kept on top of the stove. The box was empty. I should have known. I stood up, ran to the back porch to get a new box then ran back to the stove. Opening the box I took out a match then closed the box exactly as Jim had taught me. I carefully struck the blue tip against the side, then watching the flame closely and moving slowly so it wouldn't blow out, I reached my hand into the broiler unit to light the oven.

There was a sudden "Who-o-o-sh!" followed by a flash of light and burst of heat that knocked me backwards on the floor and banged my head against the lower cupboard doors. I was so shocked that I didn't move for a moment. Then I began rubbing my head and staring in wide-eyed amazement at the flame dancing its way around the burner unit. I wondered what had happened, what I had done wrong. After several seconds I began to realize that my face, hands and arms were hurting as if they were on fire. I was scared because I had made a mistake and I started to cry as I realized that the explosion had burned me. My face contorted which sent ripples of pain coursing through the skin. A strange odor was coming from the burned hair on my forearms. I later saw that I had burned my eyebrows, and also singed my bangs.

I knew I could not allow myself to give in to the pain. I had made a mistake. Mother and Jim would be angry. They would not love me. I forced myself to stand up and close the broiler door. Slowly I turned to the counter behind me, picked up the cake pans, turned back to the stove and placed the pans on top. When I opened the oven door, the heat that was building inside made my face and arms hurt even more. Tears streaming down my face I gritted my teeth, reached for the cake pans and set them on the middle shelf, evenly spaced, just like Mother had taught me. Then I carefully set the timer.

Without stopping to clean up my mess, I walked, stiff and in pain, out of the kitchen, through the dining room to the front door. I had to get to Cheryl next door. She would know what to do. With each step I felt more pain. Each movement became an agony.

I was grateful that Mother wasn't home. I knew I must have done something terribly wrong. She wasn't going to be happy with that and she was always angry when I hurt myself.

I let myself into Cheryl's house without knocking. I found her in the kitchen doing dishes.

"Cheryl, I hurt myself," I whined.

She turned and looked at me. Her eyes registered shock.

"Oh, my God! What happened?" She dried her hands on her apron as she hurried to me. She knelt down and took my hands in hers. I shrieked in pain.

"I'm sorry, honey, I'm sorry," she said dropping my hands. "What happened?" In choking sobs, I told her, "I don't know. I was lighting the oven when all of a sudden there was this big flash of light."

"We have to get a salve on your burns right away, before they get any worse," she said.

Sitting me down in the chair in her kitchen, she went to the cupboard and pulled out a bowl and poured in a half box of baking soda. She mixed that with cold water to form a paste and then began spreading the mixture on my arms. "This will make you feel better," she said. But the baking soda was not fully dissolved in the water. The paste felt like sandpaper as she began to apply it to the first and second degree burns on my arms. I flinched and screamed, trying desperately to pull away from her. But she held my arm firmly, saying, "I know it hurts but this is the only way to make your burns stop hurting."

I didn't feel better. I felt like I was being punished. I sobbed helplessly.

She carefully applied the mixture to my hands, arms and face. Finished, she brought me a glass of milk and a cookie, then asked me to tell her exactly what had happened. I went over the steps that led to the explosion while Cheryl listened intently. She then put her arm around me warmly and explained that I must never leave the gas burning for more than a few seconds before lighting the oven. What she said seemed familiar, like Mother or Jim may have said the same thing. However, I don't think they had ever explained why leaving the gas on without lighting the oven was unsafe. I thought I had been negligent for not figuring that out.

Cheryl walked me home, gave me two aspirin for the pain, told me she would clean up the kitchen and that I should lie down until Mother came back. Even though the pain was awful, I was more worried about what Mother would say. Instead of the approval and praise I had imagined for my baking, I now faced the prospect of Mother's disapproval because I had been stupid. Why had I been so careless? I should have known about not leaving the gas on.

The aspirin helped some and I fell asleep, waking up when Mother came home. Cheryl was still there and explained to Mother what had happened. I heard Mother say that she had told me to be careful and couldn't understand what was wrong with me. I closed my eyes. I was a stupid failure and now everyone knew.

A few months later, Mother had her kidney surgery, recuperated nicely and began to look for a job again. I didn't want her to go back to work. While she was home she could do things for me that she hadn't been able to before. She organized and started a Bluebird troop and became our parent-guardian, planning all functions and helping us earn badges and beads. I felt important and special having my mother be the parent that all the other girls looked up to. I wanted to believe that meant they liked me, too.

Mother also helped out with the PTA and brought refreshments to our year-end party. Having my mother be such an active part of my life made me look more normal, more like my friends whose mothers did not work. And I loved the extra attention. Besides Jim only wanted to have sex with me when Mother was gone to her club meetings which were two nights a month. I dreaded those nights, hating him and hating myself. I felt safer when Mother was home.

That summer on the occasion of my eleventh birthday Mother organized a swimming party for me, inviting the girls from my Bluebird troop and a few girls who lived in our complex. There was a large community swimming pool in the center of the complex where I swam every day. I had always been a good swimmer and that summer I learned how to swan dive, somersault and back dive. I practiced every day until I could do them, especially the back dive, better than most of the other children.

The day of the party everyone was supposed to meet at our house at noon. I stood at the door from eleven-forty-five waiting for all the guests to arrive. One by one they walked up to the door. Mother had invited fifteen girls, but only eleven came.

They probably don't like me very much, I thought, wishing I could make everyone be my friend. I wanted to cry but instead pasted a smile on my face, laughed and joked with the other girls, all the while stealing glances out of the window to see if the others might come after all.

At twelve-thirty Mother announced that it was time to start the party. I looked through the window one more time as she told us to change into our swimsuits, gather up towels and pool toys and get ready to walk to the pool. Cheryl was helping Mother chaperone us. Just as they were ushering us out the door, the phone rang. I ran to pick it up, hoping it was one of the four who wasn't there calling me to wish me a happy birthday. It wasn't. Instead a man asked to speak to Maureen.

"It's for you, Mommy," I said swallowing tears one more time. Taking the phone, she said, "Cheryl, go ahead with the girls to the pool. I'll be along in a second."

We were already in the pool by the time Mother came through the pool gate. I noticed that she wasn't smiling. I frowned, wondering what was wrong. But Mother soon smiled and began organizing the games.

We had timed races, relay races and ended with an exciting and breathless swimming game of "Marco-Polo," in which the person who is "it" is blindfolded and shouts out "Marco," to which the others who are above water respond "Polo," and the "it" person tries to locate the voices to "tag" them. When the games finished, we swam while Mother and Cheryl set out the refreshments. Hoping attention would make me forget about the four girls who hadn't come to my party, I decided to show off my perfected back dive. I climbed out of the pool and went to the board.

I walked to the end and shouted to Vickie, the member of the Bluebirds who I liked the best, "Watch, Vickie! I'm going to do a back dive!"

"Go ahead!" she yelled back and waved from the other end of the pool.

"Mother, watch!" I shouted, wanting a larger audience.

"Oh, Barbara, stop being such a show-off and just do it!" Mother said.

I'll just show her, I thought. Turning around I backed to the edge of the board, letting the heels of my feet hang over. I took several deep breaths, lowered my hands to my side and closed my eyes. When I felt ready, I opened my eyes, bent my knees and sprung, immediately beginning a backwards curve. Instead of diving in a straight line, I dove off center and as I entered the water I banged my head on the side of the pool. It felt like I had been hit with a bat.

I tried to cry out as I sunk beneath the surface, my mouth filling with water. Curling into a tight ball, I grabbed my head and moaned. For a moment I couldn't move but my body floated to the surface. Eyes closed, I heard someone shouting and felt hands grabbing me and lifting me out.

Choking and sputtering as water gushed from my mouth, I collapsed into their arms and onto the wet cement. My head hurt so much, I thought it might burst from the pain. Momentarily I was able to push myself up a little and saw blood on the concrete and on my hands. I was so scared that I started to hyperventilate. I saw visions of brain matter spilling onto the concrete and in terror, as much as pain, I screamed.

"Barbara Jeanne, be quiet!" I heard my mother shouting, "Let me see what you did!"

"Mommy, it hurts!" I cried.

"I know, I know!" she responded sounding exasperated. "Now hold still, for goodness sake, and let me see!"

I stopped struggling and crying. I didn't want to be hurt so bad that I would need stitches again, and I was terrified that I might. I held my breath and waited for her to tell me how severe the wound was.

Several seconds later she announced, "It's just a surface cut. It will need a Band-Aid, but that's all." I breathed a sigh of relief. "Cheryl, why don't you start another game with the girls while I take Barbara back to the house and clean up this mess." Turning back to me she said, "Barbara, come with me."

I stood up and noticed, for the first time, that all the other girls were staring at me. I couldn't look them in the eyes, not wanting to see the disapproval I was sure was there. Ashamed because I had messed up the dive and embarrassed because I had screamed, I looked at the concrete and mumbled, "I'm sorry, I'll be back in a minute." This day wasn't turning out at all like it was supposed to.

Humiliated, I followed Mother back to our house. She cleaned the gash and cut away some of the hair around it.

"If you had been paying attention to what you were doing instead of showing off to the other girls, this wouldn't have happened, Barbara Jeanne," she said as she applied the Band-Aid. "Besides, what about the girls who can't dive as well as you?" She was standing in front of me with her hands on her hips. "How do you think they feel when you have to show them how good you are? You should think about that," she said waving her index finger at me.

As I considered that they might feel inadequate that I could do something better than they, I felt bad. I didn't want anyone to be uncomfortable because of me. Quite to the contrary, I wanted them to like me. And now it looked like if Mother was right, I had caused just the opposite. Maybe now they hated me. I didn't want to go back to the party.

"Mommy, can I lay down for a while before I go back? I kind of have a headache," I said.

"Barbara Jeanne, this is your party, everyone is waiting for you. Now come along with me. You can lay down later if your head still hurts."

"Okay, Mommy," I answered meekly.

"You won't be able to go swimming anymore today. Your cut needs to heal over a bit first."

That was fine with me. I wasn't sure I wanted to go back into the water anyway. I didn't even want to think about the diving board.

Taking my hand, we walked towards the pool. As we approached the gate, she told me, "By the way, the call you answered was from a man who wants me to start working on Monday."

"Oh, Mommy, do you have to go back to work so soon? Can't you wait until the end of summer?" I begged, hoping she would see how much I needed her.

"He needs me to start on Monday," she said sounding a little annoyed. "Besides if you hadn't answered the phone, I wouldn't have to go."

Even though I didn't want her to go back to work, and would have done anything to stop her, she was going and it was all my fault. My birthday was totally ruined.

That night when Jim came home from work, I was in my room putting away birthday presents. I listened as Mother told him about the accident. She made a point of telling him that I had been showing off to the other girls.

"After she failed on that dive, did she go back and do it right?" I heard him ask.

"No," Mother answered, "I wouldn't let her back into the pool with the cut still bleeding a bit. It wasn't serious. I'm sure it's okay now."

"Well, she'll have to do the same dive off the board again. Otherwise, she's going to be afraid." Then he called out, "Barbara, come in here!"

I ran into the living room hoping to get a hug and a kiss and his birthday wishes. Instead, he motioned to the ottoman by his chair and said, "Sit down, I want to talk to you."

Holding my breath, I sat down and looked up at him. His face was very serious.

"Barbara, do you know what you did wrong today?" he asked.

I shook my head and tried not to cry. Why couldn't he just say happy birthday instead of lecturing me? I hated it when he lectured.

"Well, you have to find out so that you don't do that again. Let's go over to the pool while your mother is cooking dinner and you can show me."

"Mommy said I couldn't go swimming again today," I said, pointing to the Band-Aid, hoping we could put it off until tomorrow. I had messed up the dive and was afraid I could never do it right again. I hated failing, especially in front of Jim.

"She told me that your cut isn't serious, so put on your bathing suit and come with me."

I started to cry. "I can't, Daddy, I'm scared!"

"Barbara, have you ever heard the expression that says when you fall off of a horse, you must get back on right away?"

"Yes," I said in a tentative voice, trying to swallow the lump in my throat. I knew what was next.

"Well, that saying is around for a reason. You will not be allowed to go back in the pool until you are ready to do another back dive."

I was being punished for doing the dive incorrectly. Tears sprang to my eyes and I swallowed hard to keep them from spilling over. He stared at me waiting for my response. When I didn't speak, he prodded, "Well? Are you going to come with me or not?"

I wanted to be allowed to go swimming. If I kept on being scared, the punishment would continue. I was ashamed of my fear. Looking down at the carpet, I mumbled, "Okay, Daddy, I'll try."

After I changed into my suit, I wrapped a towel around my waist and followed Jim to the pool. Even though the midsummer air was warm, I was shivering. As we walked through the pool gate I saw the water looming in front of me like the cavernous mouth of some huge prehistoric monster. The diving board looked like a platform for human sacrifice. I froze, unable to move another step. Jim didn't notice.

"Get up on the diving board," he commanded. "You have to get right back on that horse. You know you can do the dive and I know you can, too. Now just get back up there like you always have and do it!"

My feet felt as if they were encased in the concrete. With every ounce of will I could summon, I forced myself to walk to the board. I stood there gaping at it, my eyes wide with fright.

"Barbara," he said in a loud, threatening voice. I jumped. "Get on the board and do it!"

Try as I might, I couldn't make the step up on that board. Finally, unable to force myself, I cried, "I can't, Daddy, I can't."

"Then you won't be allowed in the pool again until you do. If you want to be a baby, we'll treat you like one!" he barked as he turned and stomped to the gate, motioning me to come along. I followed in silence, tears streaming down my face.

For several days, we repeated that scene. He would come home from work and immediately ask if I was ready. I would hesitate and then reluctantly say yes. We would walk over to the pool. I would freeze. I was unable to dive.

Each day as I sat under the walnut tree on the other side of the fence, listening to the sounds of the other children frolicking in the pool, I would berate myself. Why can't I just do it? I would ask myself over and over. What's wrong with me? I have to get back on the horse.

Finally I would grit my teeth, set my shoulders and be determined that tonight would be the night I would do it. And each night I would fail. I hated being full of fear. If only I could make the scare go away.

After two weeks, with only one more week of summer vacation left, I vowed to myself that I would do it. That night Mother, who had started working as a bookkeeper for a toy manufacturer, came home first. I was waiting in my bathing suit, bathing cap and towel in hand. I ran to her as she walked through the door and said, "I think I can do it now, Mommy!"

She didn't have to ask what I meant. Putting her purse on the coffee table, she said, "Let's go."

On the way to the pool, I told her my plan. "If you'll let me dive once from the edge of the pool, like when I was learning, I'll do the next dive off the board."

"Okay," she said, "but don't tell your father I let you do it this way. You know how he feels about it."

"Yes, Mommy," I answered. "But this will work, you'll see."

The first dive off the edge went smoothly. I climbed out of the pool and turned to the board, which looked as scary as it had every other day. It seemed to be mocking me, saying, the side of the pool isn't the board, Barbara, that was kid stuff.

Straightening my back, and setting my chin, I forced my feet to move me forward towards the board. Step by step I walked. I was going to do it, no matter what. This time I didn't let myself stop at the back of the board. I kept myself moving, stepping right up on the board and walking to the end. Turning around I positioned my heels over the edge of the board and looked at Mother. Then I looked down at the water — and froze. Despite all my resolve, my terror was getting the better of me. I started to cry.

"Mommy, I'm scared."

"It's okay, Barbara," she said in an uncharacteristic moment of tenderness. "I'll be here if anything happens. I know you can do it, honey."

Her words surprised me. Maybe she wasn't angry with me after all. I would do this for her.

I looked down at the water again. I was still crying, but I pressed my lips together trying to stifle the sobs. I took a deep breath, held it, closed my eyes, and heard the voice inside my head shout, "Now! Do it now!"

I opened my eyes and leaned back, letting my body fall in a slow backwards arch, lifting my arms over my head. As my feet left the board I finally relaxed into the dive. When I felt the cool water envelop my body, I knew I had done it! Triumphant, I swam to the edge of the pool to where Mother was standing. As I climbed out of the water, she had a big smile on her face.

"You did it! I'm so proud of you! Daddy will be so happy!" she said with obvious delight in her voice.

I breathed a sigh of relief. It was over. I had succeeded. Mother was proud of me.

"See, Barbara, we knew you could do it all along. Now aren't you sorry you made such a big deal out of it?"

My joy and pride dissolved in a wave of shame. She was right, I had been such a bother. The dive itself hadn't been a big deal. I had been wrong all along. Wrong to show off, wrong to be afraid, wrong to carry on like I had and wrong to cause everyone such a problem. No one else would have acted the way I had. There was something wrong with me all right.

Role Reversals

The thumbtack, paint, scooter and ankle episodes all occurred before Jim's arrival in the family and demonstrated that Maureen's dysfunction existed long before Jim's entrance into the family system. With Jim's arrival, her own co-dependent disease process would escalate. When Jim pushed for Barbara to take on the heavy household chores, Maureen said nothing. Having been raised in her male-dominated autocratic family, she would never have presumed to question Jim's knowledge and ability to parent appropriately. Even though his ideas may have differed from her original approach to the type of chores the children needed to do at home and the ages at which they needed to learn those tasks, she apparently assumed that he must have known what he was doing. She also would have avoided any confrontation with him if she could.

What Maureen did not realize is that Jim was subconsciously setting up and controlling his environment so that he could drink more and become more and more irresponsible and dysfunctional. This is not an unusual situation in the alcoholic home. Maureen did not perceive that she was being placed in the position of wage earner and Barbara was being placed in the position of homemaker and spouse.

In addition Shawn was being trained to take over any of Jim's household chores. That would leave Jim with nothing to do except drink, be totally taken care of at home and at least partially supported financially. The more Barbara could do at home, the less Maureen would have to do there and the more she would be able to focus energy on her job and her earning capacity.

The alcoholic male frequently sets the co-dependent spouse up in the role of financial support while one of the children fills in as homemaker and sexual partner. This is particularly easy to do when the wife is as unsure of herself as Maureen was and would do anything to avoid dealing with emotions and conflict.

Maureen made it even simpler for Jim. She had already set the stage with Barbara by not only making it impossible for Barbara to voice objections and express her feelings, but also by insisting on the kind of obedience and perfectionism that had ripped Barbara's self-esteem out by the roots and replaced it with a people-pleasing orientation.

It never dawned on Maureen that having Barbara sweeping, cleaning, vacuuming, mopping, dusting, cleaning her own room and the family bathroom, doing the laundry and the cooking on a daily basis was age and role inappropriate. There was no way for Barbara to know this, except by asking other children and their parents. Jim made sure, however, that Barbara and even Maureen could not question his demands by telling Maureen and Barbara that this was a sign that they cared about Barbara's training and that the other parents did not care enough if their children were not expected to do the type and quantity of chores expected of Barbara. Barbara also assumed from watching the other children out playing before she could finish her chores, that she was probably incompetent and that was why the other children got out to play before her.

At the beginning of the marriage Jim was able to test Maureen's naivete and ease with which she could be manipulated. He rapidly learned that Maureen would do anything to avoid a conflict and that if he blamed Barbara for problems, Maureen would go along with it. Subconsciously, he had tested just how far he could go and found that there were no limits to his abuse and control.

The burn scene and the swimming pool episode both occurred after Jim's arrival and takeover of the family. They both point to various aspects of the growing dysfunction in the family.

The burn scene demonstrates several things: Barbara's growing spousal role, her growing need for approval, her burgeoning love affair with food, the constant harping of her negative voice, the growing assumption of the need to be perfect, her escalating vigilance and her growing conviction that her only worth came from what she did and not who she was. Through Barbara's eyes we can watch how Maureen's lack of healthy

parenting skills and her emotional and physical absence was interpreted
by Barbara as something insufficient in herself. It never came into Barbara's awareness that it was, first, inappropriate for her to be doing that
level of cooking unsupervised in the kitchen at age ten and, second, that
it was Maureen's failure in her role to prepare Barbara for any cooking by
not telling her about the gas pilot and lighting the oven. Barbara could
not really know that the reason she "failed" was that she was expected to
do chores inappropriate for her age.

Since children trust their parents for guidance, they assume that the
parents are healthy and appropriate. They have very few other feedback
systems, except perhaps school. Unfortunately our educators believe
that teaching children math and reading is more important than teaching
children what is healthy family behavior so our family dysfunctions go
unchallenged.

In the pool story Maureen repeated her previous dysfunctional treatment of Barbara's emotional and psychological needs. Blaming and shaming Barbara for getting hurt, rather than loving and supporting her,
Maureen was caught up as usual in her concern over what outsiders
thought of her and not in how Barbara felt about herself. Maureen even
went so far as to blame Barbara for "having to go to work" because Barbara had answered the phone. Obviously Maureen had been intending to
go back to work or she would never have applied for the job in the first
place. Not wanting to deal with her daughter's sadness over her loss of her
mother's companionship, Maureen diverted Barbara's pain by blaming
her for picking up the phone. In all of this, we see Maureen's growing co-
dependence, her almost total disregard for her child, her concern for her
own appearance and her need to blame everyone else for her choices in
life. Co-dependents rarely take responsibility for their lives. They pretend
that they are victims forced into the choices that they have made.

Another important dysfunction that we can see in the story is the use
and abuse of old sayings that are held as gospel when they are nothing
more than someone else's belief or when they contain, at best, only a
grain of truth. Jim abused the saying about getting back on the horse
after a fall. Instead of using it to talk to Barbara about what fear can do to
people, he used it to punish and control her. He never got into the pool
with her; he never tried to help her approach the dive gradually, from
the side. Barbara had to figure out how to work her way gradually
through the fear and then could not even acknowledge her achievement
because her parents had made it wrong for her to be afraid.

Jim's participation in the swimming pool episode also demonstrates
more of the subconscious testing of how far he could go in his control of
Maureen and Barbara. When Barbara worked on the scene I had a sense
that at least a part of Maureen would have loved to throw her arms

around her little girl and let her go swimming without punishing her fear. We see from the poolside scene where Barbara asked her mother if she could dive off the side of the pool first before going off the board and Maureen answered, "Okay, but don't tell your father I let you do it this way," that Maureen was frightened and dominated by Jim.

We also see in Jim's approach what we frequently see in dysfunctional families: cruel and sadistic abuse of a child's emotional boundaries in the name of teaching the child a lesson. In this case the lesson appeared to be "how to conquer fear." The real lesson was how abusive Jim could be and how Barbara's fear of and need for Jim's approval was greater than her other fears.

Jim was learning that he had Barbara and Maureen very firmly under his control. In Maureen's need to hide her disagreement, she further enforced his dictatorial hold over the family. He could now increase his abuse without any fear of interference on Maureen's part or any resistance on Barbara's part. He was working on breaking Barbara's will and continuing the destruction of any remaining positive feelings that she might have about herself. Coupled with the ongoing incest, this would begin to bond her to him by diminishing her choices and making her believe that no other man could possibly love her but him, and that was at best conditional.

4

When In Doubt,
Lie!

Amanda Small and I had been each other's best friend since my family moved into her neighborhood shortly before both of us entered first grade. Inseparable playmates, we joined Bluebirds together, played endless games of make-believe and "house," created countless paper doll families and took ballet and tap from Amanda's mother.

We rarely had an argument or disagreement, since we always seemed to want to do the same thing or were willing to compromise. There was one major exception when we were nine years old.

One night shortly before the wedding, Mother and Jim had planned an early evening date. Our usual babysitter, Rose, was not available, and Mother had no one else, so she decided to leave us alone for the first time. Before going out, Mother sat Shawn and me down for a talk. She told us in a serious voice that we must not let anyone come into the house and that we must not go outside to play. We were to tell no one, "but no one," that we were alone. Amanda's father was a police officer, she warned, and might put us in jail if someone found out. My eyes widened and my throat constricted as I promised I would do as she ordered. I didn't want to go to jail, and I certainly didn't want Mother to go to jail!

As Mother and Jim left the house, they made sure that we locked the door behind them and issued a final instruction to keep the door locked until they came home. We sat down in front of the television to await their return. Not long after they left, there was a knock at the door. Shawn and I debated in angry whispers about answering the door. He said that we shouldn't answer the door at all. I argued that we should at least find out who was there. I won.

I walked over to the door and without opening it, I asked, "Who is it?"

"It's me!" I heard Amanda shout behind the closed door. "Let me in."

"I can't," I yelled back. "Anyway, I can't play with you tonight so you have to go home."

"Why?" she demanded.

"I just can't, Amanda," I shouted, "I can't tell you why."

She was silent for a few moments. Thinking that maybe she had given up and was going home, I ran to the dining room and looked out of the window to see if she was gone. She was still standing on the porch looking at the door, a frown on her face. Realizing that she wasn't going to leave, and afraid that I would be punished if my mother came home and found me talking to Amanda, I ran back to the door and yelled, "Amanda, you have to go home!"

"Why?" she yelled back.

Exasperated, I shouted, "Because I don't have a babysitter, and if you tell your dad he'll put us in jail."

"What?" she said, sounding confused. "What do you mean Daddy would put you in jail. He wouldn't do any such thing and you know it!"

"Yes, he will," I disagreed. "My mother told me so."

I waited for her to say something, instead I heard her footsteps as she ran down the steps. From the window I saw her run down the driveway, then stop and look back at the house. She had tears streaming down her face.

"You're a liar, Barbara Jeanne," she shouted, "and I'm going to tell my mother." With that she turned and raced down the sidewalk towards her house.

I started to cry, afraid that I had done something wrong, though I wasn't quite sure what it was. I hadn't meant to make Amanda cry, I just didn't want to be in trouble with Mother. I would tell her I was sorry as soon as I saw her again. Wiping my tears on my sleeve, I went back to watch television with Shawn.

Several minutes later, there was another knock at the door. Assuming that Amanda was back, I unlocked the door and flung it open, planning to apologize for whatever I had done to make her cry and then beg her to leave so I wouldn't be punished for having opened the door. Instead of Amanda, Mrs. Small was standing on the other side of the door with an angry frown on her face.

She demanded to know what I had said to Amanda to make her cry. I repeated Mother's warning to me. She accused me of lying. She yelled that she would talk to Mother. With that she turned and left the porch without another word.

Behind me I heard Shawn say smugly, "I told you not to answer the door the first time. Now look what you've done. You'll be in trouble when Mother gets home."

"Oh! Shut up, Shawn," I sobbed. "What do you know anyway? I didn't lie and you know it."

He stuck his tongue out at me, turned his back and sat down in front of the television.

Slowly I closed the front door. I didn't understand. I guessed that Shawn was right, that I shouldn't have answered when Amanda came over. But even so, why would her mother think that I would lie about something like that? Didn't she know how much I loved Amanda and that I would never, ever do anything to hurt her? Amanda was my best friend, and I wouldn't have done anything to risk losing her.

A few hours later Mother and Jim came home. Before I could tell her what had happened, the doorbell rang. Mother opened the door and there stood Mrs. Small. I stood by silently as she told my mother what had happened. I wanted to find a place to hide when she told Mother about how hurt Amanda was and how Amanda had demanded to know why her father would put her best friend in jail. The last thing Mrs. Small said drove a stake of pain deep into my heart.

"I don't know if Amanda can play with Barbara anymore."

Standing like a statue behind my mother, I watched her back stiffen as she listened to the tirade.

In my mind I screamed at my mother and begged her to stand up for me, to tell Mrs. Small what she had said, to tell her it wasn't my fault. I couldn't believe Mrs. Small might take Amanda away from me. I stood behind Mother, eyes wide, arms stiffly at my side, every muscle tense and barely breathing, waiting and hoping for her to save me.

Instead of defending me, Mother began to apologize for what I had said. I stood in horrified shock as she said she didn't know what had got into me. She assured Mrs. Small that she didn't condone lying and that I would certainly be punished for making up such a story. As I listened to Mother, I realized that everyone was angry with me: Amanda, her mother and now my mother. Even thinking that I had done the right thing wasn't enough.

As soon as Mrs. Small left, Mother closed the door and stood with her back to me for a few moments. With slow and deliberate movements she turned to face me. She took a deep breath and began to yell.

"How could you say that to Amanda? Haven't I told you never to say anything that could hurt other people? Why can't you think before you open your mouth? I'm so embarrassed."

She finished by demanding that I go to Amanda the next day, instructing me to tell her that I had lied and then to apologize. Then she sent me to bed.

In bed I wept bitter tears, not so much with anger at the injustice, but in hurt and disappointment in myself. Why did I keep messing up? Why couldn't I know what I was doing or what was going to happen ahead of time. Other people didn't make as many mistakes as I did. I thought I should have been able to know exactly the "right" thing to say and the "right" thing to do. I didn't know how I was going to summon up the courage to face Amanda the next day.

I hardly slept that night. The next morning I woke up early. Breakfast was a stiff silent affair. Neither Mother nor Shawn looked at me or spoke to me. It was obvious that I had not been forgiven my transgression of the day before. Swallowing back tears, I kept my head down and tried not to draw attention to myself. I barely tasted my food. When I finished eating, I climbed down from my chair, carried my dish into the kitchen and walked out the back door. Tears that I couldn't hold back any longer cascaded down my face. By the time I had walked down the driveway and the two house distance to Amanda's house I broke into sobs. I trudged across the lawn up to Amanda's front door as if my shoes were filled with lead.

Before knocking, I stood on the porch for a moment willing myself to gain control. I swallowed hard, dried the tears on my sleeve and looked up at the door looming before me. My hand, poised and ready to knock was shaking so hard that seeing it almost melted my resolve. But Mom expected it, Mrs. Small expected it, Amanda couldn't be my friend if I didn't, and it was the only way I would have any possibility of regaining any acceptance. I took a deep breath and rang the bell. A few moments later the doorknob turned and Amanda stood before me.

She stared at me not saying a word. I could see the hurt in her eyes. My breath caught in my throat. I started sobbing again and through my tears managed to say, "Amanda, I'm so sorry. I don't know why I said what I said. I'm sorry."

Still she didn't speak, and the silence was pure torture. I assumed that she wasn't going to talk to me and, looking away and turning around, I started to leave. As my foot touched the first step, I heard the screen door open behind me. "It's okay," she said softly. "I still want to be your friend."

She was standing in front of me reaching her arms out to hug me. I fell into her arms, and my body wrenched as her sobs mingled with mine. Holding on tight, I made a vow that I would always be careful never to say anything to hurt her again.

Denial, Double Binds And Double Messages About
Lying And The Roots Of Co-dependence

A significant indication of Maureen's already existing co-dependence appeared during this episode when Maureen left Barbara and Shawn alone with instructions not to open the door and not to let anyone know that they were home alone lest Amanda's father put them all in jail. Obviously intending to scare Barbara enough so that she would not open the door, Maureen seemed to have no qualms about lying to her daughter to insure obedience. Many parents are like Barbara's mother: frightening children with threats (like the boogie man) or lies to make them behave, while at the same time insisting that children always tell the truth.

Maureen failed to see how severely dysfunctional and co-dependent her behavior was. She did not realize that she was first, setting up conditions which might create fears that are carried into adulthood; second, that she created the double bind situation of making lying wrong except when her image was at stake and, third, that she was in denial about her own lying. Barbara was told not to lie, but the example set for her was one of lying.

As a child, Barbara's emphasis was that everyone was angry with her rather than that her mother was lying to save face. Not only did Barbara learn to lie, but she also learned not to trust what Maureen might say or do. Reality became treacherous for Barbara, a dangerous obstacle course in which her survival was based on her ability to guess when Maureen expected her to lie for her and when she expected her to tell the truth.

As Barbara and I discovered together in her therapy, this episode set up some interesting conditions for Barbara. It was one of the first real obvious examples to little Barbara that the truth and her own honesty were less important to Maureen than the image she presented to the world outside her family, or her own need to see herself as the perfect mother. When she yelled at Barbara, after Amanda's mother left, Maureen was aware, at least to some degree, that what was at stake was her image. Without realizing it, her communication to Barbara about Barbara's needing to learn to think about what she said before she spoke meant, in essence, "You better learn to distinguish which lies I expect of you." Prior to that Barbara's automatic response was, as it is with most children, to tell the truth. Barbara began to adopt a determined vigilance around her communications that had not previously existed.

It has been my experience that children are basically honest in their communications. It is our so-called socialization process that teaches children to lie. Our dysfunctional culture insists on our learning to be polite, or at the very least tactful. What these phrases really mean is, "Don't hurt people's feelings by being honest."

In our dysfunctional homes the child is urged to be honest while at the same time told not to tell family secrets or embarrass the family outside of the household. Hiding family secrets is one form of lying which eventually will lead to full-blown denial. The need to look good to outsiders solidifies the family's denial of reality and ultimately eclipses the emotional health of the individual family members.

Maureen's insistence that Barbara was at fault and that she go to her friend's the next day and lie for Maureen imbedded Barbara further into the disease process. Up to this point, Maureen's disease process was actually much further along than Barbara's. As a result of this episode, Barbara's disease took a quantum leap. Barbara mentioned that later that night she cried "not so much with anger at the injustice," but rather "in hurt and disappointment" in herself. She was being trained to somehow become a "mind reader" and figure out which lie her mother needed her to tell to keep her image from being soiled.

The other dysfunctional co-dependent lessons being imprinted in Barbara from this process were that she, Barbara, somehow had the power to control other peoples' feelings, if only she could figure out how, and that she should always protect others even at her own expense. She had learned in the past that shielding her mother was important, now she was learning that rescuing her mother was more important than knowing and telling the truth or taking care of herself.

Barbara and I discovered in therapy that it was this incident in particular that set the stage for Jim's physical, emotional and sexual abuse of Barbara. This episode put the capstone on Barbara's distrust of her right to take care of herself and her abilities to understand reality. It further froze in place the belief that she was a defective person. In addition it became obvious to Barbara that her survival was dependent on recognizing that the absoluteness of the family rule about protecting Maureen's image outside of the family took precedence over telling the truth. Barbara learned that her mother gave lip service to certain rules, like "always tell the truth" but expected Barbara to sort out when that was a true expectation. After this incident, Barbara would be totally absorbed in the co-dependent trait of trying to guess what others (especially Maureen) might think or need.

Am I Having Fun Yet?

In our family beer was the primary adult beverage for all gatherings, no matter what the occasion. Practically every day Jim consumed at least a six-pack of beer if he was home and more when he stopped at the bar. Even when there was limited money, there always seemed to be enough for beer. Jim was such a good customer at the local tavern that they let him buy beer on account. Sometimes Mother complained about the amount of the monthly bill.

When I was about thirteen, Mother bought Jim a refrigerated tap-beer dispenser for his birthday. That way he could buy a keg of beer every so often from the local bar. Later she told me that she had thought he would stay home since he'd have all the beer he needed at a touch. He didn't. The only thing that changed was that now he could get away with drinking more at home since there were no beer cans to count, making it more difficult for Mother to judge when he'd "had enough."

His trips to the bar were becoming more frequent, but we could usually count on him being home on Saturday mornings. He was always up before I was, even if he'd tied one on the night before, like the day after the luau Mother had hosted for her civic club.

Mother sent me to bed about ten o'clock, but the noise from the party had kept me up well after one o'clock. Mother had to work that Saturday and was gone long before I awoke to the noise of Jim in the kitchen making coffee. I rolled over, squinted at the clock and moaned. It was only seven-thirty. I hoped he would let me stay in bed for a few more hours. I curled up under my blankets and went back to sleep.

I awoke with a start as his hand shook my shoulder. "What are you going to do, sleep the day away?" he asked, sounding annoyed. "Come on, it's time to get out of bed." As he turned to leave I glanced at the clock. It was ten minutes to eight. A few seconds later I heard him yelling at Shawn to get up, too.

Sitting on the edge of the bed, I rubbed the sleep from my eyes and wondered why he had to wake us so early. After all, it was Saturday and most of the kids I knew got to sleep until ten or eleven. But it wouldn't do any good to argue with Jim, who often said that he didn't care what the other kids did, that we were his children and that we would do as he said.

After I brushed my teeth, Shawn and I ate breakfast quietly while Jim drank his coffee and read the newspaper in his usual early morning stony silence. At one point I must have looked like I was daydreaming because suddenly Jim shouted at me, "Hurry up and eat. We've got a lot to do today!"

I gobbled down the rest of my cereal and quickly cleaned up the mess. As I put the last dish away Jim grabbed his first beer of the day, then sat in his chair in the living room and began barking orders.

"Barbara, clean up the bathroom, and make sure you scour the bathtub. Shawn, you start cleaning the pool. Report back to me when you're finished." Then he buried his head in a Western novel.

I felt guilty for resenting having to spend my Saturdays cleaning the house. Since Mother had to work, I should clean the house so she wouldn't have to when she came home. I didn't deserve a day off if Mother had to work.

After I finished the bathroom, Jim gave me the rest of my chores, one by one: Mop the kitchen floor, change the linen on all three beds, dust and vacuum the living room.

I finished at noon, just as Jim was downing his fourth beer. He inspected my work and then, sounding pleased with himself, he said, "Like I always tell your mother, I can get more work done in three hours, sitting in my chair than she can do all day!" I was glad he was happy. He said it was time for lunch. I wanted to go back to bed.

Jim, who seemed to be in a much better mood, helped me make sandwiches and soup. When we were finished eating, and I had cleaned up the mess, he suggested that the three of us spend the afternoon playing a game of Monopoly. I hated playing games with him, but if I said no, I would risk his ridicule. Whenever I refused, he said that the only reason I didn't want to play was because I always lost. He was right. Even though he told me I should learn how to be a good loser, I couldn't seem to find anything good about losing.

Whatever game we played, Jim liked to make up additional rules to augment the ones that came with the game. He did this, he said, to "make the game interesting." In Monopoly one of Jim's "to make the game interesting" rules was that if a player other than the one who landed on a property, brought it to the owner's attention, that player would then have to pay the rent instead.

Shawn and I set up the game while Jim got another beer. About a half hour into the game, I noticed Jim winking at me and nodding his head to the side in Shawn's direction. I looked down at the board and saw that Shawn had landed on one of my properties.

"Rent!" I shouted.

"You told her!" Shawn whined angrily at Jim.

"Oh, come on, don't be a crybaby," Jim said. "It's only a game."

While Jim went to get another beer, Shawn glared at me then grabbed the rent money from his pile and slammed it down on the table next to mine. Even though I felt special because Jim had tipped me off, I was uncomfortable with Shawn's anger.

Several turns later I noticed that Shawn, who was busily arranging his money in the same manner as Jim's, didn't notice that Jim had landed on one of his railroads. Wanting to get back into Shawn's good graces, I tried to get his attention. I coughed, cleared my throat, drummed my fingers on the table, and then said in a voice louder than necessary, "Whose turn is it?"

Shawn looked up, then down at the board and yelled, "Rent!"

Jim turned at me and shouted, "Just what are you trying to pull? You know the rules!"

"I didn't say anything," I protested.

"And just what was all that shit with coughing and hitting the table? You're not fooling me! Pay your brother the rent!"

Ashamed for being so obvious, I counted out the money, which was over half the money I had left. The next time I rolled the dice, I landed on Boardwalk which was still for sale. I didn't have much money left and Boardwalk was an expensive piece of property.

"I don't want to buy it," I announced.

"Whaddaya mean, you don' want it?" Jim slurred.

"I don't have very much money left," I answered meekly, instantly sorry for my decision.

"Big chicken shit as usual, huh?" Jim retorted, his mouth a disgusted frown. Turning to Shawn he laughed, "She always makes it easy for us to win, huh, Squarehead?" I hated it when he called Shawn "Squarehead," but Shawn never protested.

I hated this part, knowing that for the rest of the game Jim would yell at me for everything I did. Before the game ended, he found fault with the way I stacked money, how I kept track of properties and finally where I placed houses. At the end he was even disgusted with the way I rolled the dice. Every time my turn came my whole body would become a mass of tension until I had a headache.

The next time I went to get Jim a beer, I quickly gobbled down three cookies and poured myself a glass of milk.

An hour later, when I inevitably lost, I acted like a "good loser," hiding my disappointment. I knew I would never be good enough to win. I pasted a smile on my face and reached for a cookie. The game would have been better if I was better at playing games. If I wasn't so stupid, Jim wouldn't get so angry.

Games And Other Abuses

Alcoholism is a progressive disease. There may be brief time periods when the alcoholic might stop or slow down but, in general, without support and treatment, alcoholism marks a continual slide into hell that drags everyone in the family system along with it. As the alcoholic progresses deeper into his or her disease process, the family system adjusts more and more to accommodate the growing dysfunction of the alcoholic and the alcoholic drinking cycle. Home life often takes on a surrealistic aspect. "Am I Having Fun Yet?" is Barbara's example of how crazy the family becomes and how painful even playtime is in the home of the alcoholic.

There are several important issues to note in "Am I Having Fun Yet?": first is the alcoholic drinking cycle, second is the way Jim blamed Barbara and Shawn for his own character defects, such as being poor losers, third is the control Jim needed so that he never had to face his own emotional dysfunction, fourth is the destruction that Jim wreaked on both Barbara's and Shawn's self-esteem, and fifth are the co-alcoholic dysfunctional ways Maureen attempted to handle Jim's drinking.

If we pay attention to the nature of Jim's behavior from early morning to later in the day, we see the progress of the alcoholic cycle. Contrary to popular belief, alcoholics do not necessarily sleep long hours. In fact many, like Jim, roll out of bed early in the morning awakened by their bodies' call for alcohol.

When we first see Jim, he is up early but grouchy and nasty, as many alcoholics are before they get enough alcohol in them to feel mellow. Sitting in his chair, "barking orders" to the children, he would begin his drinking. Two beers later, he would start behaving a little nicer toward the children. Several beers later, he had moved back into the obnoxious behavior of the latter part of his drinking cycle. Living with this cycle was crazy-making for Barbara. She believed that there was something that she could do to make Jim behave differently. She believed that if she had only learned to play the crazy game better, or if she had won more, Jim would have acted differently or felt better about her. Nothing could have been further from the truth, and the havoc this wreaked on her self-esteem was enormous.

While Jim's drinking pattern is fairly typical, it is not the only pattern with alcoholics. There are many types of alcoholic patterns. Some alcoholics have a poor-pitiful-pathetic-me pattern into which they lapse during their drinking cycle. Others will do the life-of-the-party cycle. The important thing to remember is that there is nothing anyone in the family (except the alcoholic himself) can do to change that pattern — just as there is nothing that anyone can do to change another person's feelings. Unfortunately Barbara was raised in a dysfunctional home where she was led to believe that she was responsible for her parents' feelings and for shielding her parents from discomfort.

As a child, Barbara could not see that Jim's control of the rules of the game, the emotional battering she received and the blame for being a poor loser were all indicators of Jim's own immaturity. Jim could not handle losing. He had to "win" at any cost. He would lie, cheat, control, manipulate and blame the children, Barbara in particular, so that he would not have to lose face. The question is, would he have been any different if he had not been drinking?

After nine years of private practice working with alcoholics, chemical dependents and Adult Children of Alcoholic and Dysfunctional Families, I can say that I have never found an alcoholic or chemically dependent person who did not come from a dysfunctional family and who was not dysfunctional long before the substance abuse began. The drinking or substance abuse will exacerbate the problems and must be dealt with and treated first. We must consider the idea that just because alcoholism is a primary disease that will kill, it does not mean that it does not co-exist with other primary disease processes.

Years ago, during the early developmental stages of psychotherapy, alcoholism was relegated to the role of a symptom. Therapists discovered, as recovering alcoholics had found out in 12-Step programs, that by labeling alcoholism as a symptom, it was never dealt with properly. The same is now true for the dysfunctional behaviors that alcoholics demonstrate. We run a huge risk of developing severely disturbed emotional disease processes, other than alcoholism, if we do not pay attention to the general underlying addictive process. Without dealing with the underlying issues of poor self-esteem, the addictive process of avoiding feelings and blaming others, personal boundary problems, depression and chronic ego defenses, the other dysfunctional behaviors will continue, even when the drinking stops. The continuation of those behaviors is what is referred to in Alcoholics Anonymous by the term "dry drunk."

Inside every chemically dependent person is a damaged child who never grew up, a child who never had his or her dependency needs met, who never received validation for his or her emotions or never had healthy modeling of functional behaviors. The chemically dependent person may have had his or her physical, emotional or sexual boundaries violated by abusive, controlling or smothering parental behaviors. This person becomes an Adult Child and acts out the childhood pain on his or her own family, expecting others, including his or her own children, to take care of the unmet childhood dependency needs. Jim's behavior was a result of a combination of factors, including his own dysfunctional upbringing and his drinking. While Jim never would have been able to stop his dysfunctional behaviors without stopping the drinking, simply stopping the drinking would not necessarily have stopped the dysfunctional behaviors.

If we turn to Maureen's part in the family process, we see that there are several behaviors in this story that point to Maureen's enabling conduct. No matter what the financial situation was, Maureen always saw to it that Jim had his beer. She would complain about Jim's bar bill, but she never refused to pay it and never tried to stop Jim's charging by calling the barkeeper and telling him she would not cover Jim's drinking bills anymore. She even bought him a beer dispenser in hope that he would stay home more because he would have all the beer he wanted. This action enabled him further, by making it easier for him to drink even more. Maureen had apparently also slipped into the co-alcoholic's typical pattern of watching to see when Jim had enough to drink. With all of this, she never tried to talk to him about his drinking and how it affected her individually, their relationship and the children.

Bumps In The Night

By the time I was thirteen years old, Mother was so involved in her job and civic groups, that she had little time left over for me. Jim's spare time was spent drinking, watching television or entertaining his drinking buddies. Even Shawn, who had at one time been close to me, had drifted away. We rarely spoke except to argue. I had no one to confide in, no one on my side, no one who really cared.

There was no escape from the pain that seemed to intensify with each passing year, no place to hide, no privacy. I had no space that was really my own, including my own bedroom which was subject to Mother's periodic surprise inspections. The only place that afforded me any relief was the fantasy world I created in my mind. And even that wasn't safe from invasion.

Many times I stood at the kitchen sink doing dishes, gazing out of the window, becoming lost in a make-believe world where I was popular, pretty, well-liked and the center of attention. Usually, involved in my fantasy, I would stop washing dishes and stare blankly into space. The illusion would shatter when behind me Jim or Mother bellowed, "Stop daydreaming! Pay attention to what you're doing!" Like Cinderella, I hoped that someday there would be a prince who didn't drink to help me make my dreams come true.

I had ownership of nothing including my own body. Mother attended two evening meetings a month with the civic group. On those nights, invariably, Jim stopped at the bar for several hours before coming home. The memory of those nights are blurred, one on top of the other, intermingled and filled with a sense of hopelessness and despair. But their one common thread was the way they ended.

I would be asleep, awakening to the sound of the doorknob turning as Jim came into the room. My body stiffened as I waited. I knew I couldn't stop what was coming. I had no rights. Even threatening to tell Mother as I had done before, only produced a response of wicked laughter from Jim. "What makes you think she'll believe you over me?" he jeered. "I'll just tell her you're lying!" I believed that, if push came to shove, she would listen to him.

Curled up on my left side, back to the door, unmoving, hardly breathing, eyes closed, I pretended to be sleeping. The door closed with barely a sound, and after a moment, I heard Jim whisper in the darkness.

"Barbara?"

I didn't answer, holding my breath, praying he would leave me alone.

"Barbara!" he muttered, his voice more insistent than before. I wanted to shout at him to leave me alone, but what good would it do?

"Come on, Barbara, you're awake, aren't you?" His hand was on my shoulder, squeezing, hurting.

Still I didn't answer, feigning sleep, hoping he would give up and leave me alone, even though that never worked.

I felt the blanket tug as his hand slipped between the sheets, creeping across the bed, coming to rest on my waist. My body recoiled from his touch. "Barbara?" he whispered. "Come on, little sweetheart! Wake up!"

"M-m-m-m-ph?" I mumbled, trying to discourage him.

"Move over!" he commanded in an angry whisper, and the disgusting smell of alcohol reached my nose.

As he forced me onto my back, I sighed deeply and resigned myself to the inevitable. Sliding my body to the left to make room, I realized, as I always did, that there was no point in resisting. He would get what he wanted. At least he didn't beat me.

He began caressing my stomach and chest. "You know that I love you, don't you, sweetheart?" he slurred in the darkness.

I hated him. Why couldn't he love me without this? I didn't believe that I could make him love me *and* tell him to stop. Making him love me was more important so I kept my mouth shut.

"Well?" he insisted drunkenly.

"Yes, Daddy, I know you love me," I responded remembering that I had better pay attention and say the right thing, or else he might squeeze or pinch me, becoming angry if I cried out. The less I resisted, the faster he would leave. What I really wanted to do was disappear.

He started kissing me, sliding his foul tongue into my mouth. He smelled like half-empty cans of stale beer, dirty ashtrays and days-old accumulation of sweat. He held my face in his hand forcing me to submit. Bitter bile rose to my throat as I finally managed to twist away. I swallowed hard to keep from vomiting.

When his hands moved to pull my legs apart I turned my head to the side, stuffed my fist in my mouth, and waited for him to finish.

Sometimes he would make me do things that made me feel dirty and perverted, like putting his penis into my mouth. He smelled of urine and that turned my stomach in knots. One time he became too aggressive and I gagged. His inebriated laugh broke the silence. "Just like your mother," he slurred, his words cutting a wound in my soul. Tears of guilt and despair slid silently down my face.

When finally he finished, he would kiss me deeply one last time and then leave. Alone in the darkness of my room, crying myself to sleep, all I could think of was my hatred, for him, for myself, for my life.

Sometime during the night I would awake, my shivering body drenched in sweat, my mind disoriented from what I thought was a bad dream. Afraid of the dark, afraid to go back to sleep, I turned on the light, and after a few minutes to calm my shaking body, I tiptoed silently down the hall to the kitchen, my stomach churning. With only the refrigerator light for illumination, I searched the cupboards for something to eat, a bowl or two of cereal, a peanut butter sandwich, some left-over spaghetti, a box of graham crackers.

The next day at school, my private parts stung, forcing the memory of his drunken desire to the front of my mind, making it difficult to concentrate on my lessons, as all morning long I watched the clock, waiting impatiently for lunch.

"Barbara, Where Are You?"

Process work rarely moves chronologically. Because so much of the work surfaces as a result of the associative processes of the right brain, Barbara and I would often find ourselves working on scenes that were related to but not identical to the ones we had started discussing. During one of our early sessions, we had been talking about a typical "Bumps-In-The-Night" scene.

Originally the path our talk had taken led me to believe that we might start processing the guilt Barbara felt over enjoying the initial caresses and the power she had felt from being wanted, or perhaps, how she felt about her mother being so bonded to Jim that she would probably have believed him over her. As we talked, Barbara brought up a few other issues that were associated with the incest.

One of the topics was the flinching response she had whenever someone touched her on the right side near her waist, another was the conflict and turmoil she felt over wanting him to love her, yet wanting him to stop his disgusting and painful attacks, and a third was the almost constant feeling she had that a piece of her was missing. I mentioned to Barbara that there were several topics she could work on, like the guilt, the power, the conflict, the flinching or the missing piece, and I asked Barbara which issue she wanted to work on at that time. She said that since we had already worked a little on the flinch response in one of her previous sessions, she would prefer working on the feeling that some part of her was missing. We talked a few minutes about her eventually dealing with the other issues, especially the guilt and the power, and she said that she definitely wanted to work on them after she had processed the "missing piece." Since Barbara rarely avoided dealing with issues no matter how painful they were, we tabled further work on the other areas and started in on the missing piece.

I asked her to see if she could get a sense of where she felt the piece was missing from and what it might be. I had Barbara close her eyes, focus her attention inward for a few moments, scan her body and tell me when she thought she had found something. Not long afterward, she pointed toward her solar plexus and said, "I'm missing something there. I'm missing . . . I'm missing me."

"Where did you go, Barbara? Where are you?" I asked.

She answered, "I'm in the bedroom."

"Where are you in the bedroom? How old are you? What are you doing?"

Barbara replied, "I'm ten, I'm standing at the foot of the bed." She stopped, shook her head in a motion that said "no" and did not go any further.

"What's happening?" I asked.

"I don't know. I don't want to look," she whimpered.

I asked her if she would be willing to look. She said that she was. (Had she not been willing to look, we would have had to find another way to approach her problem and her process, but she was willing to go on, so we did.) Eyes still closed, she raised her face, as if to watch something. Silent tears began to flow down her face.

"He's hurting her," she sobbed.

Although I believed that I knew who the "he" and "her" were that Barbara was talking about, Barbara needed to own what was happening to her. Her language told me that she was not owning her experience, that she had disassociated from it.

"Who is he?"

"My stepfather."

"Who is he hurting?"

"He's hurting Barbara."

Realizing at that point that the part of Barbara that was speaking was still not ready to own what was happening to her, or her body, I asked the disassociated piece if she could tell him to stop hurting Barbara. The part of Barbara standing at the foot of the bed began speaking softly, but as she spoke, the anger surfaced and she screamed at her stepfather, "STOP HURTING HER, YOU RAT!"

I quietly asked, "Can you tell Barbara, on the bed, that you'll help her?"

The ten-year-old child standing at the foot of the bed began to talk lovingly to the small inanimate body in the bed. After a few moments of that, I asked Barbara if she could be the Barbara in the bed. She nodded.

Barbara in the bed, "He hurt me!"

I asked her if she would do a two-part process and begin switching back and forth between the "other Barbara" and the Barbara on the bed. She did.

Barbara standing said, "Yes, I know."

Barbara in the bed, "YOU LEFT ME!"

Barbara standing, "I was afraid. It was awful!"

Barbara in the bed, "BUT YOU LEFT ME, AND I WAS AFRAID, TOO!"

At this point, I asked the Barbara who was in the bed to tell the other Barbara what she wanted. She told her that she wanted her to come back inside. The other Barbara was not willing to do that yet.

I then asked the adult Barbara to see if she could sense how much of her was in the bed and how much was standing at the foot of the bed. Using percentages as we often did, she said about 35% was in bed, the rest was outside. The adult Barbara recognized that part of her had disassociated from the child who was being molested and that the disassociated part was not ready yet to reintegrate. I asked her if she, the adult Barbara, would spend some time at home dialoguing and talking with the Barbara who had left the body and was standing at the foot of the bed. I suggested that she support her in dealing with her fear of re-entering the violated body.

Before Barbara left that session, we discussed two things: her age in this particular process (noting that this episode was from an early time in the sexual abuse) and her confusion about being both Jim's daughter and his lover. When we began "the missing part" work, neither of us knew where the process might take us. I had guessed that Barbara would probably be working on some aspect of sexual abuse, but I had no idea how far back she would go in this first reintegration. Sometimes a survivor will start with the later material because it is freshest in her mind. Since Barbara had let herself be guided by her body, she was able to get back to an earlier period.

The last thing we talked about in that session was the tremendous confusion Barbara had experienced being both lover and daughter to Jim. Still a child when the first attack had come, Barbara needed Jim to remain her "Daddy." She would call him Daddy, even during sex, and in his diseased thinking, Jim seemed to relish having sex with both mother and daughter. Unfortunately, this dual relationship also led to Barbara's inability to separate love from sex in her relationships with men. Barbara never had a healthy relationship in which to learn affection and warmth about sex.

When Barbara returned for the next session, we went back to the part of Barbara that was in bed during that first scene. Since she had already spent time at home working with the part that had disassociated, she needed to do some similar work on the part that was left. As we worked on the pain and terror that the Barbara in the bed felt, that Barbara began to grow experientially in size in relationship to the other Barbara. When Barbara in the bed was about 65% of Barbara, I suggested that she try the merger again. She did. This time it worked. Barbara now had a sense of how her disassociative process worked and what she could do if she found herself disassociating again in other circumstances.

Human consciousness has an incredible fluidity about it. We are capable of separating from extreme trauma in many ways. "Leaving the body" is one of the forms of disassociation we use to separate from distressful situations. In this type of disassociation, the person never loses touch with reality, as does the schizophrenic, and never completely loses touch with the other aspects of personality, as does the multiple personality. Instead, the consciousness develops many subpersonalities which can and do separate and reintegrate at various times. The key is not to try to stop the process from ever happening, but to be able to recognize it when it happens and to have the tools to deal with it. It is possible, through Gestalt dialoguing techniques, to be able to work with, be responsible for and reintegrate the disassociated aspects of our personalities.

There are many ways that the dialoguing techniques may be used. Barbara's session, in which I had her deal with the disassociated part by having the two parts speak to each other, showed one particular way to use the technique. Having her go home and talk to the part that had disassociated is one variation of that process, and having her come back to therapy the next week and work on the part that was left in her body was another variation.

When she worked on the part that was left in her body, I had her go back and deal with the terror and pain to gain the strength that she needed to support a reintegration. As time passed in her therapy, Barbara discovered that she had disassociated whenever she had experienced a particularly painful or disgusting encounter with Jim. Because of this, she had to frequently repeat her reintegration process.

Once Barbara had gone through her first reintegration experience, she was able to learn to recognize various disassociative states. She saw that her fantasies were another way for her to avoid the painful reality she had to survive daily. It was solely Barbara's enormous psychological strength that had prevented her from taking her fantasies further into the realm of schizophrenic disassociation.

Having no privacy is extremely harmful to people. We need a certain amount of physical and psychological privacy in order to withdraw from the outside to integrate new material into our pre-existing self. Without that privacy, we may be forced to withdraw into insanity or multiple personalities. Continually invaded, both physically and psychologically, Barbara still managed to find the minimum amount of privacy necessary to prevent a complete withdrawal from reality.

The first reintegration process that Barbara and I did furthered her ability to go deeper into the gory details of the various "Bumps-In-The-Night" episodes that she had survived. In order to heal, Barbara had to deal with her original traumas and the ensuing pain. To do her grief work, to mourn her losses, she had to know what she was mourning. This meant finding and dealing with the horrors of Jim's invasions. Doing this work with a therapist validated her pain and her right to grieve. It also gave her additional tools with which to work with her inner child.

During the course of our work, I also pointed out to Barbara that she did not need to reserve these tools only for usage with parts that have disassociated and left the body. The tools could be used to deal with any of the negative voices that she heard in her head. The difference is that instead of using these tools for the integration of the negative voices, she would be using these tools for the recognition of, the separation from and ultimately the disappearance of the negative voice.

Surprise Attacks

Jim's drinking increased and while Mother held down an important job, Jim went from job to job, working as a pipe-fitter, an insurance salesman, a civil service job and a driver for a soft drink bottling company. Two to three nights a week, Jim stopped at the local bar before coming home. Sometimes when he missed work after drinking too much the night before, Mother would phone his boss saying he had the flu. As time went on he had the flu a lot.

On the nights he came home first, he would immediately inspect the house, looking for some infraction of the rules. He was rarely disappointed. There were two rules that I broke with increasing regularity. Rule one was: Do not turn on the television before five o'clock. Rule two was: Do your chores before doing anything else.

On the way home from school, I would chastise myself to follow the rules and not put anything off until the last minute. My first stop was always the kitchen where I would begin opening cupboard doors and refrigerator in search of something to eat, anything to fill the void in my stomach. Even though I had eaten a big lunch three hours earlier, I was usually famished.

Then I would break the television rule, watching cartoons or my favorite serial with Annette on the Mickey Mouse Club, intending to turn it off as soon as I finished my snack. Jim would only know if the television was still warm when he came home. If I could be clever, and Shawn didn't tell on me, Jim would never know.

Television was a relaxing way for me to unwind from the pressures at school where my grades were gradually sliding. I was gaining weight and Mother had said that I wasn't pretty. My clothes weren't as nice as some of the other girls. Mother said that was because I didn't take good care of the ones I had, so I didn't deserve new ones. When she bought me a skirt, blouse or dress that I really liked, I took care of that, but usually didn't do a very good job.

Most days Jim didn't come home by dinner time. Then Mother would start calling the bar. In the earlier years, he'd be home about a half hour after she called. As the years passed, it would take two to three phone calls, and sometimes even then he didn't come home. Sometimes the bartender would say that Jim wasn't there. Mother knew he was lying but never said anything to Jim about it.

On the nights that he came home after her second call, I heard Mother greet him at the door and say, "Hello, honey," in a sweet voice, as if he had come home straight from work, and everything was fine, and she hadn't been upset. She would tell him that dinner was ready and offer to get him a beer. He never refused.

While he washed up, Mother would call me to the kitchen to help her dish up dinner, and then we would all sit down at the table looking very much like a normal family. Mother, father, daughter, son. A normal family having a normal dinner. In fact, Mother and Jim would often comment that other families didn't spend as much time "as a family" as we did, implying they weren't as good as we were.

After dinner I would clean the kitchen while they watched television. Those were the happy nights. On other nights we had Surprise Attacks.

One such night started like many others. Jim came home from work at four-thirty, and the TV was warm, but I had already done most of my daily chores, cleaned the living room, always a mess when Jim had been home the night before, emptied fully laden ashtrays, dusted table tops strewn with wayward cigarette ashes, thrown away empty beer bottles and then vacuumed the carpet. After that I had straightened the kitchen and bathroom.

But I hadn't started my homework, and to make matters worse, I had forgotten to pick up his laundry on my way home from school. This meant that he didn't have a clean work shirt for the next day.

After yelling at me, then tossing his dirty shirt on the floor, he demanded that I wash, starch and iron it before going to bed, then left for the bar in a huff. On his way out the door he shouted, ". . . and have dinner ready by the time I come home!"

As his car pulled out of the driveway, I started in on myself, "Why can't you, just once, do things right? What's wrong with you?"

I had a lot of homework to do. I had to rehearse a presentation for a science project that was due the next day, and final touches were needed on the display board. I also had to finish the translation of one of Grimm's Fairy Tales for German class. It didn't matter that I didn't have time to do Jim's shirt. If I complained, he would say, "If you'd picked up the laundry, you'd have had time." I hated having to iron his shirt anyway, knowing that he always complained that I wasn't as good as the cleaners.

I cried as I put a load of dirty clothes including his shirt into the washing machine, and then started a salad and peeled potatoes. A short time later Mother's car pulled into the driveway. Not wanting her to know that I had been crying I ran into the bathroom to wash my face. Red and puffy eyes would tell her I had done something wrong.

Several minutes later, after holding a cold cloth over my eyes to reduce the puffiness, I flushed the toilet twice and turned on the faucet not wanting to arouse any suspicion. She had already changed out of her business suit into slacks when I entered the kitchen, and was busy putting the finishing touches on the meatloaf. "Did you forget to pick up the laundry again?" she asked angrily.

With a deep sigh of shame, I said, "Yes."

"What am I going to do with you?" she asked sounding both exasperated and angry. I didn't know the answer.

"I wanted to do a load of towels for you and found your father's shirt in the washing machine," she went on, explaining how she had found out. Slapping the counter with her hands she shouted, "Why can't you just remember to do the few things I ask you to do? Everything would be so much better around this house if you weren't so irresponsible."

Tears welled in my eyes. She was right, everyone would be so much happier if I could stop messing up, maybe even happier if I was dead. I wiped my eyes with my sleeve and sniffed loudly.

Turning around she yelled, "Barbara Jeanne, for heaven sake, must you cry every time someone looks at you cross-eyed?

"Finish the salad. And quit being so dramatic. You have no one to blame but yourself."

Biting my lower lip, I walked to the sink. By the time I finished, Mother was sitting with her feet up, reading the evening paper. I snuck a cookie and went to my room to complete the display board. Having trouble concentrating, twice I glued pictures in the wrong spots. The project wasn't very good, but there was no more time.

On the way to the kitchen for a drink, I heard Mother talking on the phone. I stopped in the doorway and listened.

"I know, Jim, I already talked to her . . . I know, honey, I know. I don't understand it either . . . Dinner's almost ready now . . . Okay, finish the game. I'll hold everything until then . . . Okay, honey, see you soon," she finished and hung up the phone.

"Your father's disgusted with you," she sneered. "He'd stay home at night if you did as you were told."

I didn't know what to say. I wished that she'd get angry with him. He stopped at the bar almost every night and she never yelled at him! My silence must have made her mad because she frowned, shook her head, then stood up to leave.

"The shirts are out of the dryer. Get one done before he gets here. Maybe then we can have a pleasant evening for a change."

Ironing the shirt, I thought that nothing I did would ever be good enough. Mother hadn't noticed that I had done most of the things I was supposed to. They both only saw what I didn't do. Once I tried to justify what I hadn't done by pointing out what I had done, arguing that they never said anything good about me. Jim's response had been, "When you don't do a job well, I'll tell you. When you do what you're supposed to, you won't need me to tell you because you'll know you did!" I didn't suppose there was anything I did well, because it seemed like they were always telling me what I did wrong.

As I hung Jim's shirt on the hanger after ironing it, I frowned. It wasn't crisp and smooth like it was when it came back from the cleaners. I just couldn't figure out how they did it. No matter how careful I was, it never looked right.

Looking up at the clock I noticed how much time it had taken me to iron the shirt, and Jim still wasn't home yet. Hungry, I frowned as I remembered that Mother had said he would be home soon. How long were we going to wait tonight? Other kids I knew ate their dinners around six o'clock. We rarely ate before seven-thirty or eight o'clock.

Just then Mother came into the kitchen, looked up at the clock and frowned. While I put the ironing board away, she picked up the phone and dialed the bar again. When Jim came to the phone, she smiled sweetly and said, "Honey, the meatloaf is drying out. Isn't that game over yet?"

There were a few seconds of silence as she listened, then she slammed the phone down in its cradle. He must not have said what she wanted to hear. She was finally angry with him and I was glad. She looked at me and I could see tears forming in her eyes.

"What are you staring at?" she shouted. She didn't want an answer because she kept on yelling, "Eat your dinner and clean up the kitchen." With that she stomped out of the kitchen, muttering under her breath that she just couldn't "take this anymore."

After dinner I cleaned up the kitchen. Thinking that maybe Jim would want to eat when he came home, I left the meatloaf and potatoes on the stove. On my way to my bedroom I peeked in Mother's room. She had fallen asleep. I tiptoed into her room, removed the book from her chest and switched off the light. Before beginning the final touches on the translation, I reached up to set my alarm. It was already nine o'clock, only a half hour until my lights-out curfew, not enough time to finish.

Sure enough, by the time nine-thirty came, I was only half finished. I was tempted to stay up, but thought better of it. If Jim came home and found me, he'd be angry for sure. After he spent an evening at the bar, things seemed to upset him more than usual, and his punishments were more severe. I went to sleep.

Bang! I awoke with a start.

"Goddammit!" Jim shouted. Bang! Metal against metal. "Son of a bitch!" he yelled. My whole body was taut, waiting. Please don't let him come in my room, I prayed looking at the clock. It was after one o'clock. God didn't listen. Throwing open my door, Jim flipped a switch flooding the room with light.

"Get out of that bed," he bellowed, "and get your ass into the living room!"

Resisting was out of the question. Tears in my eyes, I put on my robe, grabbed a handful of tissues and hurried out into the hall in time to bump into Mother as she came stumbling out of her room half-asleep. Giving me a mean stare, she turned and walked ahead of me into the living room. Jim was sitting in his chair with a can of beer in his hand. Mother sat on the couch next to him. They both turned to me and frowned.

"Sit down," Jim demanded pointing to the wing-back chair in the corner. "Isn't it your job to clean the kitchen after dinner?" he asked in a nasty voice.

Before I could answer, Mother said, "Barbara Jeanne, what's the last thing I told you to do? Don't tell me you didn't clean the kitchen."

I didn't say anything.

"Well, is it your job or isn't it?" Jim repeated.

"Yes," I mumbled, and looked from him to Mother, hoping she would stand up for me. She rolled her eyes to the ceiling, then gave me an angry and disgusted frown.

"Then why in the hell didn't you do it?" he shouted.

"I did," I started to protest.

" 'I did,' " he said, mimicking my whiny voice. "What about the meatloaf and the mashed potatoes? Did they grow legs and walk in there after you finished?"

"I thought you'd want to eat something when you came home," I said trying to explain why I hadn't put them away.

Looking at Mother, he asked, "Did you tell Barbara I would want something to eat when I came home?"

"No," she answered with a sigh that expressed all the annoyance she felt. Against all hope I silently wished she would stand up for me. I hadn't stopped working on dinner, my homework or his shirt until bedtime. Why didn't she say something?

Turning back to me he went on, "Did your mother tell you it was okay to leave those pans out?"

"No," I muttered. She hadn't said anything, she had been asleep.

"So what's the truth? Why didn't you clean up the goddamn kitchen?" he boomed.

"I cleaned everything else," I protested, all the time knowing this approach was probably hopeless, too, but I was so tired I was willing to try anything.

"Either you do a job or you don't!" he shouted, the familiar refrain, reminding me of his all-or-nothing standard about chores. "I'll ask you one more time, why didn't you clean up the kitchen?"

I didn't know what he wanted me to say. Mother's eyes were closed and she was massaging her temples. I had given her a headache.

"Barbara Jeanne!" Jim shouted and I jerked in my chair. "Answer my question — why didn't you clean up the goddamn kitchen?"

"I told you," I cried. "I thought you would want something to eat."

"That's not the truth!" he roared. "Now, goddammit, what is the truth?"

On and on he went, unrelenting. He wasn't going to let up until I said what he wanted me to say. I didn't know what the "truth" was. He hadn't told me yet.

Finally, slurring each word, he said snidely, "You didn't want to clean the kitchen so you made up this little lie, hoping I would be stupid enough to buy it, didn't you?"

The clue! All I had to do was agree and this attack might end. Then maybe I could get some sleep.

"Well," he said, "I'm waiting for your answer. You hate cleaning up the kitchen and you look for any excuse not to do it, don't you? You didn't care if I ate or not, you just didn't want to clean the kitchen. Just like this afternoon, you care more about watching the goddamn TV than you do about doing what you're supposed to do. I'm sick of you!"

I didn't say anything. He had said so many things I wasn't sure just what I was supposed to respond to.

"Well, I'm right, aren't I?" he insisted. "You didn't clean the kitchen because you didn't want to and it had nothing to do with me eating or not eating, right?"

"Yes," I murmured. Even though that wasn't the truth, I knew that I'd better agree or we'd be at this until I did.

"Yes what?" he demanded, and I knew he wanted me to repeat his words.

"Yes, I didn't want to clean the kitchen," I finished.

"Just as I suspected," he said triumphantly. Turning back to Mother, he said, "Maurie, this girl is impossible. What are we going to do with her?"

"Well, she'll just have to be punished," she answered, glaring at me. There was no one on my side. Maybe he was right, perhaps I didn't want to clean the kitchen and couldn't tell that I was making up excuses. I couldn't trust myself to know right and wrong.

"The choice is," Jim began, "a spanking right now or two weeks in your room."

"My room," I answered.

"Sure, take the easy way out like you always do," he said in a disgusted voice. "I can't stand to look at you anymore. Go clean the kitchen and then get to bed."

Without another word, and with tears streaming down my face, I dragged myself out of the chair and walked out of the room. Biting my lip to keep from sobbing and risking more ridicule and disapproval, I put the leftovers into the refrigerator, then washed both pans and put them away. I glanced up at the clock above the sink. It was almost three o'clock in the morning. In three and a half hours, I would have to be ready to start a new day. Even though I was thoroughly exhausted when I climbed into bed, I didn't go to sleep; instead I tossed and turned until the alarm clock sounded at six-thirty.

I received a "C" on my science presentation and failed the German translation. I walked home all the way from the bus with my head down. I told myself that I should have done a better job on the board and that I should have started the translation at the beginning of the week instead of waiting until the last minute. I knew I had to do well or face the consequence of being punished if I didn't. I vowed to study harder.

That afternoon, determined that I wasn't going to get into trouble when Jim came home, I started my chores right after I ate a sandwich, a bag of potato chips and a candy bar I had hidden in my room.

I had just finished preparing liver and onions for frying when Jim came home from work. It was Mother's club night and she would be home early to fry the liver before she went. Jim left for the bar but came home at six-thirty, earlier than usual, in time to eat dinner and say goodbye to Mother before she left.

He was giving me the silent treatment, barely speaking to me except to issue perfunctory orders like, "Pass the salt" and "Get me a beer" and "Clean up the kitchen." Finished in the kitchen I went in to take a bath, one of the few things I was allowed to do outside my room during restriction. Soaking in the hot water I wondered how long he would be angry. I hated it when he ignored me.

When I was finished with my bath, brushed my teeth and set my hair in curlers, I stopped in the kitchen for a glass of milk before going to my room for the night. With my towel wrapped around my naked body, I walked through the living room on my way to the bedroom. Jim was watching television. He looked up at me without saying anything as I passed by. He was still mad at me.

I finished my homework, re-read a portion of *The Little Lame Prince,* then turned off my light. Tired from the lack of sleep the night before, I fell asleep almost immediately even though it was only eight o'clock. A few hours later, I awoke to the sound of my doorknob turning, hearing Jim's familiar whisper. I knew he wasn't mad any longer when his hand slipped between the sheets.

The Disease Process Escalates

If you did not have an emotional reaction to Barbara's Surprise Attack story, you are either numb, unconscious or you have suffered so much worse that you don't realize that this was a horribly abusive situation. Surprise Attacks is a textbook case of alcoholism and the Alcoholic Family Syndrome. If we had only this story to draw from, we would have every component of the alcoholic's and co-alcoholic's disease process and the effects on the children.

We have fourteen-year-old Barbara who was expected to do all the household chores daily, do her homework, go to school and get good grades. Remember, the guise that her parents had previously used for having Barbara take on the housework the summer that she was ten was that they were teaching her how to run a home and do the things she would have to do when she grew up and had a family. The irony was that Maureen was not doing what she supposedly was training Barbara to do when she was married and in Maureen's position. Barbara was doing Maureen's chores so that Maureen could hold down a high-powered position and spend huge amounts of time and energy on her civic clubs. Had Barbara questioned this, she would have been told that Maureen worked hard and that Barbara was expected to "help."

What co-alcoholic Maureen could not see was that Barbara's job as a child was to go to school, do her homework, pick up her room and participate with all the family in the general upkeep of the household. What Maureen and Jim expected of Barbara was not only age inappropriate, it was severely abusive. To expect a fourteen-year-old to cook, clean, keep house, go to school and get good grades, do her homework and be in bed with the lights out by 9:30 borders on sadistic. As we saw in an earlier chapter, Jim had actually manipulated his wife into setting Barbara up to take over her mother's responsibilities so that Maureen could take over Jim's responsibilities as the main wage earner.

Barbara's inability to do "her chores" was made worse by her eating disorder. Driven by her compulsion to eat, she would spend many of her afterschool hours binging and "going unconscious." As the abuse increased, compulsive eating also increased. Also tied into this downward spiral of helplessness, compulsivity and shame was the ongoing incest that drove Barbara further into her eating disorder.

Maureen never realized that Jim had manipulated her into cooperating with his diseased needs. Barbara's family portrait in Surprise Attacks has Jim doing nothing but going to work, drinking until he was drunk and crazily ranting about the household. (In therapy Barbara described Jim, during her time at home between the ages of ten and eighteen, with five job changes, brief periods of unemployment, no advances when he was employed and working less and less as years went by.) Maureen would go to work, come home and sometimes put the finishing touches on the dinner or throw a wash in for Barbara. More often than not, she would retire to her room to read with a splitting headache or sit in front of the television. At other times, she would be out with her civic group.

Maureen could not see that she had fallen into the trap of the Alcoholic Family Syndrome. Daily she would return from work focusing on whether her alcoholic husband was going to be at home or at the bar. With Jim's manipulation, Barbara would be scapegoated as the reason for Jim's going to the bar and drinking, and the focus would be shifted to Barbara. Maureen was so accustomed to blaming other people, Barbara especially, for her own feelings that she could not recognize that Jim was the only one responsible for his drinking, and that no one but Jim, himself, could stop the drinking.

Jim's alcoholic disease process was fairly obvious. Using any excuse available to drink, or making one up if one was not at hand, he used Barbara as an emotional pin cushion, a place that he could stick his drunken rages any time he pleased. In total denial about his own shame and completely incapable of dealing with his own pain or the truth, he blamed Barbara for his misery and his life not working. And Barbara took it all because she was raised in what Alice Miller has called the "poisonous pedagogy," which dictates that children must obey their parents at all costs and that children are responsible for the anger of their parents.

To some people not knowledgeable in the co-alcoholic syndrome, Maureen's disease process might be less obvious than Jim's. Hurt, angry, demoralized and abandoned by a husband who preferred bars and drinking to her company, Maureen disowned her pain and avoided confronting the realization that her second husband was not only alcoholic, but was at least as abusive to her daughter as her first husband had been. By throwing herself into her work and climbing the corporate ladder, she could hide from the turmoil at home. She became a workaholic, often staying at work late at night and on weekends. She also joined women's civic clubs, frequently held office and was even named Woman of the Year twice in a row. Of course, she could do all of this outside the home while her child took on all the wifely chores of running the household, including being a bed partner for Jim. Maureen looked good to the outside world while her home was in shambles.

In addition Barbara told me that she found out from a neighbor who sat for Barbara that Maureen had started taking small amounts of tranquilizers and sleeping pills. Because doctors have very little training, if any, in medical school on psychological and emotional problems or on alcoholism, it was not unusual for them to prescribe drugs without really dealing with the emotional background of the patient. The drugs simply became another way for Maureen to hide from the pain and the disease in herself and her family. The drugs also assured Jim of undisturbed sex with Barbara at night, even with Maureen right on the other side of the wall.

Maureen, as well as Jim, used Barbara as the Family Scapegoat. Unable to take responsibility for her own life and dysfunction, refusing to see Jim's alcoholism and his need to be responsible for his own life, unable to see the need for professional help, Maureen blamed Barbara for everything in her family that did not work.

Toward the end of her therapy, Barbara attempted to tell her mother about the incest. Recognizing how far into her disease process Maureen was, Barbara did not expect much support or communication, but what she got was still a shock even with all her own degree of healing and preparation. Maureen blamed Barbara for bringing her anguish and making her life a lie. Today after even more healing, Barbara laughs at the irony of the statement. "What Mother doesn't know is that her life really was a lie, but not just because of the incest."

According to Barbara many years later in recovery, Maureen was able to begin seeing more clearly the life that she had with a fourth-stage alcoholic who worked very little, stank from the smell of stale cigarettes, beer, sweat and infrequent washing, was sullen, withdrawn and nasty when sober, loud and abusive when drinking.

Today Barbara recognizes how diseased the family was. Back then she believed that there was nothing wrong with the family except her. Having grown up in dysfunction, knowing only unhealthy expectations and the denial of emotions, she believed that she should have been able to do all the housework, keep up with her homework, function in school the next day, protect her mother from the incest and do all this after those insane Surprise Attack sessions without any feelings. The fact that her parents insisted on a nine-thirty lights-out curfew was more than ludicrous, it was a vicious lie. It perpetuated the pretense of a normal childhood. Since other children her age probably went to bed at approximately the same time, a nine-thirty bedtime was one of the ways Barbara's parents kept up the myth of normalcy.

The family's subscribing to the "poisonous pedagogy" made Barbara less than a menial laborer. Barbara could not quit as a worker can and did not even believe that she had the right to protest. By the time Barbara first worked on these scenes in therapy, she could allow herself to get angry with her stepfather. It was not until much later in her work, after much discussion and processing, that she could really give herself permission to have the anger that she felt toward her "sainted" mother.

For years Barbara believed that she was in the wrong. She had never questioned her mother's behavior until she had been in therapy. Remember, Maureen's treatment of Barbara, prior to Jim's entrance into the family, already led her to believe that she was defective as a person. Add to that the guilt and trauma of the incest and the perpetual emotional battering from Jim, and Barbara was dragged into a continuous downward spiral of self-blame and self-loathing.

Prior to therapy, Barbara had never doubted that she was wrong, never saw the farce involved in the family sitting down for a meal together if Jim made it home for dinner. She had never realized that in a healthy family, a child would not even have to deal with, let alone be expected to clean the filthy aftermath of a parent's evening drinking at home. She had never questioned the injustice or the sickness involved in the Surprise Attacks or the fact that her mother allowed Jim's drunken treatment of her child. She never saw how Maureen pretended to be the homemaker by making sure she put the finishing touches on dinner, by frying the liver or doing the meatloaf. Barbara had bought into Maureen's pretense that Maureen was the perfect mother and Barbara was the only defective part of the family. Barbara believed that she had deserved the abuse and blame that was continuously heaped upon her. It was not until therapy, when she recognized the severity of her mother's dysfunctional need to avoid feelings and discomfort and have peace at any price, that Barbara realized that she was the price Maureen had paid to avoid confronting herself. Barbara was a human sacrifice.

During one therapy session when we went back to the scene in the kitchen when Maureen was chastising Barbara for being dramatic Barbara finally broke into a rage.

Pounding furiously on the futons in my office, she cursed and screamed at Maureen for her part in the destruction of Barbara's self-esteem. Barbara told Maureen that she hated her for never praising her or supporting her and for letting Jim abuse her, and for expecting her to be the homemaker when she was only a child and needed to do her schoolwork. She told Maureen that she was crazy for allowing the Surprise Attacks to continue and for not seeing the insanity in Jim's treatment of her. Barbara had finally broken through emotionally and could finally stop minimizing the role her mother played in the family dysfunction. It took many more years of work for Barbara to be able to get angry at her mother in reality and not just in a process.

From Barbara's ending of the Surprise Attacks episode, we are also able to see how Barbara had connected sex with acceptance. In her eyes when Jim was mad at her, he would ignore her. At times after his angry tirades, she would actually try to entice him to bed with her. If he approached her sexually, she then assumed that he was no longer mad at her and at least momentarily accepted her. This set Barbara up to sexualize her behavior around men and to assume that the only way she would know that she was accepted would be if a man wanted her sexually.

5

"You Slut!"

Soon after I entered the ninth grade, Mother received a call from her cousin, Tom. Grandmother and Tom's mother had been sisters and each had one child, Mother and Tom. Both only children, they had grown up as close as brother and sister. Mother and Tom were still quite fond of each other.

Tom was having a difficult time with one of his sons, my cousin Frank. Frank had been having problems in school, had even been in trouble with the police, and Tom was at his wits' end. Nothing he had tried seemed to work. Realizing, perhaps, that he was not capable of getting through to Frank, Tom was considering sending Frank to military school. He wanted to know if she knew of any in our area.

"We have a good family," Mother started after she had gathered us together that night. We all nodded in agreement. "We do things together." Turning to Jim she said, "I think we're good parents. Barbara and Shawn are respectful, they never have problems in school, and all our friends tell us how well-behaved they are. I want to help Frank. He'll straighten out with some good discipline. It would mean a lot to me if you would agree to let him live with us. A cold impersonal military school isn't the answer. Besides Tom has never asked my help before, and I want to do this."

She fell silent, looking expectantly at Jim, then Shawn and finally at me. I wanted Frank to come to live with us. He had always been my favorite cousin. We were only a few months apart in age and very fond of one another, never lacking for things to talk about.

As we grew older, Frank had become a bit smitten with me and I liked how I felt around him. So far he had done nothing overtly romantic, just friendly hugs and pats. I didn't want him to be in trouble or to have to go to some stuffy military school.

Looking up at Mother, I said, "I think it would be neat if he came to live with us."

Shawn chimed in with, "He can stay in my room, and I'll help him make friends at school." Shawn was fifteen and very serious.

Mother looked at Jim. He nodded and said, "I think we can help the boy, but I want to make sure of one thing. We all understand that this is not just fun and games. Frank's been in lots of trouble but here he's going to have to follow the rules. He pulled the wool over his father's eyes, he's not going to be allowed to do that in my home!"

Turning back to us he cautioned, "You two will have to be on your best behavior so Frank will understand that we are a family where the children behave and do as they're told. You will have to follow all the rules to the letter. Do you understand?" he asked.

Both Shawn and I nodded eagerly. Mother had tears in her eyes. "Thank you," she said to all of us. "I know we can help him."

The first few weeks Frank lived with us, he and I went everywhere together. He waited at the edge of the baseball field after school each day so we could walk home together, his arm around my shoulders. I relished his attention. I flirted with him outrageously, and soon he returned my attentions very seriously.

Our adolescent passion ignited, we pursued each other in earnest. Unfortunately we weren't aware that we were on a collision course with pain as sure as two runaway freight trains. Within weeks we began a sexual relationship that continued for months.

We began to live for stolen moments when we were in the house alone, Saturday afternoon walks to the park to kiss and pet behind the bushes, walking the dog at night and groping for each other in the alley behind the store. Without ever saying anything, we knew that we couldn't let Mother and Jim in on this new dimension in our relationship. Guilt and excitement were a part of every waking moment. I needed and liked his attention yet wondered painfully if he only liked me for my body. Sometimes in the midst of the heat of heavy petting sessions, I would hate myself.

Concentrating on schoolwork was out of the question as I rode an emotional roller-coaster. Along with the new relationship with Frank, I still had to endure

Jim's periodic visits to my room at night whenever Mother was gone. Job stress had resulted in Mother's use of occasional tranquilizers or sleeping pills, and her deep sleep emboldened Jim to visit my room while she lay sleeping in their bed on the other side of the wall.

Late one winter night after Frank had been with us for several months, and Christmas and New Years had come and gone, Jim entered my room while I was studying. With a frown on his face, he said, "Put down that book, I have to talk to you." His voice sounded ominous, and I wondered what I done wrong. His brow was deeply furrowed, eyes narrowed into slits, jaw set. I started to shiver.

"I'm going to ask you one question," he said, his voice shaking with anger. "You better tell me the truth. I'll only give you one chance."

Gulping for air, eyes widening in terror, I waited in silence for him to continue.

"Do you understand?"

"Yes, Daddy," I answered in a voice shaking with fear.

Then came the question.

"Barbara, have you slept with Frank?"

The world stood still, I couldn't speak or even breathe. I felt dizzy. Somehow he'd found out! Mother would hate me! They'd send me away. Please God, strike me dead before I have to answer!

"Answer me!" he bellowed.

There was no escape from this trap. Breathing a deep sigh I resigned to my fate. With tears in my eyes I mumbled, "Yes."

His face registered first intense rage and then, to my surprise, hurt. I expected anger. Why hurt? But the hurt faded quickly and was replaced by pure hatred.

"You slut!" he whispered caustically, effectively stabbing a knife through my heart. Life was over. He hated me! Wordlessly he walked from my room, slamming the door. Sobbing, I threw myself down on the bed.

Soon muffled voices filtered into my room, Jim was in the living room with Mother. I couldn't make out what they were saying. And then I heard Mother scream, "NO! It can't be! Are you sure?" She was sobbing.

Within seconds Jim stood in front of me again, hatred still in his eyes. "Your mother thinks you misunderstood," he said. Then he took a deep breath, "When I asked you if you had slept with Frank, did you understand that I meant having sex with him?"

In too much pain to speak I could only nod my head.

He turned and left. From the living room came Jim's angry voice and Mother's sobbing voice. I was a slut. How could I ever face Mother again? Seconds later, I did as she came into my room and stared at me, her eyes red and swollen, tears streaming down her face.

She sat down on my bed and tried to speak but could only sob. It was my fault that she was hurting so much. I wanted to reach out to her, to hold her, to comfort her but I was afraid that she would reject me, push me away, and I didn't think I could stand that.

When her sobs subsided, she looked at me and asked, "How could you let this happen?"

"I'm sorry, Mom," I cried, looking away. I couldn't stand to see the pain in her eyes, knowing that I had caused it. How could she ever forgive me?

To my surprise, she reached out for me and wrapped her arms around me. She held me for several minutes while we wept together, patting my shoulder and rubbing my back. From the back of the house we could hear Jim yelling at Frank.

"Your father is so upset, Barbara, I'm afraid for Frank. Jim has already hit him once, I think he could really hurt him. Tom is coming to take him home in a few hours, and," she sobbed, clinging to me, "I don't know how I'm ever going to face poor Tom." We didn't speak for several minutes, each of us lost in our own pain.

We heard doors slamming and more loud voices. "Pack your fucking clothes and get the hell out of my house," Jim raged at Frank.

Mother was shaking. "I can't believe Frank would do this to me after all I tried to do for him." I was astonished. She wasn't blaming me. She was blaming him!

We heard more shouting and abruptly Mother stood up, her eyes wide with fear. Motioning to me she said, "You wait here, I have to go calm Jim down!" With that she left my room. When she came back several minutes later, her face was ashen. "I've never seen him like this, Barbara. I'm frightened."

I was scared, too. Was he hurting Frank? It wasn't Frank's fault. Men had needs. Jim had told me that. I had just taken advantage. It was my fault. I was the one Jim should be hitting.

Holding me in her arms, Mother asked, "Barbara, has Jim ever touched you?"

"What?" I asked, not believing what I'd heard.

"Has Jim ever touched you," she repeated, "You know — like Frank did?"

"No," I said quickly. I had to make her stop thinking like that! Did she suspect, after all? If she knew the truth, she'd send me away for sure.

"I just can't understand his reaction to all of this. He's out of control. That's not like him," she said. I had never seen her so scared. I didn't believe she really wanted to know, and I didn't want her to know how bad I was.

She left my room when Tom arrived. It was over quickly. They left within minutes. Frank was gone. I never saw him again. I didn't even have a chance to say goodbye.

Several hours later, I fell into a light sleep. Early the next morning Mother told me I wouldn't be going to school and she wasn't going to work. She was going to take me to the doctor to make sure I wasn't pregnant.

"I just had my period, Mom," I protested, hoping she would change her mind. Wasn't it bad enough that they knew, did we have to bring Dr. Gallagher into it, too? Was there no end to my shame?

"Well, your father and I want to make sure that you're not confused, maybe you don't really understand, maybe it didn't go as far as you think it did. Dr. Gallagher will be able to tell us. I want to make sure you're okay and healthy. Now stop arguing and go take a shower while I make the appointment."

Turning away from her, I walked into the bathroom without letting her see the tears in my eyes so she wouldn't accuse me of being too dramatic. Even standing under the hot shower I couldn't stop shivering and sobbing.

I had never been examined "down there." Kind and gentle Dr. Gallagher, the doctor who had soothed hurts and fixed me when I was sick. Was he going to put his hands between my legs, too? How much more was there to endure? Always fond of me before, now he would know me as a slut, like Jim said. How would I bear it? Trying to convince Mother to change her mind was pointless. I finished my shower, combed my hair and dressed in silence.

On the way to the doctor's office, Mother held my hand. Tears dripped down my face, so seldom did she show any tenderness. Sitting in the waiting room, I buried my head in a magazine, refusing to look at anyone, sure they knew what I had done. I jumped when the nurse announced my name, and nearly tripped over my own shoes standing up. I followed her into the examining room with my head down, and was horrified when I realized that Mother had followed me. She was going to watch! Wasn't this embarrassing enough without that?

"Take off your clothes and put this on," the nurse ordered tersely, handing me a hospital gown that tied in the back. Fighting back a renewed threat of tears, I took off my shirt, pants, socks and shoes and started to put on the gown.

"Your underwear, too, Barbara," Mother said.

That did it! No longer able to force back the tears, I started to sob. "Mom, I can't. Please don't make me do this!"

"Barbara Jeanne, I've already explained why we have to go through with the examination," she said sternly. Then smiling, she said gently, "It's really not that bad, and I'll be here."

I couldn't tell her that having her in the room was part of my distress. Taking a deep breath, drying my eyes and summoning my courage, I unhooked my bra and removed it and my underpants as well. Mother helped me tie the gown after I climbed up on the cold, hard examination table. For the first time I noticed the metal stirrups at the end of the table. I turned away and shivered.

Mother read a magazine and I continued to shake while we waited for Dr. Gallagher. When the door opened, I jumped. Looking at the doctor's face, I started to cry again.

"Well, Maureen," he said, addressing Mother and ignoring me, "I didn't expect we'd be doing this quite so soon." Then he put a comforting arm around her shoulder, and continued to act like I wasn't there.

"She's a minor, so you and my nurse will have to stay here while I examine her," he said, sounding very professional.

"I understand, Doctor," she answered.

"Good! Well, then, let's get on with it," he said actually beginning to sound cheerful! The nurse came in carrying a green drape and a metal tray covered with a white towel. She walked to the end of the table, and said, "Lay down on the table and scoot down until your bottom is at the edge."

I did as she instructed, then closed my eyes. She lifted first my right leg and then my left, placing them in the stirrups. I kept my knees together, trying to keep from being exposed. She covered my legs with the drape, then reached under it and pulled them apart. "Doctor can't examine you with your legs together, honey," she said. "Now don't move!"

Biting my lower lip to keep from crying, I kept my eyes closed. How was I going to be able to stand this? Dr. Gallagher walked to the end of the table and said, "This won't hurt and it'll only take a second," his cold hands pulling my legs farther apart. Something cold, hard, big and wet slipped inside me, and I flinched.

"We really should get heaters for these things," Dr Gallagher laughed like this was some big joke. I hated him!

Relentlessly he continued this invasion of my body. I wanted it to be over. I felt hungry and sick at the same time. In the midst of his examination, I remembered that I hadn't eaten breakfast and stopped thinking about what was happening and started to think about what I would eat when we got home. A bowl of cereal to start, then maybe some toast and peanut butter. If Mother went to work, I could spend the afternoon alone. I would take a bubble bath and maybe take a long nap after lunch.

"Well, she's definitely not a virgin," Dr. Gallagher announced matter-of-factly, interrupting my thoughts, "and I would say she's been quite active. I don't think she's pregnant, but it might be too early to tell. Let me know if she misses her next period."

I had never been more humiliated. How could he say that to my mother? I would never talk to him again!

Replacing the drape, he handed me a wad of tissues without speaking to me. Looking at Mother he said, "Maureen, why don't you come with me and we'll have a little talk, while Barbara gets dressed. She can wait for you in the lobby."

Wiping tears from her eyes, Mother stood up and let the doctor escort her out, his arm around her shoulder. Fumbling with the tray, the nurse told me to get dressed then left the room. Using my fist to stifle sobs that I could no longer hold back, I lay on the table for a few moments trying to get control. Finally, I forced myself to sit up. I was slimy and wet between my legs. I reached down with the tissues and wiped myself. Maybe I should have been used to being violated and invaded, but I wasn't. I felt dirty. Dressed, I took a few more deep breaths and walked back into the lobby.

Mother wasn't there yet so I sat down in an empty chair close to the door, picked up a magazine and pretended to read it. Several minutes later the office door opened and Mother came out. Her eyes were all red and puffy. Dr. Gallagher was standing next to her, his arm around her shoulders.

"Everything's going to be all right, Maureen. Stop worrying," he said.

"Thank you, Doctor," she said, her voice shaking.

She walked over to me and took my hand.

"Come on, honey," she said, "let's go home."

In the car she said, "I had no idea. Really, I didn't know. How many boys have there been?"

"Only Frank, Mom," I lied. "Honest, only Frank!" I went on praying she would believe me and just let it go. Apparently she did for her next words were, "Okay, honey, but we have to talk. I can't take the time now, I'm late for work. We'll talk over the weekend."

She dropped me off at home without getting out of the car, telling me that I didn't have to go to school, but to be sure and do all the chores so Jim wouldn't be upset when he came home. After I finished with my work, I baked a pineapple-upside-down cake, Jim's favorite dessert. Then I made a batch of fudge and ate all of it myself. Afterwards, I took a hot bubble bath and then took a nap.

When Mother came home from work that night, much earlier than usual, I had already sliced tomatoes, onions and pickles, had formed hamburger patties, set the table and made a big tossed salad for dinner. When I saw her car pull in the driveway, I ran outside and gave her a big hug as she climbed out of her car. I was sorry for all the pain I had caused her but I didn't know how to tell her. I hoped that everything I had done would tell her how much I loved her, how sorry I was and that I intended to change.

"You haven't greeted me at the car in a long time," she said warmly returning my hug, patting my hair and kissing the top of my head. "I like this, it makes it so much more pleasant to come home."

She seemed pleased with everything, announcing that I had done such a good job that there was time to put her feet up and read the newspaper before it would be time to start dinner. I felt warm and safe, and very relieved. Maybe

she loved me, after all. Jim came home and didn't go out to the bar at all that
night. No one said anything about Frank. In fact, we never mentioned his name
again.

Mother and I never did have that little talk. Two nights later we had another
Surprise Attack. By the end of the following week Jim was back in my bed.
Nothing had changed. I believed nothing ever would.

Learning To Live With Trauma

By the time Frank came to stay at Barbara's household, the individual
and family disease process was so advanced that the Surprise Attacks
were occurring on an average of two to three nights a week, Barbara was
overeating continuously and Jim had moved into the latter part of the
third stage of alcoholism where his alcohol tolerance had peaked. In
addition Jim's sexual relations with Barbara were occurring at least bi-
weekly, Maureen was out of the household most of the time with either
work or her civic activities and coming home exhausted and tense and
occasionally taking sleeping pills and tranquilizers to relax, and Shawn's
and Barbara's relationship had evaporated. The levels of psychological
and emotional violence were astronomically high, and Maureen's and
the family's levels of denial so great that it is not a surprise that Maureen
believed what she said that day they decided to have Frank come to stay,
"We have a good family."

Maureen was doing what many co-dependents do, justifying her home
situation with the external proof of, "We do things together . . . Barbara
and Shawn are respectful, they never have problems at school and all our
friends tell us how well-behaved they are." Believing that these externals
proved a positive environment, Maureen was able to remain totally out
of touch with the reality of the nightmare she was living at home.

Given what we know about Maureen's family background, it is highly
probable that her cousin Tom's family was suffering from some form of
severe dysfunction too. The difference in Frank was that he was fighting
back with his behaviors. His trouble at school and with the law was a cry
for help that was louder and more obvious than Barbara's silent pain
and overeating.

A number of years ago one of the drug addicts that I worked with had
come in for his fourth session. As we continued delving into his childhood
we found both verbal and emotional abuse. When I asked if he knew that
he was an abused child, he was shocked because he thought that his
parents' treatment of him was normal and that he had been bad and had
therefore deserved that treatment.

In 1981 Jael Greenleaf presented a paper at the National Council on Alcoholism, for the Annual Alcoholism Forum in which she noted: "Children are not born with standards for evaluating behavior, social skills or moral values. They learn what they see and they do not learn what they do not see." [1]. Greenleaf went on to say that in child abuse "there is one person who is not appalled by the beating — the child. The child, having no other experience, has no yardstick to define the situation at all; it simply is."

Living with incredibly abusive circumstances and hearing Maureen say, "We have a good family" and "I think we're good parents," Barbara's perception of her own badness and inadequacy was confirmed once again.

There was no place within the family for Barbara to find out how severely diseased the situation was. In fact, what we see in Barbara's family is a clear demonstration of learned tolerance to high levels of pain and dysfunction. As with most of the Adult Children that I have worked with, one of the things that Barbara had to learn in the recovery process was to lower her tolerance levels. She had to learn not to tolerate verbal, emotional or physical abuse.

Tolerance, simply defined, is the amount of stress a person will take. Adult Children are raised with such high stress in their dysfunctional families that they tend to tolerate more than is physiologically, as well as psychologically, healthy for them. Frequently, they will come into therapy and tell me that they recently discovered that they have severe back problems or tumors and that their doctors have said that they would have discovered the problems earlier if they had not had such high tolerance for pain. They must be taught to lower those tolerance levels and stop allowing themselves to live with incredibly excessive levels of emotional toxicity and physical and psychological pain.

In order to learn to live in a more healthy manner, with less toxicity, Barbara had to learn that her boundaries had been programmed by living in her dysfunctional family and that she had become habituated to pain, abuse and emotional and developmental neglect.

When Barbara came into therapy with the idea of resolving her incest issues, she had not yet recognized that the abuse she had suffered was much more pervasive and far-reaching than she had believed and that it had affected her in ways that she had not yet been able to see.

The therapeutic process created an environment in which she could learn to recognize the abuse and lower the tolerance levels. In the first few months of her therapy, Barbara had talked about learning to better tolerate being with her family. What she had not realized was that she was asking to learn to tolerate more dysfunction from her family, to cope with Jim's violent obnoxious behavior and her mother's blame and scapegoating. When I asked Barbara what made her want to do that, she said that she had thought that she would have to face the problem in order to heal. I said that facing the problem was being able to see and tell the truth about it. I pointed out that if someone handed her a glass of orange juice with arsenic in it, and she knew that it had arsenic in it, she would be foolish to drink the orange juice. She would not expect to train her body to learn to take arsenic, so why would she want to raise her already high tolerance levels even more? Instead, she would walk away from the arsenic-laced orange juice. She said that she had not realized that she could do that. I pointed out to her that her reaction came from being governed by rules taught to her by the parents who had abused her.

We know that Barbara's great-grandparents and grandparents were extremely religious and rigid. Her grandfather had been physically abusive to his daughter, Maureen, and today Maureen would probably still say that it was not abusive for him to have had her go out and cut a switch from a tree so that he could hit her with it. According to Barbara, Maureen grew up believing (as her family believed) that children were inherently bad and needed to be broken.

Tom, Maureen's cousin, was raised in the same dysfunctional system. His mother and Maureen's mother were sisters raised by Barbara's great-grandparents. The great-grandparents' family dysfunction was being handed down generationally through the daughters and granddaughters to Barbara and Frank. Only Frank was fighting back. We don't know what was actually happening in school, but we do know that at the time that Barbara, Frank and for that matter, I was growing up, the dysfunctional thinking that permeated homes was being perpetrated on children in classrooms by the dysfunctionally raised adults who had become our teachers. Children raised in severe abuse tolerate high levels of abuse from new adults (like teachers) who come into their lives, especially if the children are raised to believe that they were never allowed to question authority.

Coming from her own dysfunctional background, Maureen would also have had very high tolerance levels for emotional abuse. Barbara once said to me that she heard her mother say that Jim was okay because he did not hit her the way her first husband had. And Barbara grew up believing that because she had a choice between a whipping and going to her room, she actually had it good at home and that the insane Surprise Attacks were a result of her failures and therefore her fault.

Helping Barbara to lower her high tolerance levels for psychological and emotional abuse and physical violence was not an easy task. Like most Adult Children, she had been trained to believe that the abuse was normal and right and her mother had certainly made it acceptable. In therapy Barbara realized that her mother could not see how abusive and repressive her home had become, nor could she see that by allowing Jim to perpetrate those drunken tirades on Barbara, she was allowing him to perpetrate them on the entire family. Even though Barbara received the direct verbal abuse, the entire family had to suffer through those two o'clock in the morning blow-ups. Like alcoholism, abuse and repression are progressive disease processes. They sneak up on us, getting worse and worse as our tolerance slowly creeps up to higher and higher levels.

Learning to lower tolerance levels is also a way of learning to set healthy boundaries. As Barbara began to get in touch with her emotions and to learn to express her needs, she began to formulate new ideas about herself and her boundaries. As she learned more about the nature of boundaries, she began to see that boundary setting was actually a continuous process. She had to learn to be flexible without being too diffuse. She had to learn that she had certain rights just as others did and that she did not have to take the kind of abuse she had been used to taking when she was growing up.

If we look at Barbara's relationship with Frank in terms of her boundaries, we discover several things about Barbara and her boundaries. Barbara had a desperate need for Frank's attention. Her reference point for evaluating herself was always outside of herself, outside her personal boundary. In addition she had already been trained to include in her boundaries the sexualization of her relationships with men. She had learned that she had at least some power over men with her sexuality. This lesson continued with her relationship with Frank.

During many therapy sessions, Barbara and I explored her desperate need for attention from men. As she worked through some of those issues, she discovered that it had actually stemmed from the need to have her natural father love her. The sexualization process had come later with Jim's molestations. Once that was in place, however, Barbara was forced to face the consequences of that process in any of her ensuing relationships, beginning with Frank.

Rather than having a romantic teenage liaison, Barbara and Frank threw themselves into a full-blown sexual affair. Barbara recognized, at least in part, her desperate need for attention and her use of her sexuality to get that attention. Her thoughts about herself and Frank reflected her turmoil. Added to that was the fact that she had no one she could talk to about any of this. Without a lot of friends, sexualized beyond her peers, raised to keep the family secrets, Barbara had nowhere to turn for advice or support.

Jim's Reaction

Given Maureen's head-in-an-ostrich-hole form of denial, it is fairly easy to understand how she would have missed all the signs of the budding affair. In all fairness Jim actually missed the signs, too. It was his sister who had seen the sexual overtones between Barbara and Frank.

Once alerted, Jim had to find out if there was anything happening between the two teenagers. His insanely jealous reaction over Barbara's relationship with Frank went beyond hurt. He was enraged because he somehow believed that he owned her. She was his property. Whether we like to admit it or not, this belief is not unusual. Even in non-sexually abusive families, parents believe that they have a right to decide what their children can be or not be and can learn or not learn (even in the schools) because they believe that the children are their possessions. This precipitates the "This is my child and I can do whatever I want" mentality that fosters violent, abusive and controlling and invasionary behavior on the part of parents. Of course Jim's feelings were hurt because Barbara found someone else attractive, but it went beyond that. His greater fear was of losing his grip on her. Calling her a slut, after all the years of sexually using her, was a form of abuse that Barbara could not even recognize at the time. All she could see was that he hated her.

In her monumental book, *The Chalice and the Blade,* Riane Eisler documents the origins of this severely dysfunctional concept of human ownership. According to Eisler (and thanks to some enormous archaeological breakthroughs) this dysfunction did not begin during our supposed savage prehistoric past, as previously believed. Eisler demonstrates that the early period was not a time of violence and barbarism. Instead what has recently been revealed to us was a world with ". . . a long period of peace and prosperity when our social, technological and cultural evolution moved upward: many thousands of years when all the basic technologies on which civilization is built were developed in societies that were not male dominant, violent, and hierarchic."[2]

The origin of human ownership, hierarchical family systems, an authoritarian social structure and its accompanying "might means right" mentality began with waves of barbaric invasions several thousand years ago that swept across the highly developed, peaceful art-loving lands of central Europe. These invasions brought with them an emphasis on destruction and dominance, brute strength, warfare and human debasement through conquest. In order to support this hierarchical structure, families had to imitate the basic order of society. The peace-loving, nurturing, egalitarian families of pre-invasion Europe were eventually destroyed and replaced by the patriarchal, violent, control-oriented, slave-taking hordes of barbarian invaders. Our dysfunctional families are the direct descendants of the bloody violent waves of dominance and death-oriented tribes that swept across Europe destroying art and beauty and human equality.

It appears that what Alice Miller calls "poisonous pedagogy"[3] is a direct result of that heritage of violence. It is also because of this heritage of savagery (which resulted in a tremendous regression from our original life-nurturing evolutionary past) that there are so many fathers today who believe, as Jim did, that they own their children and that they have a right to their daughters' (and sometimes their sons') bodies. Jim was not alone in his attitude back then, and there are many parents today who still believe that they somehow own their children and that their children owe them absolute unquestioning obedience.

As Barbara began to deal with Jim's inhumane attitude toward her sexually, she also began to realize that practicing alcoholics (or for that matter practicing addicts of any kind) do not have loving relationships with people because of their love affair with their addiction.

Through much hard work, Barbara came to recognize that Jim was not capable of loving her and that his inability had nothing to do with her. Barbara spent many tearful sessions imagining Jim in the chair opposite her and telling him how badly she had wanted him to love her and not sexually abuse her. When she placed herself in Jim's chair and allowed herself to imagine what he was experiencing, Barbara realized that the person she had hoped she would find was not there. What she found sitting in the chair was the shell of a human being, wracked with terror and rage and pain and drowning in his alcoholic stupors.

"Poor Mom"

In this episode we once again find young Barbara worried about Maureen and living out the family rule of taking care of Mother. We see the extent of the family disease process when we are faced with an adolescent Barbara who has just been emotionally battered by her insanely jealous stepfather but who is so concerned about her mother's pain that she has the desire to reach out and comfort her mother. It never came into Barbara's awareness that she was the child, and Maureen was the adult and that taking care of her mother's feelings in this drama was just another instance of the family dysfunction. Instead what we see is Barbara's surprise that her mother would comfort her and not reject her.

Barbara had never seen Maureen place the blame on anyone but Barbara so she was shocked when her mother blamed Frank instead of her. She did not realize that Maureen's denial had to place the blame outside the family if at all possible.

However, no matter how strong Maureen's denial had been, Jim's rage was so insane that even Maureen's denial could not totally gloss over it. When she asked Barbara about the obvious possibility of the cause of Jim's jealousy, Barbara, guessing accurately about Maureen's need to *not* know the truth, told Maureen what she really wanted to hear, that Jim had never touched Barbara. Maureen was already too bonded to Jim by this time to allow the truth to surface.

Continuing The Trauma

What followed after Frank's removal from the household was a continuation of the trauma for Barbara. Barbara told me that she believes that the visit to the doctor's was upon Jim's instigation. Jim, of course, knew that Barbara was not confused, but he also would have seen another chance for humiliating Barbara.

What happened in the doctor's office was another instance of the dysfunction rife in all walks of life, including the medical profession. Is it possible that Barbara's perception of the doctor's cold aloof treatment of her was a distortion? It's possible that she was mistaken but not probable. Barbara's picture is too clear. Through her eyes, we see an older male doctor who has turned from the tears of a fourteen-year-old child (who appeared to have been breaking his norms) in order to comfort the mother who agrees with his norms and therefore is to be cared for and pitied. Then with the unfortunate insensitivity of some male doctors, he tells Barbara that the examination won't hurt and makes a joke that totally disregards the fact that he has a terrified, sad, fourteen-year-old child on the table for her first gynecological examination.

I've worked with many adult women who report insensitivity and a negatively judgmental attitude from their male gynecologists, and I personally have had to deal with judgmental and condescending attitudes from some gynecologists. It is incredibly degrading to be in a physically vulnerable situation and to be treated like a piece of meat, and it is disgraceful for a doctor not to recognize how emotionally and psychologically abusive this kind of treatment can be. Barbara handled the humiliation in the best way she knew how, by avoidance. She began to focus on what she would eat when she got home. This process of avoiding the emotional trauma by focusing on eating had already become enormously self-reinforcing. Leaving the examination to daydream about food was one more instance of reinforcement.

The fact that Maureen and Barbara never had their little talk should surprise no one at this point. What Barbara has not told in this story is something that Barbara had told me in therapy — that her mother was not the one to tell Barbara the "facts of life." Maureen had turned over to Jim the job of telling the facts of life to "the children," both Shawn and Barbara together. Imagine the scene of Jim telling both children about sex with Barbara sitting there having been molested by Jim sexually for quite some time. It is probable that Jim manipulated the situation so that he would be the one to tell Barbara to insure that she wouldn't somehow blurt out the details of their relationship. Even if that were his reason, it does not make the situation any less abusive. And what could possibly have compelled him to tell the children together? There appears to be a certain sadistic element in the situation. In addition, it would be almost inconceivable, except that we now know the lengths to which Maureen's desire to avoid discomfort has already gone, that a mother would turn the task of telling her own daughter about sex over to a stepfather.

This episode ends with Barbara finally receiving a hug and a pat on the head marking Maureen's long-awaited and infrequently received stamp of approval. Since she had not gone to school that day, Barbara managed to get everything done in time.

During the therapy session when Barbara repeated to me Maureen's final statement that Barbara had done such a good job that Maureen would have time to put her feet up before she "started dinner," I asked Barbara if she would go over in the other chair and repeat the statement as if she were Maureen. She did. When she came back and sat in her own chair, she was quiet for a moment, realizing what her "mother" had just said. Then she began to seethe, her face tightening and her eyes narrowing. Verbalizing a string of very healthy expletives, Barbara said, "You had some damn nerve. I had dinner all ready. All you had to do was turn the damn broiler on. I did all the work. You rarely did anything at home except watch television or read a book unless you were going around ranting about me not being able to do things to your satisfaction. I'm furious."

Through months of hard work on herself, Barbara was beginning to see her mother's subtle lies and to feel some healthy emotions about the situation.

Adulteress

One afternoon shortly after my fifteenth birthday in the summer of 1962, I was visiting our neighbor across the street, Beverly Miller. Beverly was a housewife married to a city building inspector. They had two children, Bill and Cindy, who I babysat on occasion. Beverly had taken me under her wing that summer. Knowing I wasn't allowed to have friends at my house during the day, she seemed to understand how lonely I was. She took pity on me, often inviting me over for lunch or to help bake cookies.

A devoutly religious Baptist who was active in her church, she was given free tickets to hear a nationally known evangelist who was holding a week-long revival meeting. Beverly planned to go every night and invited me to join her as many times as I wanted.

The first night I went was youth night. The preacher talked of the evils of sex and alcohol, then warned against disobeying parents, teachers or ministers. We must follow the commandments and honor our parents if we wanted to escape the eternal fires of Hell. I shivered, both from the excitement of his emotional oratory, and at the thought of someday having to answer for my sins.

At the end of the meeting he invited the audience to come forward and be saved. I wanted desperately to go forward, to be saved, to escape eternal damnation, but if I did Beverly might guess that I was a terrible sinner who had already had sex and not want to be my friend anymore.

That night I told Mother all about the evangelist. I talked in excited tones about the stadium, the people and how wonderful this man was. She listened without comment, then quietly said she would like to go with us the next night.

The meeting started the way the other one had. The choir director led us in several hymns. Then a hushed silence fell over the stadium as the preacher walked out onto the stage. Lifting his hands to the heavens, he shouted, "Hallelujah! Praise God!" The audience shouted back in return. Dropping his arms to his sides, he closed his eyes and bowed his head. Had I known the topic of that night's meeting ahead of time, I might have chosen to stay home, have a headache, have the flu, get hit by a truck, anything to avoid the words of doom that blasted my life to pieces in the calm of a warm summer breeze.

A pregnant silence filled the warm evening air. The entire assembly waited, pulses quickening. My heart skipped a beat. I sat on the edge of my seat, Beverly on one side of me and Mother on the other. When I was sure I could stand no more anticipation, he slowly raised his head, placed his hands on the pulpit, and slowly gazed at the thousands of people waiting for his inspiring words. Suddenly his shouts pierced the silence like a knife.

"Brothers and sisters!" he began. "I'm here tonight to shout in the face of evil, to warn you against the lowest sin of all. A sin so vile, so depraved, so wretched, so vulgar, that mere thoughts of it damn you to the fires of Hell for all eternity, as sure as there is a Satan and as sure as Satan is at work in this world."

My shoulders stiffened. What sin? And have I committed it? Suddenly uncomfortable, an uneasy tension passed through my body as I waited for him to continue, not at all sure I wanted to hear what he was going to say.

" 'What is it, Brother?' you ask. Well, I'm here to tell you, children of God." He paused again for effect. Picking up the Bible and waving it in the air, he took a deep breath, lifted his head up and screamed, "That vile, depraved, wretched and vulgar sin is . . . Adultery!"

Murmurs of agreement rose into a crescendo of shouts, while I melted into my seat, hoping for a violent earthquake to swallow me up. I knew what adultery was. Jim was married to Mother, not to me, and that meant that having sex with me was adultery. I could hardly catch my breath, and my eyes widened in horror as I realized that Jim had been committing a sin. And then I thought, what about me?

The pastor answered my question. He said that women who knowingly "lay down" with married men were repeating the transgression of Eve by leading the man into sin. He said that God would judge the woman more harshly than the man. Committing a sin was wicked, he said, but seducing another into sin would invoke God's harshest vengeance.

I sat unmoving, eyes wide and unblinking as he continued to drive daggers of unrelenting accusation deep within my soul. My deepest fears were being confirmed by this holy man of God. I was to blame for everything. Jim might be a sinner but I was more guilty. I should have been able to stop him.

I began to shiver, unable to catch my breath. I wanted to scream, to run and hide, to die, to shout, to cry, but forced myself to sit still, praying for the nightmare to end. I hated myself more in that moment than I had at any other time in my fifteen years.

As he finished his sermon with a prayer asking God to reach into the hearts of those gathered together on that warm summer evening, I couldn't control my emotions any longer and began to cry. As he had on the night before he called upon sinners to come forward, confess their disobedience of God's laws, and beg His forgiveness. I started to sob. Noticing my distress, Beverly put her arm around my shoulder and said in a soft voice, "Barbara, dear, what's wrong?"

This show of tenderness and concern nearly sent me into hysteria. I began to choke and cough.

"Do you want to step forward, dear?" she asked pulling me to her and and cradling my head in her shoulder.

I nodded, and started to stand up.

From my other side came my mother's cold voice, "Barbara Jeanne," she said in a tone that sounded like a warning, "you don't really want to do that, do you?"

Talking past me to Beverly, she said, "Our religion doesn't believe in public confession."

I didn't want to do anything wrong or outside "our religion" even though I wasn't really sure what our religion was. Mother hadn't gone to church on a regular basis for several years. True, she had encouraged me to attend Sunday School, and had supported my membership in the youth choir, but neither Mother nor Jim attended services except on special occasions. I had never received any instruction about public confession.

Looking back at me, Mother said, "Now stop being dramatic, Barbara. Besides, if you went up there with all those other people, we would have to wait for you and that wouldn't be fair, would it?"

I looked down at my hands and shook my head. I was ashamed. I hadn't thought that wanting God's forgiveness would inconvenience anyone. Besides, God probably wouldn't forgive me anyway.

On the drive home I sat in the back seat with my eyes closed pretending to be asleep. I made a bargain with God. I would make Jim stop if God would forgive me and not condemn me to the fires of Hell.

In bed that night I plotted how to convince Jim that we had to stop this "affair." Playing out one scenario after another, I imagined telling him that I was afraid of getting pregnant. I could threaten again to tell Mother, even though I knew I wouldn't. I could just pretend to be sleeping each time and maybe he would leave.

In spite of my determination, I was confused. The truth was I wasn't sure I wanted him to stop. I had always hated the sexual part, but I still wanted him to like me. Letting him have his way made me feel accepted. Would he understand or would he be angry?

On and on the internal battle waged until I fell into a fitful sleep just before the first rays of dawn lit the morning sky. At breakfast, I remembered that Mother would be going to her club meeting that night. There was no more time to plan. He always came to my bed on club nights. That night would be no exception.

Jim went straight to the bar and didn't come home until ten o'clock. I was already in bed reading. As he passed my door on the way to his room, he mumbled, "Turn off your light, it's late." He sounded like he'd had a lot of beer. I turned off my light and pulled my blankets up around me. Shivering despite the warm night air, I wasn't sure I could go through with it. I rolled over onto my left side, curled up in a fetal position and tried to fall asleep, but each nerve in my body was on heightened alert, and each sound as he moved about his bedroom sounded amplified in my ears.

About fifteen minutes later I heard his door open and then his footsteps as he walked down the hall into the kitchen. The sound of the cupboard door opening and closing, the clinking of a glass, the sound of liquid as it filled a glass all told me that he was drawing a beer at the tapper. Slowly, not making a sound, I rolled over on my right side. With my door open I could see into the living room from my bed. Opening my eyes just a bit I watched as he came into the living room, turned on the TV and sat down in his chair. In the flickering light coming from the television screen I saw that he was naked. Usually he wore his undershorts around the house at night, but tonight he was totally nude. He placed his beer mug on the table, reached down for a pack of cigarettes and a book of matches, struck one and lit the cigarette.

I closed my eyes again. Maybe I had a reprieve. Maybe he didn't want me tonight. Slowly I rolled back over on to my left side, curled up again and tried to go to sleep. Less than five minutes later, I heard him turn off the TV. Moments later my bed creaked and shifted as he sat down next me.

"You're not asleep yet, are you, sweetheart?" he whispered in the darkness.

I didn't answer, hoping he would go away.

"Barbara?" he whispered more insistently.

Still I kept silent, unmoving, hardly breathing, praying that he would believe that I was asleep and just leave me alone. I didn't want to face this. Every muscle, every fiber of my being was on red alert, tense, coiled, waiting for his touch. I felt sick.

"Come on, honey, I know you're awake. Move over," he ordered, pulling the blankets down to expose my shoulders. I groaned, pretending to be asleep. But he didn't give up. He pulled me over to face him.

"Daddy . . ." I started to complain.

"Stop whining and move over so I can lay down!" he demanded angrily.

"Please, Daddy," I begged opening my eyes, "leave me alone."

"Just what are you trying to pull, pretending to be asleep."

"I don't feel good," I said. I wasn't lying, I felt awful.

"You looked all right a little while ago. What's wrong with you?" he asked, feeling my forehead.

"I don't know, I just feel sick," I answered.

"You don't have any fever," he insisted. "What's this bullshit about?"

I took a deep breath. This was it. There was no turning back now if I wanted to keep my promise with God.

"Daddy," I started, "we have to stop doing this." There, I said it.

"What do you mean?" he said sounding angry.

"You know," I said. "You have to stop coming into my bed."

"Why do I have to do that? What's the matter? Have you got a boyfriend or something?"

"No."

"Then what is this crap?" He was beginning to shout. I was afraid he would wake Shawn.

"It's just . . . you just . . . I don't want you to come in here. anymore!" I stammered. I couldn't figure out the right thing to say.

"You seemed to want me to three nights ago!" he complained.

"I didn't want you to then, either. I never wanted you to," I said, not knowing what else to say. There didn't seem to be any nice way to do this. He would probably hate me, and there was nothing I could do to stop that.

"You little bitch!" he shouted, then stood up abruptly, walked out of my room, into his and slammed the door.

I started to cry. Every part of me wanted to beg his forgiveness, tell him I didn't really mean it and invite him back to my bed. But I had made a pact with God. Gritting my teeth, I buried my face in my pillow and cried myself to sleep.

The next day he was sullen and nasty when he came home, then went directly to the bar. Two nights later we had a Surprise Attack because I put glasses in the cupboard that had soap scum on them.

Over the next several months he tried a number of times to make me have sex with him. Two times he succeeded and left me feeling worse than I had before the revival meetings. After both occasions I apologized to God and renewed my vow. The rest of the time I was able to rebuff him, usually by groaning loud, scaring him away.

Six months later, two months shy of my sixteenth birthday at the end of my sophomore year in high school, the attacks stopped altogether. The last time he came into my room, I had reached the point of total saturation. I could take no more. I threatened to kill him if he ever touched me again. He stopped at the bar on the way home from work and stayed until they closed for two solid weeks. Even though I had kept my pact with God, my life didn't get better.

Who Is The Sinner?

As John Bradshaw pointed out in *Bradshaw On: The Family,* the Lutheran mandates . . . "That all authority was from God and must be obeyed as a divine command" meant in the extreme that "one must obey authority, even if it is judged wrong."[3] Beyond obeying authority even when it is judged wrong is that people raised in this type of system probably stop thinking for themselves and cannot even come to the conclusion that authority might be wrong. Using the suppressed and controlled emotions of the rigidly religious, evangelical preachers have had crowds, mesmerized to the point of hysteria, believing the dysfunctional idea that children should obey their parents and wives should obey their husbands at all costs. What these rigidly religious people, women especially, fail to see is that the hierarchy was set up by men for the purpose of control, dominance and supremacy. Even in light of the Jim Bakker and Jimmy Swaggart fiascoes the fanatically religious cling to their disease process.

In *The Chalice and the Blade* Eisler brilliantly depicts the rise of the dominator model of social order with its concomitant rise in a male-dominated view of spirituality with its insistence upon the denigration and ownership of women and children.[4] This necessitates an environment in which women are blamed for men's "weaknesses" and children, like Barbara, hear not only from the mouths of their violators that "men have needs" so women should be responsible for not taking advantage of those needs, but also from the evangelical pulpits that women are to blame for any transgression a man might perpetrate.

It is horrifying that anyone, particularly women, would believe this degrading philosophy, and it is incredibly sad that in Barbara's situation it was only this belief that she was a terrible sinner that gave her the courage to stop Jim's sexual abuse. It is a severely diseased mind, the mind of an addictive personality, that would expect someone other than the perpetrator to take responsibility for his actions. It is this mentality that we see in the religious judgment that the female co-participant in adultery is blamed for the entire situation, or in Barbara's case, where the child-victim is blamed for the perpetrator's crimes.

While Barbara's assumption that the evangelical preacher would blame her for the situation was never directly researched, it is likely that her evaluation was accurate. When Barbara and I were doing an incest segment for our radio show, *Mental Health Magazine,* we received a call from a listener who had been raped and incested as a small child. Years later when this woman went to her minister for help, he told her that she should pray to God to forgive *her for her sins.* Our listener had verified the existence of this diseased thinking process in certain religious leaders.

Maureen's reaction to the revival situation was somewhat predictable. Fearing embarrassment and uncaring about Barbara's true spiritual needs, Maureen blames Barbara for being dramatic and inconveniencing her. There was no indication from Maureen that she was aware of anything troubling her child. It had taken a stranger to notice and be concerned about Barbara's distress and probable spiritual needs.

The one positive thing that came from the evening was that Barbara, after much conflict because of her desperate need for Jim's attention and approval, was able to stop his sexual abuse. Driven by the fear of the eternal fires of Hell, a fear apparently greater than the fear of the disapproval of her stepfather, Barbara sought to stop her "sinful behavior."

When Jim entered her room one night shortly after the revival meeting, he was met by a child's plea for understanding. His dramatic reaction this time when she called him "Daddy" makes it clear that he did not want to be reminded during this sexual assault that his role was supposed to be that of her father and guardian. He certainly was not used to being rebuffed or disobeyed. Desperately trying to keep his control and perpetuate his lies to himself, he retorted, "You seemed to want me three nights ago." His statement indicated that in his diseased thinking process, he was pretending that Barbara had some say in the matter from the beginning.

Unfortunately for Barbara it wasn't until months later when she was old enough and strong enough to threaten to kill Jim if he ever touched her again, that he finally stopped. Then demonstrating the usual irresponsible behavior of the alcoholic, he spent "two solid weeks" closing down the bars in a self-pitying demonstration of revenge. No longer able to dominate Barbara sexually, Jim launched into even greater emotional and psychological abuse until Barbara left home.

Incest And Sexual Addiction

There are several important topics being discussed today by mental health professionals working with addictions that may shed some light on Barbara's family. We have begun to recognize that there exists at the root of all addiction an underlying addictive process, that if that process itself is not dealt with then, there is a high probability that serial or multiple addictions will make an appearance. This means that rather than having one addiction to contend with, there are several addictions which may appear in the addict's life, either simultaneously or one after the other.

In her treatment manual for incest families, Adele Meyer has listed substance abuse as one of the common characteristics of incesting fathers,[5] and John Bradshaw has said that almost all incest offenders are pedophilic sex addicts.[6] Pedophilia, child molesting, is now viewed by many addiction experts as a form of sexual addiction. Keep in mind that while not all sex addicts are pedophiles or incest perpetrators, and not all incest perpetrators with a single deed are sexual addicts, there is a high correlation between sexual addiction and incest, due to the components of shame, secrecy and impaired thinking found in both. There is also a high correlation between alcoholism, sexual addictions and incest.

According to Patrick Carnes:

> Many people attribute sexual excesses and even incest to the power of alcoholism. The reality is that alcoholism often is a concurrent illness with, rather than the cause of, the sexual addiction. Many alcoholics have discovered that the treatment of one addiction does not cure the other. There is a growing documentation about the interaction between the two addictions. It may be that one of the greatest, unacknowledged contributors to recidivism in alcoholism is the failure of treatment programs to treat multiple addictions.[7]

In Jim's drinking binge reaction to Barbara's rejection of his further sexual abuse, we certainly see the interaction of the two disease processes at work. Actually there are three addictive processes at work. Denied his sexual outlet, Jim turned to increased abuse and rage, which had also steadily escalated over the years along with his increased drinking.

Sobriety alone will not create true healing in an alcoholic. Several of my recovering alcoholic clients have reported the huge difference between dry alcoholics in their programs, who may have been dry for years but who have done no therapy, and those who have spent time doing deep emotional and inner child work. What is frequently seen, in those who have done no emotional work, is a lot of "white knuckling," toughing it out and keeping dry, with a lot of support from program friends in the face of strong urges to drink that have not dissipated even after years of being dry.

For those recovering alcoholics who have been doing their deep process work, continual "white knuckling" does not seem to occur. That does not mean that the recovering alcoholic will never have to face down the urge to drink, but it does mean that the urge shows up less frequently and with less intensity and can be dealt with by using deep process tools.

Since the belief in one's own badness is a component in all addiction, just stopping the drinking or for that matter, stopping all the dysfunctional behaviors (like incest or sexual addiction or bouts of rage) is not enough. In the 12-Step programs the 4th through the 10th Steps deal with directly facing our human shortcomings, removing ourselves from the isolation we had placed ourselves in because we had believed ourselves bad for those shortcomings and making amends for the wrongs we had done others.

When I work with a recovering addict, I usually have them work on something I call *remorse*. *Remorse* is the pain or the grief we feel when we recognize that we created the circumstances in which another human being had pain. I frequently remind those I work with that talking about the pain or grief or any of the other emotions is not the same as experiencing them. Learning to experience emotions to completion is very different from talking about them or using them to manipulate others. Real recovery includes regaining the ability to feel again.

If a recovering alcoholic is also an incest perpetrator who may have stopped the incest but has not directly confronted the wrongs done to the child, it is unlikely that the alcoholic's recovery process will hold. Working the 12 Steps is certainly a beginning, but without confronting the emotional traumas involved in that process, recovering alcoholics, who are also incestors, will have a difficult time staying sober as they approach Steps 4 through 10.

6

"We're Only Trying To Help You!"

Many times during those two weeks when Jim spent every night at the bar, Mother was reduced to tears and "a splitting headache," retiring early to her bed. Left alone, I blamed myself.

One night, listening to Mother's sobs on the other side of the wall, I wished that she could understand that none of this was her fault. Wanting to make her happy I tried to do extra things around the house instead, like baking a cake or doing extra chores. But I always seemed to mess something up.

A few days before I had washed the walls in the hallway from ceiling to floor to please Mother, who hated fingerprints and smudges. As I filled the bucket with hot water, added detergent, then carefully scrubbed all the marks until every inch was sparkling clean, I imagined how happy Mother would be, how proud of me.

About seven o'clock that evening, I was alone in my room reading when I heard her car pull in the driveway. Jim wasn't home, having stopped off at the bar. Just as I heard the lock turn I noticed some dirty clothes next to the bed. I grabbed them quickly, opened the closet door and tossed them inside. Mother hated messy closets and made frequent inspections of mine but if my room looked presentable on the outside, she sometimes didn't look further.

As her footsteps approached I looked up, my smile freezing as I saw a frown on her face.

"Where's your father?" she demanded, without saying hello.

"I don't know, Mom," was my trembling reply.

Without another word, she stepped into the room, turned right and opened the closet door, plummeting my hopes of being told I was wonderful. I waited for the barrage I knew I couldn't stop.

"Barbara Jeanne! Look at this mess!" she shouted, her face red and her eyes bulging. "How many times do I have to tell you to clean your closet?"

"I, uh . . . " I stammered, wanting to tell her that I had been busy washing the walls.

Instead of listening, she picked up the dirty clothes and threw them on the bed. "And look at the way your good clothes are just stuffed in here," she yelled ripping the rest off hangers, and pitching them on the pile. I stepped slowly backwards until my shoulders touched the wall, swallowing hard to stop myself from crying.

"And what am I going to find in your drawers?" she hissed. "Are they the same pigsty as the closet?"

I held my breath as she opened the top drawer on the right. As usual I had stuffed clothes and things in the drawers. Mother made me clean them about once each month, but I never kept them organized for very long.

Her shoulders stiffened as she examined the contents of the drawer: underwear, a wadded sweater, dirty shorts and a magazine.

"Why, Barbara? Why?" she screamed. "Why do you have to be such a slovenly pig? Just once I'd like to open these drawers and find them clean. Why must you make me do this?" Without waiting for a response she dumped the contents on top of the other clothes. Then she heaved the other drawers one by one, until the whole bed was a tangled mass of shirts, pants, underwear, socks, school papers, books, keepsakes, miscellaneous candy wrappers and one empty cookie box.

"Clean up this mess and then go to bed!" she shouted, as she walked to the door.

"Aren't you going to say anything about the hall?" I asked, as she was about to close the door. I wanted to make her feel guilty.

"What about the hall?" she asked without turning around.

"I scrubbed every inch of the walls today and you didn't even notice!"

"No one asked you to do that!" she fumed. "And it doesn't make up for this!" she yelled, pointing at the bed. "If you could just learn to do just what you're told, maybe your father would want to come home at night." With that she slammed the door.

I stood against the wall, tears streaming down my face. Staring at the mountain of clothes, I knew she would never be happy with anything I did. Maybe she didn't want me to do well. Throwing myself down beside the mound, I muffled my sobs with my hands.

Several minutes later I sat up, grabbed a handful of tissues from the night-table, dried my face, blew my nose and started putting the clothes away, taking care to fold them neatly and organize closet and drawers to please Mother. It was after ten o'clock when I climbed into bed, too tired even to cry myself to sleep.

Two days later as I listened to Mother's sobs filtering into my room, I felt confused. All of this was my fault and I couldn't tell her. I couldn't fix it, no matter how much I wanted to. I felt awful and had no one to talk to about it. The only thing that made life easier was my love affair with food.

A regular baby-sitting job on Tuesday and Thursday nights afforded opportun-ities to eat without worrying about what Mother would say. A "retail sales" class meant that I worked the snack bar at school during "nutrition" breaks, earning credits in lieu of pay. Each day I "bought" two doughnuts, hot chocolate and a chocolate shake. At lunch I ate a full meal in the cafeteria. After school, baby-sitting earnings were used to buy candy. Even though I was still fairly active physically, I gained seven pounds in two weeks. All my clothes were stretched to the limit. I hid a burgeoning body with sweat shirts and over-sized sweaters.

After a few months of eating like this, Jim's snide comments about my continuing weight gain became a daily occurrence. Eventually, he convinced Mother to do something about me lest I end up like Cousin Mary, overweight and the focus of Jim's "fat lady" jokes.

Mother was seeing a diet doctor at one of the several weight clinics which had sprung up around Southern California. They were staffed by nurses and doctors who performed minor physical examinations and dispensed a variety of pills (Dexedrine, diuretics and vitamins) along with a diet plan. Following the instructions Mother took somewhere between twenty to thirty multicolored tablets and capsules each day.

One evening after dinner, Jim summoned me into the living room for a talk with he and Mother. He motioned to me to sit in the wingback chair.

"Your mother has something to say to you," he said nodding to her. I held my breath, wondering what I had done wrong.

"Well, honey, . . . uh . . . well," she stuttered, sounding uncomfortable and embarrassed. "Your father and I . . . Well, we've been talking about it and we think you're getting kind of . . . well . . . fat!" she exclaimed, hardly able to look at me.

I sucked in my stomach and tried not to cry. The room felt hot and stuffy. She was right and I knew it. Even so, I protested, "I'm not that fat!"

"Barbara," she said, "be quiet until I'm finished." Jim shook his head, rolled his eyes towards the ceiling, sighing deeply.

Mother took a deep breath and continued. "All your things are way too tight and you look ridiculous. It breaks my heart to see you ruining good clothes that I paid for with hard-earned money!"

I lowered my head, wanting more than anything to disappear. For weeks I had been too embarrassed to look in the mirror. I was beyond merely stretching clothes out of shape. I was splitting seams and zippers on skirts and dresses, popping buttons on blouses, breaking fasteners and straps on bras. Almost everything I owned had been mended or safety-pinned to accommodate my expanding body.

"You've needed new clothes for a while now, I know," Mother said, as if reading my thoughts. "But I can't justify spending good money when you're just going to ruin what I buy."

I bowed my head in shame. I didn't know why I was always so hungry. I liked to eat sugar, sweets, bread, pasta, meat, almost everything. In fact, there was very little I didn't like to eat.

"Here's something else you need to think about, little sweetheart," Jim broke into my thoughts. "No boy is going to ask you out when you're so fat. All the other guys would laugh at him."

I gulped for air that wouldn't come and tried to swallow. My face flamed and my body broke out in a cold sweat. How could I ever go to school and face anyone again? The thought of being made fun of because of my fat was more than I could stand. Tears of shame spilled down my cheeks.

"Oh, for chrissakes, stop crying," Jim shouted.

I started to sob. I knew I shouldn't eat so much, but I didn't know how to stop. Hardly an hour passed when I didn't think about food. I never intended to overeat when I started, but it seemed to take a lot of food to make me feel full.

"I'm sorry, I'll try to do better!" I cried, hoping that I could make them understand how awful I felt. Then maybe they would leave me alone. I wanted to eat.

"Maurie, I give up," Jim said in a disgusted voice. "How can we help her when she cries like a baby about everything?"

I held a deep breath, and bit my lower lip but try as I might, I couldn't stop the tears.

"Barbara, don't you know that we're only trying to help you because we love you?" Mother said. "Besides, your father wants to give you a reward if you lose some weight." Turning to Jim, she said cheerfully, "Tell her, honey, it was your idea!"

I looked up warily. Jim's ideas, which were supposed to be for my "own good," usually only hurt or humiliated me.

"Here's the deal," Jim said, "Your mother's going to take you to her doctor. If you lose at least twenty pounds, I'll give you seventy-five dollars for new clothes. How does that sound?"

I was silent for several moments, considering his offer. This must be important because seventy-five dollars was a lot of money. Our grocery budget was twenty-five dollars a week. Even though we didn't buy the best cuts of meat, that was enough to satisfy four healthy appetites. Three weeks' grocery money could buy a lot of clothes. That was the good news. But the bad news was that I would have to lose twenty pounds, and I wasn't too sure I could do that.

I looked at Jim, then at Mother. To avoid more criticism and possible punishment, the only choice was to give in. There was no way out. There never was.

"How long do I have?" I asked.

"We'll go by whatever the doctor says, but remember the quicker you lose it, the sooner you'll have the money!" Mother answered. "So, how about it, honey, will you at least try?"

"Well, okay, I'll try," I sighed, wondering how long it would take for me to fail.

"Good girl!" Mother said, smiling, "You already have an appointment for tomorrow night!" She'd had every intention of winning.

The next evening Mother drove us both to the clinic where a nurse measured blood pressure and pulse, then took my temperature. Then came the part I had dreaded all day, standing on the scale. I weighed one hundred thirty-eight pounds, twenty-two pounds over what the chart on the wall said was my "ideal" weight.

Folding my arms across my chest, I closed my eyes to hide my tears. I didn't want to listen to or look at anything more. My failure had been exposed to a total stranger and I wanted to die.

The torture wasn't over. The nurse measured my neck, chest, waist and hips, announcing each number in a loud voice. I peeked at Mother and saw her bow her head, close her eyes and sigh. I wanted to vomit.

Before we left, the nurse told me which foods I was allowed to eat, and gave me six envelopes of pills, each containing a week's supply of that particular formula, and each with instructions on how many to take each day. I listened without saying a word, jaw clenched, trying to concentrate. Inside I was a knot of anxiety. How could I tell them that I didn't trust myself, that they shouldn't trust me either? I was certain I would disappoint them. Even so, I told myself that I would try as hard as I could.

As we left, the nurse told me that I should be able to lose at least five pounds in the next week. I smiled and tried to look happy, trying to pretend everything was fine. I was good at pretending.

Our family had two major rules about eating. One was that I had to eat a portion of every dish whether I liked it or not, the rationale being that I was being trained to be able to go anywhere and eat anything a hostess served without complaining. One night Jim had forced me to sit at the table until two o'clock in the morning demanding that I eat a bowl of stewed tomatoes, his favorite vegetable. I hated them and they made me gag. As soon as I swallowed the last spoonful, I ran to the bathroom and threw up.

The other rule was that I had to eat every last bite of any food I put on the plate myself, whether or not I was full. If they put the food on my plate I only had to eat a few bites. This, of course, was about "those starving children in China."

Now there would be no more potatoes, pasta or bread, cookies, ice cream, doughnuts or candy. The next morning I took a red pill, then a yellow one, blue one, blue and green capsule, green capsule, and a red and white capsule. I hoped they would work.

On the way to school I looked over the list of permissible foods. Biting my lip and taking a deep breath, I vowed that I would follow the list to the letter all week long. My vow lasted for almost two days.

The evening of the second day I baby-sat for the Murphys next door. As they were leaving, Mrs. Murphy told me to help myself to the chocolate chip cookies in the cupboard, my favorite. I started towards the cupboard when an alarm sounded in my head. Diet!

Darn! I walked out of the kitchen, and joined ten-year-old Susan in the den, to watch television and do homework. I was doing an algebra equation when Susan left the room, only to come back with a big glass of ice cold milk and cookies.

"Want some?" she offered, holding out a dish with six cookies. I could almost taste the chocolate from the smell.

"No, not now," I said, gritting my teeth.

"Are you sick?" she asked with a puzzled look on her face.

"No, I just don't want any," I said through pursed lips.

I heard every bite, every crunch, as she ate. Closing my eyes for a few moments, I took several deep breaths, forcing myself to concentrate on homework.

Sitting on the sofa after Susan was tucked in bed, I noticed the empty plate and milk glass on the table. I frowned, angry that I had to clean up her mess. At the next commercial I carried the dishes into the kitchen, passing by the open cupboard where the cookies were. It wouldn't hurt to have just one, would it? I shook my head and forced myself to walk to the sink.

I wanted one so bad and wished I didn't have to be on a diet. Why couldn't I eat what I wanted and not gain weight? Lots of thin people ate cookies. One wouldn't hurt. Besides, who would know?

The nurse at the clinic expected a five-pound weight loss by the following week. And Mom would kill me if she found out. But how would she know? I had followed the diet to the letter for two days. After all I still had five days to undo any damage. I deserved to have one cookie! Maybe even two! But that's all — two!

I filled a glass with milk and grabbed three cookies. Staring at them I said out loud, "Okay, three, but that's all."

Back in the den I ate all three cookies hardly stopping for a breath. Then I licked the crumbs off the napkin.

With the cookies and crumbs gone, thoughts, silenced while I ate, came back with a vengeance. What if Mother checked up on me? She didn't do that often, but I never knew when she would. I jumped up, gulped down the rest of the milk on the way back to the kitchen, washed the glass and put it away. Then I grabbed two more cookies.

Mother didn't check on me that night, and I made several more trips for "one more cookie" until half the bag was gone, and I felt guilty. In bed that night, I knew I had failed. Only two days into the diet and I had made a mess of everything. What was wrong with me? I went to sleep vowing not break the diet again.

My vow lasted until the snack period the next morning. I opened my purse for a quarter to buy milk and seeing the envelopes of pills, realized that I had forgotten to take the morning dose. I only had five days. How was I ever going to lose weight if I couldn't even remember to take the pills? I was so discouraged that I ate two doughnuts during the snack break. What difference did it make? I was going to fail anyway. I always failed. Nothing ever worked for me.

I didn't weigh myself until the day before my next appointment. One hundred forty pounds! Not only had I failed to lose five pounds, I had gained two more! What would the nurse say? Worse yet, what was Mother going to say, and what would she do? I was terrified. I didn't know how I was going to lose seven pounds overnight. I decided to fast until the appointment and hope.

Drinking water helped quiet the nagging hunger during the morning. Hiding in a bathroom stall during lunch insured that I wouldn't be tempted to eat. By dinner time I was famished and had a raging headache. For the family dinner I prepared chicken for frying, peeled potatoes and tossed a salad, forcing myself not to eat so much as one piece of lettuce.

As I was setting the table for dinner, I remembered that one of the pills that the nurse had given only to Mother was a "water" pill, to help Mother shed excess water weight gain. A ray of hope! If I took one, maybe I could lose another pound or two!

I looked in the bathroom. Nothing. I searched Mother's bureau. Nothing. Where could they be? I knew she didn't take the bottle with her because she filled a pill case each morning. Where were those damn pills? I finally found the bottle of little yellow pills in a drawer of the dining room hutch. "Take one a day as needed for water retention," the label read. Bingo! I put one pill in my mouth, then carefully put the bottle back.

I decided to go ahead and eat a little bit of dinner. I ate a small piece of chicken and some salad with no dressing. No one commented on how good I was being. Feeling sorry for myself, I remembered that they only noticed when I did something wrong.

I tossed and turned all night making frequent trips to the bathroom. The next morning I found that I had lost four pounds overnight! My smile faded to a worried frown as I realized that was still only a net loss of two pounds. I had to lose five. In desperation, I took another water pill before leaving for school.

The morning was spent straining to concentrate on lessons. Before lunch I got a pass to the nurse's office. I wasn't really sick, but I didn't want to face the smell of food. I had to maintain the fast. On the walk home from the bus I bought four candy bars to eat after the doctor's appointment, when the threat of facing the scale was relieved for another week.

On the way to the clinic that evening I broke out in a sweat. Nauseated, I opened the window, took a deep breath and closed my eyes, praying that the scale wouldn't let me down.

"Only three and a half pounds," the nurse said as she adjusted the slide bars. "Did you go off the diet this week?"

"No," I lied.

"Are you sure?" Mother insisted. "Not even at school?"

"No, really," I protested, hoping they would never know that I had lost five and a half pounds in two days.

I was still sweating even though the building was cool. I tried to look attentive as the nurse explained the diet again, droning on about carrots, celery, hard-cooked eggs and cottage cheese. All I could think about was candy, potatoes and bread.

Mother told me just not to think about food, making it sound so simple. "You mustn't think about the cookies in our cupboard either," she went on, "those are for Jim and Shawn. After all, we can't deprive them because we're on a diet." She thought that if she was doing well, so could I. But I knew I would never be as good as she was, no matter what I did or how hard I tried.

By the time I finished doing the dishes after dinner, had tried to study for an hour, I had a grisly headache. After dutifully kissing Mother and Jim good night I went to bed. Twenty minutes later, when I was sure they thought I was asleep, I quietly opened the nightstand drawer. One by one, I ate all of the candy bars, wishing there were more. Before drifting off into a fitful sleep, I vowed to fast the next day.

But I didn't diet the next day or the next. The repeated pattern of the week before yielded only a two-pound weight loss. When Mother noticed that some of her water pills were missing and accused me of taking them, I denied it. After that she put the pills in her purse and took them with her. The next time I weighed, I had gained a pound. Disgusted Mother stopped taking me, saying she wasn't going to waste hard-earned money. If I didn't care about myself, she didn't either. Unhappily I wondered if she ever had.

When Helping Is Hurting

After cutting Jim off from sex, Barbara was still faced with living with an alcoholic parent who was in the latter stages of alcoholism. By that time everyone in the family had also moved into the latter stages of the family disease process. Her wall-washing story poignantly describes the continuing pain of a sixteen-year-old whose desperate need for some sort of maternal acceptance was constantly denied. It also points out Barbara's own growing co-dependent attempts to make things right for her mother.

Barbara's focus, as usual, was placed on attempting to please and somehow make Maureen feel better. Starving for some word of kindness, acceptance and approval, Barbara scrubs the hallway walls but leaves her drawers and closet in disarray. On the surface this appears to be the reason for her mother's anger and disapproval. Actually there was nothing that Barbara could have done at this stage of the family disease process to lower Maureen's rage reaction. Even if Barbara had cleaned her drawers and closet, Maureen would have had to find something else as an excuse to rant at Barbara.

Maureen's own disease process had worsened to the point where she had lost almost all of her softness as a person at home. Any of her pent-up irritations over her job and her constant state of disappointment, hurt, anger and frustration of living with Jim's alcoholism were taken out on Barbara. Her treatment of Barbara had become more and more abusive, with no recognition that her rage was the result of her growing sense of impotence around Jim. As alcoholic Jim's behavior worsened, co-alcoholic Maureen's became more desperate. Frantically looking for some semblance of order, Maureen sought to dominate in areas that "appeared" controllable, such as Barbara's drawers and closet, or even Barbara's weight. Maureen felt safe about taking her rage out on Barbara. Being the family scapegoat, Barbara was the logical target for Maureen's anger and attempts at control. Maureen already knew that Barbara could not and would not fight back, so Maureen's rage over her impotence with Jim was easily dumped on Barbara.

In the later years of Barbara's adolescence, Maureen had turned as mean as Jim. Rampaging through Barbara's closet and drawers, calling Barbara a slovenly pig, Maureen took no responsibility for her own violent outbursts. Her language with Barbara demonstrated the extent of dysfunction and enmeshment in the family. Accusing Barbara of "making her" rip through Barbara's room like a fiend, Maureen could not see that Barbara had not forced her to be the frenzied harridan she had become.

Maureen certainly never realized that Barbara needed (as all children developmentally need) a place that she could call her own. Usually the child's "own" place is the child's bedroom, but Barbara had no privacy there either. Just as she had learned to tolerate huge amounts of pain and dysfunction, Barbara had also learned to tolerate invasions into areas where she needed to have some boundaries. Barbara did not realize that she had given up her body and space boundary rights, so when Jim and Maureen broached the topic of diet, it was not uncharacteristic for Barbara to believe that they had a right to invade in this area as well.

Rather than love and support for Barbara's eating problem, Jim and Maureen tried bribery and coercion. In her communication to Barbara about the diet doctor, Maureen exhibited a frightening absence of any support or compassion. When I first heard Barbara play Maureen in a two-chair process involving the diet doctor scene, I sat silently watching. Playing Maureen, Barbara's face tightened in stern disapproval as she repeated her mother's words, "It breaks my heart to see you ruining perfectly good things." I had been caught off guard because hearing the beginning phrase of "It breaks my heart," I had wanted to finish with some healthier ending such as: "to see you in such pain" or "to not be able to help you." If I felt any doubt about what Maureen had said, the look on Barbara's face as she played Maureen told me I had heard correctly.

By the time Barbara reached this particular scene in therapy, she had been taking back some of her personal power and had been breaking up her negative context about herself. I had recently had her do a "fairy godmother" process in which Barbara acted as a loving fairy godmother to the inner child. Drawing on that experience and the other self-support she had developed, she moved over to the Barbara chair and said with tears in her eyes, "You're so sick, Mother! You're so sick that you can't see how sick you are — You can't see my pain, you can't see that I'm more important than the damned clothes and my damned appearance and your damned appearance. My God, you're so sick!"

The Addictive Eating Cycle

Anyone who has suffered from any form of overeating knows how painful this addiction is. Twenty-five years ago, the 60s medical diet mentality followed the lines of traditional medicine with its "pill-for-every-ill" thinking. Many 60s dieters were unfortunately destined to become "speed freaks" and diet-pill addicts due to the lack of real knowledge about both diet pills and eating disorders. Although Barbara was to go on from her initial contact with diet pills to flirt with many other drugs, her substance of choice remained food.

The day after the rape Barbara was driven by her terror and pain into eating like a construction worker who needs huge amounts of food to fuel hard labor. Barbara did not know that she had triggered an eating disorder. Nor could she have realized that in addition to her dysfunctional need to use food as a way to "numb out," she had also received numerous mixed messages over the years about food that made for much confusion around eating.

Receiving at least small approval for cleaning her plate of all the food she had taken herself and for eating a portion of everything that someone else had served to her even when she didn't like it, Barbara never sorted out the real reason for having to eat that way until she came to see me. During therapy, Barbara realized that the rules were designed so that Jim and especially Maureen would never have to be embarrassed by the children's refusal to eat something at someone else's house. Maureen was frequently embarrassed herself when guests did not like something she had served, and Barbara remembers hearing her mother making the guests wrong for having said something about not liking one of the menu items.

The other confusion around eating came when Jim would insist that Barbara eat all of something that had been served to her, like the stewed tomatoes. Before therapy, Barbara didn't realize that Jim's enforcement of the rules was arbitrary and whimsical and that his need for the rules had more to do with control than with teaching Barbara anything that might have to do with her health.

By the time Maureen and Jim approached Barbara with the idea of the diet, Barbara had already reached the third stage in her eating disorder. She had been out of control with her food intake for years. Her life had become unmanageable as it revolved around food and where, when and how to get it. Using Barbara's "Surprise Attacks" story, we could go back and watch Barbara's addictive cycle at work when she came home from school. Every day after school, Barbara knew that she had chores to do. Each time she had got into trouble the day before for not completing her chores, she would vow to come home and get them done. By the time the school day ended, Barbara was "famished." She had usually been into her *preoccupation* with how, when, where and what she would eat after school by the time she finished lunch. Once she got home, her behavior went into her *ritual,* her routine for getting her food. Sitting in front of the television, she would *eat compulsively* until either Shawn came home or it was almost time for Jim to come home. Then realizing what she had done, she would move into *despair* about her powerlessness once again.

When Maureen and Jim approached Barbara with their proposal for dieting, Barbara already knew that she was out of control with food. She had been hiding behind oversized clothes and avoiding looking in mirrors. She knew that her appearance had gone downhill, but all she really wanted was to be left alone to eat.

Putting Barbara on a diet with the doctor, without any understanding of her process or the pain she was experiencing, merely pushed Barbara further into her eating disorder. Not only did her addictive eating cycle escalate, Barbara became more and more devious about her eating habits

and what she was eating. She started fasting, taking diuretics and hiding
her food intake to look like she was doing something about her weight.

Eat, Sleep And Go Numb!

The end of the senior year of high school is a mixture of melancholy and
anticipation. For me there was only pain and thoughts of food. The strain of
living with parents, who I constantly disappointed, and a brother, who barely
spoke to me, left me with only enough strength to drag myself through each
day. I would not have survived without my favorite class — Advanced Drama.

There were twenty students who had passed the required audition, and Mr.
McMillan treated all of us well. He chose the two plays we performed that year,
and I auditioned for one of the leads. I was chosen for understudy and the next
favored position, Student Director. I was thrilled at the attention and acknowledgment. When everything seemed to be eclipsed by failure, this was a
welcome ray of sunshine, a moment to be special.

I abandoned my usual seclusion, my grades stabilized and I didn't spend as
much time eating or thinking about food. My appearance improved and I even
washed my hair two times a week, instead of just once.

Mother and Jim became even more inflexible about strict adherence to
house rules than they had been before. Involvement in the play was not an
excuse to neglect chores, and their anger seemed even more intense when I
did. I hated coming home after rehearsals. If I argued, Jim accused drama as
the cause of me developing an "attitude."

The production itself was a great success, but when it was over, I went back
into my old cocoon of protectiveness: eating, reading and sleeping. Grades,
hygiene and appearance dropped again. There was little left but to hope that
college would be better.

It had been over a year after Mother had given up trying to help me, and my
weight rose to one hundred and forty-two pounds, an all-time high. Half-
hearted attempts to diet on my own had met with negligible success. Self-
control lasted two days at the outside. I imagined that schoolmates were
judging me for my lack of willpower. I began hiding my binges, consuming
snacks privately in a stall in the bathroom. Dresser drawers were a repository
for candy wrappers, potato chip bags and cookie boxes. Baby-sitting earnings
and allowance went for two things — busfare to school and food. And when
I spent too much money on food, I walked the three miles to and from school.

The mirror became my enemy. I looked in it only once each day, to run a
comb through my hair. I used no makeup. My hair was usually stringy and dirty.
I wore the same underwear and soiled clothing for days in a row and wore

nylons with runs and snags or none at all. I hated the way I looked but did nothing to improve, and hurried from class to class, head down, hiding from the world.

I moped around the house alone each afternoon, wandering in an aimless pursuit of something, anything to divert attention from the pain of constant failures. The kitchen became my haven, as was watching television, taking hot baths, reading novels or sleeping. I couldn't seem to make myself do homework, even though I was in danger of failing at least two classes which would delay graduation.

I didn't have anyone I really considered a friend or confidant. I had a best friend, Samantha, the one person who had loyally stood by me since tenth grade. Even so, I never really trusted her. She seemed to like me, to want to talk to me, but I never believed she or anyone else really cared. I knew from my mother that people only said what they wanted you to hear or that people only said something nice to make you feel better.

Facing the start of each new day became more and more difficult. All I wanted to do was stay in bed. Faking illness was nearly impossible with Mother. Only a fever was a good excuse to stay home. My life of crime began: I started ditching school.

The first time was the most difficult. The next day my hand was shaking as I presented a forged note to the attendance clerk. I needn't have worried. As I held my breath, the clerk gave the note a cursory glance, then handed me a re-admit slip. I marveled at how easy it had been. The second time was a little less scary and each successive time was easier until I was averaging a full day each week.

Near the end of the year, about six weeks before graduation, I had gained so much weight, I only had two skirts and blouses that fit. I was ashamed to be seen by anyone.

One Friday morning I decided to ditch, which would give me a three-day weekend. I hadn't studied for the Government test scheduled for that morning, and reasoned that the extra time could be used to prepare for the make-up. I walked out of the door as Mother left for work. I had developed a pattern. I walked the usual way, passed by the bus stop, sat on a bench in a nearby park until after the bus had come and gone. After waiting an extra fifteen minutes, I walked home.

After letting myself in, dropping books and purse on the couch, I headed straight for the kitchen where I ate several bowls of cereal and peanut-buttered toast. My mind, which had been filled with reproach for not going to school and for missing the test, quieted down. I didn't study right away, after all there was the whole weekend.

I took a hot bubble bath, then settled in front of the television with a box of cookies, a cup of hot chocolate and a romance magazine, and promptly fell asleep. I awoke in the early afternoon, and filled the time with lunch and television until three o'clock. Shawn would be home at four. I cleaned up the evidence and put on my school clothes once again, a pattern I had developed to avoid arousing Shawn's suspicion in case he said anything to Mother or Jim. He snitched on me at any opportunity.

The following Monday morning I remembered that I had forgotten to study for the test. I decided to put off going to school for one more day, repeating the pattern of the Friday before. Lots of other students were sick for several days. Besides that might make my "illness" seem more legitimate. I would return on Tuesday. But Tuesday was a repeat of Monday as was Wednesday and Thursday.

Each night I made up a new lie about how school had been that day, like "Samantha had on a pretty new blouse today," or "We had a killer quiz in German today," little smoke-screens to ensure that I wouldn't get caught. Normally I didn't talk very much about school, believing that no one really cared anyway.

On Thursday morning, the phone rang at about ten o'clock. I jumped up and was about to answer it when an internal alarm sounded freezing my hand in mid-reach. How could I answer the phone if I wasn't supposed to be home? What if it was Mother? Or the school? I sat down, shaking and holding my breath. When it stopped after six rings, I convinced myself that it had been a wrong number.

The phone rang again at ten-thirty, eleven, eleven-thirty, twelve, one-thirty, and for the last time at three. By then all I could think of was how foolish I had been to think I could get away with five days of truancy. How was I going to explain? I tried to convince myself that I was just being silly. I would act as normal as possible when Mother and Jim came home, and I would go back to school on Friday, no matter what, and I would never ditch school again. Then thoughts of impending doom resurfaced and the cycle repeated.

To keep my mind occupied, I cleaned the entire house from top to bottom. When Jim's car pulled into the driveway at four-thirty, I was a nervous wreck. Taking a deep breath, I forced myself to sit down on the sofa and pick up a book. The car door slammed. Words blurred, muscles tensed. As his footsteps approached the door I tried to determine if they sounded angry, wondering if Mother had called him. Did he know? Did she know? His key was in the lock. In a second I would know. I looked up and smiled as he walked through the door. If he didn't know, I didn't want to arouse suspicion.

"Hi, Daddy," I said cheerfully.

"Get me a beer," he ordered.

Dropping the book on the floor, I jumped up and hurried to the kitchen. He kept his empty beer mugs in the freezer to make sure they were always chilled. I took one out and went to the tapper to draw a beer. I didn't know he had followed me into the kitchen.

"How was school today?" I heard him ask from behind.

My throat constricted and for a moment I couldn't answer. He never asked me "How was school?" I had been caught. Even so, I clung to a thin and worn thread of hope, just in case I was wrong.

Forcing myself to breathe, I answered, "Fine, Daddy," and handed him the beer. The smirk on his face drove away the hope.

"How many days has it been since you've been to school, Barbara Jeanne?"

It was time to pay the piper. I knew that lying would just make things worse. Tears rose from my constricted throat, spilling unchecked down my face.

"I'm sorry, Daddy," I sobbed.

"I don't care about sorry," he said sharply. "Tell me how many goddamn days it's been since you last went to school!"

"Five," I whispered.

"What?" he shouted.

"Five," I answered, a little louder.

"Where the hell have you been for five days?"

"Right here," I answered, "here at home."

"No, you haven't. Your mother called, I called and the school called, and no one answered the goddamn phone. Tell me the truth," he raged, "where have you been?"

"Honest, Daddy, I was here. I heard the phone ring."

"Then why didn't you answer it?"

"I don't know."

"You disgust me," he hissed, "get out of my sight while I decide what to do with you."

In my room I sat on the bed sobbing uncontrollably. Of all the terrible things I had done, this was the worst. To be sure, the punishment would be severe. Shortly before my sixteenth birthday he had announced that I was too old to be spanked. He could restrict me, but what else was new. It seemed like I was always on restriction for one reason or another. He could make me drop out of Drama, which he said had made me "mouthy." What would he do? I didn't have to wait long. Within minutes he stood before me, a mug of beer in his hand.

"Start packing," he ordered.

"What?" I asked, unable to believe what I'd heard.

"I said start packing. I'm going to call your father and tell him to get you. You're not going to make our lives miserable any longer. I want you out of here tonight!"

"No, Daddy, no," I begged. "Please! I'll do anything!"

"You're a liar and a cheat and you deserve to live with a lying cheat," he hissed, referring to my natural father's well-known penchant for dishonesty and history of trouble with the law. "Get moving! Now!" he shouted and walked away, leaving me staring at the empty doorway in shocked disbelief. There was no worse punishment.

I hadn't seen or heard from my father in years. The only thing I knew about his recent whereabouts I had discovered accidentally when, in a search for my birth certificate, I had found another document stating he had been confined to the prison ward of a mental hospital. He had been accused of molesting his stepdaughter, information that had been devastating for obvious reasons. That and memories of his cruelty made the thought of being forced to live with him fill me with a greater sense of despair than I had ever experienced before. I tried to blot the thoughts from my mind. Without realizing what I was doing, I reached to my night-stand, opened the drawer, took out a candy bar and ate it unconsciously.

Standing up I took two steps to the closet door, opened it and stared inside. I was disoriented for a moment, unable to remember what I was supposed to do. Then I heard Jim turn on the television in the living room, and reality crashed in around me once more. I had to pack. Reaching inside the closet, I grabbed an armload of clothes and threw them on the bed, then stood staring at them, unable to move. I couldn't do it. I couldn't! I would rather be dead.

Dead, how peaceful that sounded. No yelling, no hating, just a welcome nothingness. Believing that was the only answer, I went to the bathroom and closed the door. Opening the medicine cabinet I searched the shelves for some drug to wash away the pain. The strongest was a half-full bottle of aspirin. I'd heard about people who killed themselves with twenty or thirty pills. I grabbed the bottle and unscrewed the lid and spilled out a handful. After filling a glass with water, I swallowed thirty tablets, four at a time.

On the way to my room, I looked into the living room at Jim and announced, "I'm not going to live with my father; I'm going to die. I just took thirty aspirin." Without waiting for an answer, I walked into my room, lay down on the bed, waiting for death, hoping Mother would come home first so I could see how sorry she would be.

Before I could feel any of the effects, she was home. She talked with Jim for several moments and one time the muffled voices turned to shouts as I heard her yell, "How could you decide anything like that without talking to me?"

Then she flung open my door and shouted, "Why do you have to be so damned dramatic?"

I didn't answer.

"Come with me," she ordered, grabbing my arm and dragging me into the bathroom. She poured Epsom Salts into a glass half-filled with water and then handed the noxious liquid to me.

"Drink this down, all of it," she ordered.

Within seconds a wave of nausea overtook me and I vomited into the toilet. She stood beside me, not saying a word as over and over again I heaved, until my stomach was empty and the toilet was filled with partially dissolved aspirin. When I was finished, she handed me a washcloth.

"Clean yourself up, then go to your room. You won't be going anywhere tonight, so just go to bed and keep quiet."

I lay awake all night wondering what new horror would greet me the next day. I didn't have to wait much past dawn to find out. Mother walked into my room without knocking and told me that she would be driving me to school where she would sign me back in, and then have a conference with some of my teachers. In the afternoon, I would be examined by the district counselor.

I dressed in silence, forgot to brush my teeth, ran a quick comb through my hair, then waited on the porch until she was ready to leave. The only time we spoke on the way to school was when Mother asked me why I had done it. I mumbled that I didn't know.

The whole morning was a daze. Sure everyone in school knew what I had done, I spent lunch sitting in a stall in the girls' bathroom. About halfway through the first afternoon class I received a note summoning me to the counselor's office.

I handed my note to the secretary, who motioned me to the wood bench outside a closed door marked "Sr. Counselor." I wondered if they were going to kick me out of school. Part of me hoped they would. Then at least some of the pain would end.

After several minutes, the door opened and a kind-looking, balding, middle-aged man with wire-rimmed glasses motioned me inside. He invited me to sit in the chair opposite him. I sat down, put my hands in my lap and looked down.

"Barbara," he said and I jumped. "Barbara, do you know why you're here?"

"No," I answered.

"All of us, your parents, teachers, and I want to help you."

I started to cry, wishing that were true. If only he could know how much I wanted to believe what he said. No one could change that unknown something that had always been wrong with me.

"Is there something going on at home you'd like to talk about?" the counselor suggested.

I shook my head.

"What about school then? I've been reviewing your records and noticed that your grades have been dropping steadily. Is there something wrong here, other than not studying?"

"No," I repeated, "nothing."

"How about a problem with one of your teachers? Or did you have a fight with a boyfriend?"

A boyfriend? Was he kidding? Couldn't he see how fat and ugly I was? What boy would want to go out with me? Everyone except me already had a date for the prom. No one would ask me.

"I don't have a boyfriend," I muttered.

"Well, there must be something. You've been truant from school, your grades are dropping and I'm concerned. You can tell me what's wrong. I just want to help you."

He sounded concerned, but I didn't trust him. Besides the "problem" was me. Everyone knew that. He just wanted me to admit it.

"I don't know what's wrong," I cried, "I just didn't want to go to school."

"Well, if you won't tell me, I can't help you," he sighed sounding exasperated with me. I made everyone mad.

"I'm going to recommend a Senior Letter be placed in your file," he went on. "If you miss school one more time without your parents' approval between now and graduation, you'll be expelled. Do you have any questions?"

"No," I mumbled.

"All right then, you may go."

That night at home, I learned the results of Mother's conferences. Mr. McMillan, the Drama coach and my favorite teacher, had told Mother that in his opinion I was "an accomplished liar." I was devastated. The one person at school whom I had hoped was on my side had turned on me. The punishment from my parents was three-fold. I was on bedroom restriction for a month, I would not be allowed to miss school for so much as one day, no matter how sick I was, and if I talked back even once, I would be sent to live with my father.

Just when I had thought things couldn't get worse, they had. The balance of my senior year in high school was worse than before my five-day "vacation." I barely passed most of my classes, with the exception of Drama where I received an A. During the graduation ceremonies, many students cried in sadness at the ending of an important part of their lives. My tears were tears of relief, an agony was finally over. While the others enjoyed Grad Night, I sat alone watching television. As graduation gifts, many of my fellow classmates received trips, cars, money for college, luggage or other gifts acknowledging their accomplishment. Mother and Jim gave me a clock radio. It was all I really deserved.

Fourth Stage

The brief but disastrous period with the diet doctor pushed Barbara into the final stages of the addictive cycle. Attempting to diet, alone and without emotional support, Barbara became more convinced that her inability to lose weight was because she was defective. She did not realize that she was dealing with an addictive process that was similar to Jim's alcoholic process.

Having first chosen to use food to hide from the terror and pain of the initial rape and continuing sexual and emotional abuse, eating had become Barbara's drug of choice. When the family slid further and further into the Alcoholic Family Syndrome, Barbara slid further into her eating disorder. When at age sixteen, she finally put a stop to Jim's sexual abuse, the family had already been so enmeshed in the Alcoholic Family Syndrome, and she had been so enmeshed in her eating disorder, stopping the sexual abuse had little effect on the eating. In fact stopping the sexual abuse became an excuse for Jim's increased drinking and rage and pushed the family deeper into its disease process.

By senior year Barbara was in her own fourth stage and suffering from chronic depression. She perceived herself as more worthless than before because she now saw herself lacking in all self-control. Her appearance took on the look of a drunk. Her clothing was soiled, her nylons had runs, her hair was unkempt, her underwear hadn't been changed for days. She had no one to talk to and no one she trusted, not even her friend Samantha. Barbara had isolated herself for several reasons. She felt worthless and unlikable, but she also had been manipulated into isolation by Maureen's disease process.

Neither Barbara nor Maureen realized that Maureen's communication about people only saying what you wanted to hear or only saying things to make you feel better was really a communication about Maureen, herself, and how she operated her life — lying to people to look good. What Maureen's statements served to do was to make Barbara very wary of trusting people and therefore isolate herself even more. The context through which she viewed others was actually her mother's warped image of reality.

For a brief period in her senior year when Barbara had become Student Director, Barbara's depression lifted a bit and she took better care of herself. Her grades stabilized, and she was less driven by her eating disorder. Interestingly, although not unexpectedly from a clinical perspective, her minimal improvement was greeted at home with harshness and negativity. Jim's accusing Barbara of developing an attitude and Maureen's and Jim's insistence that her chores come before her participation in the school play were examples of the family disease process at work.

Rigid control of family members and resistance to any one member's possible recovery are necessary for keeping the dysfunctional family system in place. The family unit exerted pressure on Barbara to stay in the disease. Any recovery or positive growth had to be stopped by the family.

Frequently parents will bring a child into therapy who is the identified patient in the family. If the abuse at home has not been physical or sexual (and the county decides not to intercede) and the parents refuse therapy themselves (as they so often do), they will eventually pull the child out of therapy as soon as any real healing is evident. This keeps the diseased family's homeostasis.

When Barbara took her week off from school, she was well into the advanced stages of her disease and suffering from chronic depression. So her "suicidal" reaction to Jim's insistence that she go live with her natural father should have been no surprise. Maureen was so deeply embedded in her own disease by that time that her reaction to Barbara's suicide attempt with harsh cold anger was not surprising. It certainly did not surprise Barbara.

The School Counseling Situation

Twenty-four years ago when Barbara was in high school, counseling was frequently done on a part-time basis by teachers who had never been trained in counseling theory or therapy. We don't know whether the school's "Senior Counselor" who had summoned Barbara was actually trained in therapy or not. We do know, from what Barbara described in her interview, that her thinking continued along its usual dysfunctional lines (of believing that if she could only straighten up, maybe they would like her better). The counselor, therefore, had no perception of the disease process at work and no tools to work with a severely pained chronically depressed adolescent.

It is not unusual for school counselors, or any counselors or therapists, to be poorly trained and inadequately perceptive. Many people in the helping professions, including counselors, psychiatrists, psychologists and psychiatric nurses, are themselves non-recovering co-dependents whose own need to be special and needed and in charge and right is more important than the client's health.

The scene in the counselor's office went from bad to worse because the counselor apparently did not have the tools or the training to deal with Barbara. When Barbara told him that she didn't know what was wrong and that she just didn't want to go to school, she was in essence telling the truth. She believed that she was defective, but she thought everyone knew that. She could no more have told him that what was going on at home was the problem than she could have told him about the incest. It never even entered her awareness that these things, as well as her eating disorder, were the root of her problems.

Many years ago when I was finishing my internship, I was called by the father of a fifteen-year-old girl who was more than one hundred pounds overweight and who had attempted to commit suicide. Having gathered a brief history over the phone from the father, I knew that the girl had been to several counselors at various counseling clinics and had been told that they could not help her. The girl was hopeless.

When her father brought her in and left, I asked her to sit on the couch which was catty-corner to the chair I was using. I began asking her a few questions. Getting no response from her, not even an eye flicker, I got up and sat down on the sofa next to her, folded my arms over my chest, emulating my young client, and began talking as if I were she, thinking out loud.

"I'm not going to talk to another one of them — they can't help me anyway — they already said so."

Moving to my counselor's chair, I addressed the space where I had just been sitting imitating the girl.

"You probably think that I can't help you because several counselors already told you that they couldn't help you. Well, they were right. They couldn't help you. They didn't have the tools, but I do. I can help, but only if you want to be helped and only if you participate."

Finishing my counselor part, I again moved to the sofa, crossed my arms and said, thinking out loud again, "I'm not going to speak to her. She's just like all the rest. She doesn't understand."

Back and forth I went, continuing my dialogue the entire time. As with a lot of my work with people, much of what I said in that session came intuitively. At one point during the session, when I was role-playing the girl, I said, "This woman's crazier than I am."

The girl barely moved the entire session. When it was time to go, I stood up, announced the end of the session, and went to let the girl's father into the office. I told him to bring her back next week, same day and time.

He brought her back the following week. She entered exactly as she had the week before, staring down at the floor with a sullen look on her face. I sent her father out. The minute that I closed the door, she looked up at me with a shy smile on her face and said, "You really are crazier than I am." With that introduction, we began down the long recovery road together. I am almost certain that if that girl had suffered one more counselor like Barbara's school counselor, she might have attempted another suicide and this time perhaps have succeeded.

Fortunately for my young client, we had given her help before she was totally lost. Sadly for Barbara, her recovery did not begin as early as this girl's had. Her suicide attempt was brushed off by Maureen as Barbara's dramatics, and the counselor had not been able to spot any of the warning signs of chronic depression or an advanced eating disorder. Barbara was cast adrift to flounder about in her pain for several more years.

PART II

Welcome
To Healing

7

Stepping Out Of Chaos

Recovery For Incest Survivors, Adult Children Of Alcoholics And Co-dependents

One of the first pieces of cognitive information that I gave Barbara was about a psychological game called the Drama Triangle. While I firmly believe that true insights come from doing deep levels of process work, I also know that sometimes it helps to have a framework of understanding in which to place our daily situations. Frequently the healing process can be made easier when we can understand, look for and learn to step out of the systems and patterns that run our lives.

When I began my work with Barbara, there was very little Adult Children of Alcoholics and Sexual Abuse literature available. I knew that Barbara had been raised to lie to herself and others about what she was feeling and what motivated her. She was raised to play psychological games with herself and others. I decided that I would give her a framework for understanding her dysfunctional psychological processes. The framework I chose to teach her was the Drama Triangle. It was obvious to me that Barbara's family literally lived in the Drama Triangle, that Barbara had been thoroughly indoctrinated and habituated to this most chronic and pervasive dysfunction.

When Stephen Karpman published an article in 1968 on the "Drama Triangle,"[1] he briefly described what is, in my opinion, one of the most damaging psychological processes that we see today. After recognizing the value of the Drama Triangle, I began working together with Dr. Arthur Melville in 1978 to clarify the Triangle so that it could be used as a major teaching tool in the understanding of dysfunctional families. We added some information to the basic Triangle to develop a more complete model of human dysfunction. We also found that while the original Triangle could be used to describe the complicated interactions of psychological games, it did not pay enough attention to the acknowledgement or completion of the emotional processes that keep people caught in the Triangle. So Dr. Melville developed a tool called the Feeling (Emotion) Diamond based on the recognition of the four basic emotions of Joy, Fear, Sadness and Anger. We began to use that in conjunction with the new information that we had added to the Triangle to support people in moving out of drama and chaos in their lives.

Because the Drama Triangle can be used to describe the various characteristic processes of all dysfunctional families, including addictive families, I decided that it would be the perfect tool for Barbara. By understanding the roles designated in the Triangle, the way they interact, and the rules that ensnared her in the Triangle, she could learn to avoid becoming entangled in it and the drama that it precipitates.

Since Barbara came from a family suffering from alcoholism, incest, emotional violence and chronic co-dependence, she was aware of the chaos and drama that was part of growing up in a dysfunctional home. Having been raised in a dysfunctional family, she found that she was expected to act out a particular role in the family for the family's benefit. She was expected to be inauthentic. She was not allowed to be in touch with who she was, how she was feeling and what was truly motivating her.

Being raised in a dysfunctional family meant that she was very familiar with the Drama Triangle, although she had never had a name for what she was experiencing. All she knew was that she felt awful and nothing ever seemed to turn out the way she had hoped or expected. What she was experiencing, without knowing it, was the result of being caught in the Triangle and having to play out the various roles and moves governed by its nature.

After more than six sessions of deep process work, I taught Barbara the Drama Triangle. I explained to her that the Drama Triangle is the representation of a complex interactional process involving the three participating roles of Victim, Persecutor and Rescuer. The Triangle is based on blame and guilt and is put into operation whenever *any* type of *lie* or *denial* occurs. Without blame, guilt or lies, there would be no Drama

Triangle and no chaos. Instead there would be healthy responsible relationships based on honest and clear communications.

If you look at the Triangle in Figure 7.1, you will notice that it is placed
upside down on one of the points, rather than on its side. This configuration emphasizes the pivotal position of the Victim. To understand the
Triangle, it would, therefore, be best to start with that position. Before
exploring the Triangle in depth, it is important to remember that participating in any role in the Triangle does not mean that you are a bad
person. It means that you are caught in the dysfunctional programming
that you grew up with in your families.

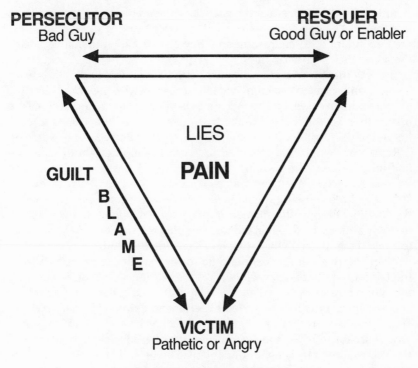

Figure 7.1. Drama Triangle

Victim

The Victim position is the key role in the Triangle because it is the
position around which the others revolve. People operating in the Victim
position take no responsibility for their actions or feelings. They truly
believe that they are life's fall guys, and that everyone in the world is

"doing it to them." They continually look for someone or something else to blame for things not working in their lives. Victims can frequently be identified by their usage of such language as: Everyone, anyone does it to me; you, they (the government, mother, father, boss, spouse, children, etc.) do it to me; poor me.

There are two basic types of Victims: the Pathetic Victim, and the Angry Victim. The Pathetic Victim plays the pity ploy, using woeful "poor me" looks and the desolate language of self-pity, while the Angry Victim pretends to be powerful, using angry "I won't let you do it to me," "Look what you did to me," "You're not going to do that to me again," or "You're bad" types of language.

Both types of Victim are looking for someone to blame for the emotions that they are having and also for their lives not working. In addition they are looking for a Rescuer, someone they can "hook" into taking care of them and their responsibilities.

The way that the Victims manipulate others into doing what they want is with blame and guilt. Victims will find someone who they can blame for their lives not working. If that person believes the Victim and accepts the blame, then he will feel guilty and try to remedy the situation. As soon as he tries to fix things for the Victim, he moves from Persecutor to Rescuer.

Remember when Maureen lied to Amanda's mother about what she had told Barbara. She took no responsibility for her lies and expected Barbara to rescue her from her own lack of integrity. Barbara had to apologize for something she had never done. Maureen was so steeped in the Victim role that she blamed Barbara for exposing her own lack of integrity and demanded that Barbara not only rescue her with an apology to Amanda, but rescue her by never discussing the truth.

Whenever we want someone to lie for us in order to protect us from the consequences of our own lies, we are playing Victim and expecting the other person to rescue us. By telling the truth, Barbara had set up circumstances in which Maureen experienced extreme embarrassment. Therefore, in Maureen's eyes, Barbara was her Persecutor. At the same time, Barbara felt like the Victim and actually became one when she rescued Maureen by lying for her and placing herself in the Rescuer role. Maureen did not realize that any of this action was taking place; she was operating on denial and avoiding pain and embarrassment no matter what the cost. The defense mechanisms that trigger participation in the Drama Triangle are subconscious and become part of our personalities very early in our lives.

Barbara's Christmas charity story is an example of how Maureen would blame others as Persecutors and expect Barbara to act the part of the Rescuer. Maureen, whose experience in life was one ongoing Triangle, was very upset when the church sent Christmas gifts to her home. Unable to take responsibility for her financial distress or her embarrassment about it, she blamed the church for seeing her as one of "those people." She easily drew the children into the Triangle by returning the things to the church and expecting the children to rescue her by not discussing the situation so that she would not have to deal with her own emotions. This also stopped the children from having their emotions and placed them in the Victim position after rescuing Maureen by not expressing what they wanted for Christmas.

In both Victim cases Maureen was totally unaware of operating in the Triangle. In both cases she maneuvered Barbara with blame and guilt. In the first case, she openly blamed Barbara for being her Persecutor. In the second case she blamed the church for being the Persecutor and implied forthcoming blame to the children if they did not rescue her with silence.

Victims, like Maureen, use open or implied blame to try to manipulate others into rescuing them. If a Victim can get a person to feel guilty, *that person* will rescue the Victim in order to avoid being cast in the bad person, Persecutor role. Once the person feels guilty and rescues the Victim, the Rescuer is now *hooked* into the Triangle.

If you look at Jim's role in the family, you will see that he played, as raging alcoholics do, the Angry Victim. Jim blamed Barbara specifically for his going off to drink in the bar and, generally, for his life not working. Barbara believed him and tried desperately "to do better" so that Jim would not go bar-hopping and Mother would be happy.

Look at the sexual example Barbara presented. Barbara was frequently told by Jim that men had sexual needs that they could not control (and were, therefore, the victims of) and that women were responsible for taking care of those needs, whether they wanted to or not. He also trained her to feel guilty for *his* desires. He blamed her for his sexuality, just as the evangelist had blamed women for men's infidelities. This type of male-dominated religion operates from the Drama Triangle. Men do not have to be responsible for their sexuality or sexual dysfunction if they are the poor Victims of their sexual urges and if they can blame women as their Persecutors. It was easy for Barbara to believe that about herself because she already believed that she was the "Bad Guy" Persecutor. She, therefore, was desperate to reach the position of "Good Guy" by rescuing or taking care of everyone else.

Rescuer

As any recovering co-alcoholic knows, the role of the Rescuer is a highly addictive role because it is the position of the "Good Guy." Because of the way most people are raised, whenever they feel guilty, believing that they have been "bad" and have done something wrong, they will try to get out of the guilt by moving into the Rescuer "Good

Guy" position. People do not like to be labeled "Bad Guys" so they actively seek the position of Rescuer — "Good Guy" and because it affords them some relief from the guilt, they get addicted to it.

We are raised from birth to believe that we must be "good." We are trained by the standards of our parents, our churches and our society that in order to be good, we must take care of other people physically, emotionally or spiritually, even at the cost of our own being. We are drilled with the idea that to take care of oneself is to be selfish, that selfishness is bad. Therefore, when the Victim approaches us with blame or tales of woe, we are already prime targets for the manipulative hook of guilt. We already believe that we *should* take care of other people's problems, and that if we do not, we are bad. Because we do not wish to be cast in the Bad Guy Persecutor role, we jump in to rescue the Victim, even when it is not in our best interest and not integral with the truth about who we are and what we want. This position of Rescuer in the Triangle fits the traditional role in the Alcoholic Family Syndrome of the enabler, the co-dependent. This is the person in the family who enables the alcoholic to continue the disease process by not insisting that the alcoholic be responsible for his actions.

When we looked at the concept of selfishness, we found that most parents who train their children not to be selfish were likely to be co-dependents who were actually operating out of their own selfishness. They may have wanted the children to share their toys to make the parents look good to others. They may (as Maureen did) have refused charity and denied some of their children's needs in order to meet their own need to avoid embarrassment. They may have stopped their children from communicating feelings to them because they lacked the ability to deal with the emotional reality. All of these examples are forms of parental selfishness hidden under the guise of teaching children not to be selfish, and all of these set children up for the role of Rescuer in the Triangle.

If a child did not do what the parent wanted, then the child was labeled "bad" and cast in the role of the Persecutor. Taking the position of Rescuer, therefore, affords a person some relief from guilt and gives the person the opportunity to pretend that he is acting unselfishly and for someone else's good. This creates the momentary high that makes the Rescuer position so addictive. The Rescuer does not realize that he is motivated by selfish reasons. He does not want to feel or appear to be a bad person.

There is another important point to understand about Rescuers in the Drama Triangle. Because of the very nature of the Triangle, *Rescuers must have a Victim*, someone to take care of, someone to control, someone, who by their very need, makes the Rescuer feel good. When people are co-dependent and therefore addicted to the Rescuer role, they will find that they actually have a need to rescue. In order to fill that need, they will have to have a Victim around that they can "help." If there isn't one available, the Rescuer will attempt to make one.

In general, *Rescuers need to be needed,* and they need to be in control and be right, no matter what the cost. Being in control and being right allows the Rescuer to avoid dealing with any emotions or discomfort. In all addictions the addictive substance or behavior, in this case Rescuing, is used by the addict to avoid feelings.

Rescuers are so determined not to feel and not to pay attention to anyone else's feelings that they do not realize that the underlying communication that is transmitted to their chosen "Victim" is: You are insufficient. You are inept. You cannot take care of yourself. You are not good enough, therefore, I should be in charge.

When I work with people who choose the Rescuer-enabler position as their first choice in the Drama Triangle and who tell me how much they like to "help" people, I usually do a little exercise with them to let them experience how degrading it is to be in a position of being inept and not good enough. Rescuers are usually so involved with the "high" of feeling good because they have helped someone, that they fail to notice how awful the person being rescued is made to feel in the process.

Often I will ask the Rescuer to imagine being the other person, while I play the role of the Rescuer and verbalize key phrases, such as, "Here, let me do it for you!" or "Isn't it better to do it the right way?" I will especially look for phrases that the Rescuer uses when rescuing others or phrases that their own parents may have used when rescuing them.

Still another important aspect of the Triangle that is pertinent to the Rescuer role is the one-for-one rule that says that *every time someone rescues another person, the Rescuer will end up the final Victim in that particular play.*

Here is how it happens. When you allow yourself to rescue a Victim, you are not acting in your own best interest. You are either taking care of someone else in order to try to feel good about yourself or to avoid feeling guilty. If you are looking for the emotional high of helping others, instead of the healthy action of taking care of yourself, you will jeopardize your own well-being and end up the Victim. In either case, you end up victimizing yourself, but blaming them.

Often the person starting the maneuvers in the Triangle as a Rescuer is a Rescuer-Martyr who will end up as Victim-Martyr. This is the person who "helps" someone out with strings attached. This person has a hidden agenda, an expectation that is never openly communicated nor agreed upon and is rarely, if ever, achieved. The Rescuer-Martyr believes that if he does something nice for people, they should feel obligated to do something nice for him. This sense of obligation gives the Rescuer-Martyr a false sense of control over people. Without necessarily saying it out loud, the Rescuer-Martyr is thinking, "Look at all that I've done for you. You owe me."

From Barbara's perspective, Maureen's favorite position in the Drama Triangle would have been Victim-Martyr. Although Maureen would probably have perceived herself as starting in the "Good Guy" position, she also would have agreed that she was being victimized by Barbara.

The scapegoating of Barbara was the family's way of setting Barbara up as the Persecutor. Barbara believed that it was her job to rescue or fix the whole family's problems. After being designated as the family scapegoat or "Bad Guy," Barbara tried to find the "right thing to do" to fix the family pain, never realizing she was not responsible for their pain and therefore could not fix it. When Barbara cleaned the walls in an attempt to make her mother happy, Barbara was trying to be the "Good Guy." Her attempt at rescuing Maureen's happiness ended up with Barbara as the Victim.

By never telling Jim how she felt about his drunken tirades, his stench from infrequent bathing, his long nights at the bars, his sullenness when he wasn't drinking, his insane surprise tirades, Maureen was taking on the role of the Rescuer-Enabler. Because she never confronted Jim, he never had to deal with her pain nor the consequences of his behavior. Maureen withdrew into her work and community activities, while Barbara and Shawn ended up being victimized by both Jim's behavior and Maureen's withdrawal. At the same time Jim, acting as the family Persecutor, perceived himself as life's Victim.

Persecutor

The role of the Persecutor is the role of the "Bad Guy," the villain. It is the one role that few people consciously choose as their starting place in the Triangle. In fact, it is the role that keeps the Triangle going because people in the Triangle are attempting to avoid that position by moving into the Rescuer role or by perceiving themselves as Victims. No one likes to see themselves as the "Bad Guy." Even criminals in prison want to be seen as the Victims of society, rather than society's Persecutors. The Persecutor role is the one that Victims use, along with blame, to maneuver others into rescuing them. What makes this position truly unique is the fact that *once you are in the Triangle and you decide to leave it, you must leave from this position.* In other words, when you remove yourself from playing the Triangle, anyone still playing will perceive you as the Persecutor.

When Barbara had been in therapy long enough to allow herself to leave the Drama Triangle, she was once again perceived by the entire family as the Persecutor. When she finally told Maureen about the incest, Maureen rescued Jim by blaming Barbara for making Maureen's life a lie. Barbara left the family Triangle, but the family continued to see her as the scapegoat, the family "Bad Guy."

Positioning, Maneuvering And Rules In The Triangle

Now that you have a basic understanding of the positions in the Triangle, there are a number of key points to consider remembering.

1. *The Triangle is based on lies.* Tell a lie to yourself or someone else, whether it is a lie about data or a lie about your emotions or your experience, and you move immediately into the Triangle and the addictive process.
2. *All shoulds are a lie.* Therefore, shoulds will throw you into the Triangle. (An important piece of your healing process is learning how to go about getting your needs and wants met after you learn to distinguish them from your shoulds or the things that other people have told you are your needs.)
3. *All positions in the Triangle cause pain* — so no matter what position you are in at any given moment in the Triangle, you will be in pain.
4. *There is no power in the Triangle.* When you are in the Triangle, you are operating from powerlessness and irresponsibility no matter what position you are playing.
5. *Everyone has a favorite starting position* which is usually either the Rescuer or the Victim. Few people choose Persecutor as starting position.
6. *Once you are hooked into the Triangle, you will end up playing all the positions, whether you like it or not,* because of the nature of the Triangle. You may have perceived yourself as a Rescuer who wound up as someone's Victim while, at the same time, that person perceives you as the Persecutor.
7. *Guilt is the experience that hooks you into the Triangle,* and therefore you need to learn a few points about guilt:

   a. Guilt is a signal that someone is attempting to pull you into the Triangle.
   b. In order to stay out of the Triangle you need to learn to give yourself permission to feel guilty without acting on that guilt. In other words, do not let the guilt push you into the Rescuer position.
   c. Learn to sit with the guilt and be uncomfortable. This experience called guilt is a learned response; it is not the same thing as being out of integrity with yourself.

8. *The "escape hatch" out of the Triangle is located at the Persecutor position.* Telling the truth and feeling your emotions opens the escape hatch out of the Triangle. In other words, in order to leave the Triangle or for that matter to stay out of it, you have to

be willing for others (the Victims or the other Rescuers) to perceive you as the "Bad Guy" and then go through whatever
emotions surface as a result of their perception. This does not
mean that you *are* the "Bad Guy;" it does mean that others
choose to see you that way. If you are not willing to be seen as
a Persecutor you will get hooked into rescuing and place yourself
back, or keep yourself in, the Triangle. If you are already in the
Triangle and wish to leave, *you have to be willing for the others
in the Triangle to see you as the Persecutor.*

When you are in the process of leaving the Triangle, you are in
the process of telling yourself the truth about your feelings, your
motives and the situation in general. You are willing to experience whatever feelings you are having and are willing to let
others experience their feelings without your having to rescue
them. If the other people in the Triangle are willing to tell the
truth and experience their feelings, the Triangle disappears. If
they are not, as is more often the case, then you leave looking
like their Persecutor.

Let me give you an example. When you have a person in your
life whose behavior is addictive and who lies to you frequently,
and you attempt to confront that person with the truth and with
how you are feeling, you may find that person blaming you for
wanting to get at the truth. Imagine that this person is always
late for events that the two of you schedule together. Although
you are afraid, you resolve to set the situation up so that this
person's lies about getting together on time do not affect you.
You decide to meet him at scheduled events, rather than going
with him, so that you won't be late. This person will probably
experience this at the subconscious level as a loss of control, will
become frightened, play Victim instead of being responsible for
the consequences of his previous behavior, make you wrong for
taking care of yourself and blame you for trying to be in control.
You may have to leave the relationship in order to continue to
take care of yourself. When you leave under those conditions,
that person will see you as the Persecutor. This does *not* mean
that you are the Persecutor even though this person perceives
you that way.

9. **You can play the Triangle alone with yourself.** (Once you have
been raised in a dysfunctional family, you do not need anyone
else to push you into the Triangle.)

a. The way you play the Triangle by yourself is by listening to
the negative voice inside your head that beats you up, "puts
you down" and constantly *shoulds* you.

b. Remember, *shoulds are a lie.* They have nothing to do with who you are. They are someone else's interpretation of what to do and what is good.

c. When you play the Triangle with yourself, your should-er will persecute you so that you will feel like a Victim. At the same time you will be feeling guilty. This will trigger the belief that you are the Persecutor. The guilt will drive you to "rescue" someone (or some situation), even when no one except you is there attempting to manipulate you into the Rescuer position.

10. *When you actively participate in a relationship with someone who lives in the Triangle, you must be very careful of the hooks.* It is difficult to be around people who constantly operate in the Triangle and not get hooked in yourself, especially if your personal boundaries are not clear and you have not learned to recognize the Triangle.

11. *Your internalized should-er is also the voice that pushes you into the Triangle when others around you are in and attempting to hook you.* The *should-er* is the false-self, the part that is actually someone else who you believe is you. It is controlling, negative, rigid, perfectionistic and righteous. Without that part of you operating, you would not participate in the Triangle.

12. *Being in the Triangle is not being alive;* it is a living death. It is a life of pain, inauthenticity and lack of love and acceptance.

13. *Suicide is the ultimate Victim act, the ultimate act of self-pity.* When the Victim perceives that he cannot get anyone to come to the rescue anymore, and he does not have the courage to seek new alternatives, he may turn to suicide.

14. *Telling the truth and experiencing your emotions is the only way out of the Triangle.* To do that you have to learn to know and define your boundaries and take responsibility for recognizing, experiencing, expressing and completing your emotions.

Let's look at a few more examples of the Triangle positions and how they relate to co-dependence and the Alcoholic Family Syndrome. I once worked with a young woman who entered therapy as an acknowledged Adult Child of an Alcoholic. When I asked her what her purpose was for being in therapy, she said that she had come in to work on herself and her co-dependence. After relating that healthy-sounding purpose, she proceeded to spend a large part of the session telling me about her husband, who was not living up to her expectations. He would stay at home, depressed, and not go out job-hunting. In her estimation her unhappiness was based on his behavior, and he needed fixing. She said that she kept trying to push him to get a job. When I probed further, I found out two things: first, that he was not an alcoholic, and second, that he had abandoned the career that he had liked because she was embarrassed by it.

When I pointed out to her the co-dependence involved in what she was telling me, she was able to recognize her need to control matters in order not to feel uncomfortable, but she did not want to change. Although she had come into the session stating that she wanted to work on *her* co-dependence, what she was really hoping to do was to get me to help her find a way to change her husband.

When we explore this scenario relative to the positions in the Triangle (which the three of us did later on), we find that her husband, in an effort to rescue her, to take care of her embarrassment and to avoid guilt, left his job in a career that he enjoyed. He ended up experiencing himself as the Victim-Martyr and her as the Persecutor. She, on the other hand, saw herself as the "Victim" of her husband's unacceptable career and had hoped to get me to rescue her.

When she came into my office, she did not realize that she was trying to bring me into the Triangle. She was not even aware that she lived in the Triangle. She didn't see that she was trying to fix him in order to avoid dealing with herself. Toward the end of the first session, I told her that in order for me to work with her, she would have to be willing to let go of trying to control his life, starting with letting go of controlling his career. She told me she couldn't do that. I told her that it was okay, and this would be her last session. I would not work with her as long as her primary goal was to fix him.

She sat there stunned. She had really thought that I would help her by showing her how to fix him. I watched the fear rise in her eyes when she realized I was not going to do what she wanted, which was to rescue her.

She sat for several minutes more, and then she took an important step in her recovery. She agreed to be *willing* to let go of trying to fix him. She went home and told him that she was willing to stop running his career, that he could go get any job that he wanted. He did. This was the first time that they had been able to consciously step out of the Triangle.

It was obvious to me when this woman came in that she had only a superficial understanding of co-dependence. With the help of the Drama Triangle and the Feeling (Emotion) Diamond and much deep process work, this woman was quickly able to recognize when her co-dependence was operating.

Of course, Barbara's family was a prime example of what it is like to live in the Triangle. Lying about almost everything from emotions to reasons for drinking, to motives for making Barbara the scapegoat, to the incest, the family was in constant turmoil and drama. Blaming Barbara for everything, Angry Victim Jim placed Barbara in the Persecutor role, while manipulating her into rescuing the entire family from having to deal with themselves and reality. Barbara often experienced herself in all three roles simultaneously. Blamed as the Persecutor, desperate to set things right and rescue her mother from any pain, she also experienced herself as the Victim of Jim, specifically, and life in general.

The Feeling (Emotion) Diamond

As a result of my own deep emotional process work, I have found a way to simplify and support the emotional healing process. As human beings we are all born initially with the ability to experience all emotions and have the potential to distinguish the various emotions from one another. Through our dysfunctional upbringings, we suppress those abilities and are forced to go back and relearn how to identify, experience and express our emotions. In order to make that process easier, I begin by teaching about the four basic emotions: Joy, Fear, Sadness and Anger.

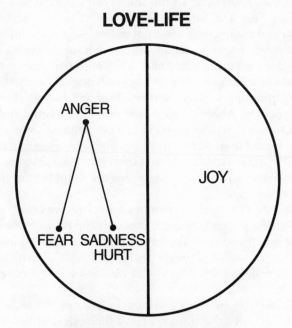

LOVE-LIFE

ANGER

JOY

FEAR SADNESS
HURT

Figure 7.2. Experience Circle

First, let us look at an Experience Circle. (See Figure 7.2.) Assume that this circle represents a portion of life. Among the many types of experiences that we have in life are the emotions. Emotions are an important part of the experience of Self, and they provide the energy for living. The four basic emotions are Joy, Fear, Sadness and Anger. Looking at the circle, you will notice that Joy is placed alone on the right side of the circle. This is done because many people seem to believe that Joy is the only good emotion and Fear, Sadness and Anger are bad emotions. This is not so. *All emotions are good.* Fear and Sadness and Anger are good. While emotions can provide the energy for actions, they are *not* the actions.

For example, we have a tendency to confuse the emotion called Anger with the action of violence. We do this because our dysfunctional families do not teach us the difference between emotions and actions and because for many of us in our dysfunctional homes, violence often followed Anger or took the place of it. We believe then that violence and anger are the same thing and that our anger is, therefore, bad and must be avoided. We amass huge amounts of anger and when we can hold no more, we burst forth in violence or react with passive aggression. If we learn to experience our anger when it happens, we do not need to use violence.

If you look at the left side of the circle, you will notice an interesting configuration. Fear and Sadness are on the same line while Anger is above them and connected to both of them. Fear and Sadness/Hurt are primary emotions. Anger is a secondary one. Because anger is a secondary emotion, it does not mean that Anger is less important than the others. It means that Fear or Sadness/Hurt or both will trigger first, and then Anger is triggered from one or both of them. Fear and Sadness/Hurt are soft receptive emotions. Anger is a hard emotion; it is powerful and dynamic. It is our protective defensive emotion and often the only way we know to defend our boundaries. Although Anger does not trigger first, once it is triggered, it must be experienced and completed (not acted out) in order to return to and complete the Fear and/or the Sadness/Hurt from which the anger was activated.

If you have been taught (as men in particular have been taught) that Fear and Sadness are bad, Anger is probably the only emotion that you will experience. If you have also been taught that Anger is bad, you will suppress that as well and begin to behave with passive aggression. Unable to directly express Anger, you will seek indirect covert ways of expressing it.

Because most women have been taught that Anger is bad, women shut down on Anger and either turn it against themselves or become victims of everyone else's Anger.

To further simplify understanding the emotional process, Dr. Melville developed the Feeling (Emotion) Diamond (see Figure 7.3). He took the circle that we were using and created a diagram to demonstrate the way the emotional process operates.

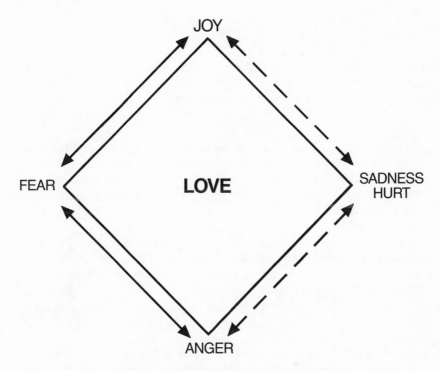

Figure 7.3. Feeling (Emotion) Diamond

When you look at the Diamond you will see that at the top of the Diamond is Joy, which is where all of us wish to be. There is nothing wrong with wishing to experience Joy. The problem comes when you believe that you should be there all the time, and then you try to hold onto it and avoid feeling Fear, Sadness and Anger. Trying to hold onto Joy (or anything else) removes you from reality and the ability to live in the moment. You have to be able to *experience* your Joy and *complete it* in order to stay present in the moment. If you truly allow yourselves to live in the moment, you will discover that you will have the opportunity to experience not only the other emotions, but all the richness that life has to offer. As you progress through your healing process, living in the moment becomes easier.

Looking again at the Diamond, you will notice that when you leave Joy you will go to either Fear or Sadness/Hurt or both. If you complete and release those emotions, you can return to the place at the top to await Joy. If you do not complete and release the Fear or Sadness/Hurt, you will either store them or convert them to Anger. When you store Fear or Sadness/Hurt, you will find it difficult to return to Joy, and the more Fear and Sadness you store, the more difficult it will become to experience any Joy. Since most people believe that being happy is right and being sad or angry is wrong, you walk around with a huge phony smile on your face, pretending to yourself and everyone else that you are happy.

If your emotional process also includes converting the Fear and/or Sadness to Anger, then you will also walk around with large amounts of incomplete Anger. Looking at the Diamond, you will see that there is no direct pathway between Anger and Joy. In order to return to a place of Joy, you must therefore not only complete and release the experience of Anger, but you must also go back and experience the actual Fear and/or Sadness from which the Anger was triggered. Only then can you return to a possibility of Joy.

Also remember that when the level of Anger stored reaches the point at which you can no longer contain it, the Anger will burst forth, either as rage or violence or, at the very least, passive aggression. You are like a storage vat. There is just so much volume available for the storage of emotions. That is why storing and controlling emotions eventually stops working. There simply is no more room available, the pot boils over and the lid is blown off.

Another important point to remember is that if you are not experiencing some form of Joy (such as happiness or contentment), you are going to be experiencing some form of Fear, Sadness/Hurt or Anger in various combinations. There are very few people on the planet today who are so advanced in their process and so present in the moment that they experience no emotional response to their reality. Most people who claim to feel "nothing" when they are in the middle of difficult circumstances feel nothing because they are either having an emotional response but are in denial about it or they are so disassociated from their emotions, they are numb. Because Western cultures tend to prize intellect and degrade emotions, people often use this as an excuse to intellectualize all human experience and behave and communicate (as Virginia Satir has said) like living computers, very reasonable with no show of emotions.[2]

If you are an Adult Child, you have had such poor emotional models and have gone through so much dysfunction, you have shut down your ability to experience your emotions. That does not mean that the emotions are not happening; it does mean that you are out of touch with them. As a consequence you are probably having several *other* types of experiences, ranging from anxiety attacks to addictive urges, all of which result from the inability to experience the true emotions that are there.

If you are in recovery, whether it is a 12 Step or therapy, you are probably beginning to discover emotions and experiences that you never thought possible. If that is not the case, you need to do something other than what you are doing so that you can move your process along. Learning about the emotions and learning to experience them are not the same thing. You may have learned that you have emotions. You may even be able to recognize them but that does not mean that you know how to experience them. Learning to recognize emotions is like coming upon the ocean and learning what it is. You see the ocean and, then you sit down and watch it. In order to experience it completely, you have to go in and swim.

Using The Emotion Diamond To Stay Out Of The Triangle

If you wish to stay out of the Triangle, you must learn to tell the truth about what emotions you are feeling and take responsibility for them. Remember that no one else is responsible for your emotions. No one else can fix them for you or change them for you. People may support you in experiencing them, but ultimately no one but you can complete and release them.

Frequently your dysfunctional families are so repressive, you cannot identify certain emotions or distinguish them from other types of experiences. When you tell the truth about what you are feeling, no longer take on the guilt that others try to place on you, and are willing to feel the fear and sadness when being accused of being the Persecutor by people who stay in the Triangle, you will step out of the chaos in your life. By being responsible for acknowledging and experiencing your emotions, you are also being responsible for your addictive process. Using the Diamond will give you some support in accomplishing that task.

1. Whenever you discover that things in your life are not working, you can assume that your addictive process has been activated and you are caught in the Triangle.
2. Ask yourself which position you are in at the moment. Is this your primary choice in the Triangle?
3. How did you get there? What lie did you tell yourself or someone else?
4. Which emotion(s) are you avoiding? This is where the Feeling (Emotion) Diamond is applicable. As I said before, if you are not experiencing some form of Joy, you are experiencing some form of Fear, Sadness/Hurt or Anger. Are you having Anger? If so, you must experience it and complete it, not act it out. Then look for the primary emotion from which the Anger triggered. Is it Fear, or Sadness/Hurt or both? Again, experience that and complete it.

Remember that emotions must be experienced not intellectualized. You cannot think your way into an experience. No matter how much I describe to you the color red in scientific terms of wave length and intensity, you will still not have the actual sensory experience of the color red if you have been blind since birth. Intellectual understanding of something is not the same as experiencing it!

If you answer the question, "What emotion are you avoiding?" by identifying a response such as disappointment, you have discovered a complex experience that combines the emotion of sadness associated with an unmet expectation. Remember, it takes time after all the years of suppression, to find and feel your emotions. Find someone who can help you experience your emotions.

Some people seem to be able to identify the emotions but not seem to complete them. There are several possible reasons for that.

1. You may have mislabeled an emotion so that you can't really experience or complete it.
2. You may be having more than one emotion and experience activated at once. You will need to identify all of them.
3. You may need to *process* the tapes and the scenes that have surfaced with your exploration.
4. You may be *running* your emotions on yourself or the others in the Triangle. If this is the case, you will probably find yourself in the Victim position and will have difficulty removing yourself from the role or the Triangle.

   Here is what *running* your emotions is about:

   Let us look at the Experience Line (see Figure 7.4) below as if it were the range between the inability to experience emotions (on the left) which I call, in jargon, "stuffing it" and the ability to experience and express emotions in a healthy way (on the right) which I label EXP.

Figure 7.4. Experience Line

When you are stuffing emotions, you are denying, ignoring or disassociating from your emotions. You may be going numb. The emotions are occurring but you are not in touch with them. You may have been raised in a family where only one emotion was acceptable. It might have been Sadness or Anger or Fear. If this is so, you will translate all your emotions into the one the family has made acceptable. Until you discover what the real emotions are, you will not be able to complete them.

At some point in your healing process, you will begin to have a sense of what the emotions are and how they feel. This is the point at which you may begin running them. What happens is that you make some contact with the emotion, but you still do not take responsibility for experiencing and completing it. Instead, you use the emotion to try to manipulate someone into the Triangle to rescue you from your emotion. You will blame others for your emotion and expect them to do something to take it away. You are attempting to control with your emotions. You are running them or making them right so that you do not have to feel them.

You will probably sound like this: "I'm hurt (or angry or scared) and it's your fault" or, "I'm feeling . . . (fill in the blank), and you should do something about the situation." Or "What you did made me feel . . . (fill in emotion) and now you have to stop, change, etc., or I can't get through my feelings."

While it is perfectly acceptable to request that someone change certain behaviors, it is still not the other person's responsibility to fix your emotions. You must learn to complete your emotions whether the other person changes or not, otherwise you will become addicted to controlling other people's behavior so that you will not have to experience your own emotions.

Let us look at another form of running emotions. If you were raised in a family where only one emotion was acceptable, anger, for example, everyone will walk around with that emotion. As soon as you begin to feel any other emotion you will convert it to anger, not because you have something to be angry about, but because that is the way your family acts. If you are sad, you will act angry. If you are scared, you will act angry. You may not even experience the anger. It has become an act for you, and you have learned to use the anger act to control yourself and others. This is one of the ways you develop a false-self.

When you are further along in your healing process, you will be able to recognize your various emotions. Then you will begin to express them to others in order to get further in touch with the emotions and *not* to try to make someone else responsible for them. Remember, this is a process, and you may slide back and forth along the Emotion Line until you are in touch with your emotions and the way that you deal with them and can express them clearly and cleanly in order to complete them.

When you are operating anywhere to the left of the experiencing and expressing end of the Emotion Line, you will find yourself operating in the *Drama Triangle*. As you learn to experience and express your emotions in order to have them and complete them and not to run them on other people or try to get some results from people, you will find yourself less and less in the *Drama Triangle* and less and less in your addictive process.

8

Boundaries

As a result of learning to experience her emotions, Barbara had begun to define her boundaries and recognize who she really was. The process work gave her the opportunity to experience how, when and with what she had obstructed her abilities to experience her life. It also gave her the tools with which to reclaim her life. As we went along in her process, there were certain new words that I taught her that were relevant to her growth. When we have new experiences, having a new vocabulary helps us to hold onto the new experiences. Some of the words Barbara learned and experienced were *boundaries, context versus content, Self* and *false-self.*

Boundaries And Limits Of Experience

Barbara learned that she, like all Adult Children, was suffering from the gradual shutdown of the ability to experience herself, her surroundings and her life. This was done through progressively more and more confining conscious and subconscious decisions about who she was and what was acceptable and what was not. With these decisions, she created a contextual structure that determined the way she related to herself and reality. Like Barbara, we all create boundaries through which we view ourselves and reality.

The decisions about those contextual structures and what we will allow ourselves to experience comes as a result of the interactions that we have within our family systems. The decisions we make about who we are, or rather who we "think" we are, also come as a result of the interactions we have with the family.

If our parents are dysfunctional, their reflection of us is distorted. We then make decisions about who we are and what our boundaries should be based on those distortions. When we decide that we are bad (as Barbara had believed) and that everything we do is wrong, then no matter what we do in life we will always be bad and never do anything right.

To change those early distortions we have to recontextualize ourselves. That is, we have to change the boundaries we have developed about who we are and what is acceptable. Changing those boundaries is not as easy as it sounds. It cannot be done by simply understanding the concept and recognizing what particular context we hold about ourselves. That is only the first step in the process. We must go back, re-experience and complete the early traumas out of which we created those decisions. Then we can go back and rebuild a new context about ourselves with new boundaries.

Context Versus Content

If you can grasp the difference between context and content, you will have little difficulty with the concepts associated with boundaries because a boundary is a contextual structure. The context which we hold about ourselves is the governing framework out of which we operate; content is the material we experience within that framework. The context we create governs or frames the way we respond to the content. The content may be anything from emotions or thought patterns to events and happenings that we experience. While the context usually functions subconsciously, it may be brought to conscious awareness. The content, usually conscious, may also be subconscious.

Barbara's overall governing context about herself was that she was a bad person *who did not know what was right* in the world and *who had no rights* in the world. This set her boundaries up in such a way that she was constantly invaded by or enmeshed with others, looking to them to tell her how she did and whether she was acceptable. No matter what Barbara said or did or felt, it was always governed by the perception of herself as bad and the world as right. Whenever Jim or her mother judged Barbara or her actions as bad, her "I'm bad" context made them right. Once this context had solidified, Barbara saw everything around her contributing to making that context right. If anyone ever said anything nice to Barbara, most of the time she would not believe them because her "I'm bad" context would not let her. Because Barbara had also taken from Maureen and incorporated the belief that people only said what they wanted you to hear, Barbara could use this to distrust people. Since she could not trust them to tell the truth, and since she needed to twist everything that people said to her to fit her negative context about herself, Barbara would have rarely believed anything nice that was said about her.

Self As True Context

It was not too difficult to show Barbara that her context about herself was "I am bad." She already had a direct experience of that. What was much more difficult to teach her was that *Who* she was was not that bad person. This meant she had to learn the difference between the Self and the false-self. What Barbara believed to be the Self was actually the false-self (see Figure 8.1). I had explained to her that the Self, the Being, is the experiential energy context, the Source, for each individual life. The Self is good, loving, lovable and whole, and the Self, or Being, is that part of us which is in direct contact with our Higher Power. Although I spoke to Barbara about the difference between the Self and the false-self, I knew that until she had a greater experience of the false-self and how it worked, she would have difficulty experiencing the true Self.

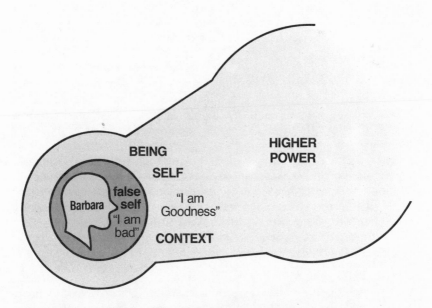

Figure 8.1. Context (Self vs. false self)

I explained to Barbara that the Self has at its disposal tools for living focused in physical reality. One of those tools is the mind. The mind is an intermediary between the Self and physical reality. It is the mind that interacts with and is programmed and affected by living in the family system, and it is the mind that develops the false-self, the false-image, as a result of living in a dysfunctional family. Unfortunately, it is also this false-self which the mind has created that then creates the boundaries or contexts through which we experience the world and attempt to experience ourselves. Once this happens, the true Self is buried and the false-self, set up by the mind, governs the way we participate in and view the world. What complicates the situation even more is the fact that the false-self and the mind do not know that the false-self is not the real Self. Only the real Self knows that, and the real Self can't communicate it to the false-self because the false-self blocks that information so that it can continue to survive.

When we are operating in the false-self, we have left the Self as the context for our lives and moved into negative false-self as the context. We become isolated from *Who* we are and cannot make contact with our Being or with our Higher Power. We believe that we are the negative false-self and then because that is a painful belief, we avoid dealing with that negativity. We move further and further away from the Being and our capacity to discover our Self. So we are caught in a void, a darkness. The healing process is one in which we can reclaim *Who* we are and make contact with our true Self and therefore with our Higher Power.

In order to reclaim the Self we must first change the negativity of and take responsibility for giving up the false-self of the mind. If we go back to the wounded child within and help the child to heal, we can make large parts of the negative false-self disappear. Through healing the child within, we can gain access to the Self and, therefore, contact with our Higher Power. It is through healing the wounded child that we can rediscover our true potential.

When Barbara found and healed her wounded child, she was able to separate from and make more of the false-self disappear. It became easier and easier for her to recognize that critical negative voice of the false-self and more natural for her to look for the voice of what she first called her "fairy godmother" and later her true Self.

Boundaries As Context

If you have come to realize that you aren't who you thought you were and you don't know who you are, you are suffering from boundary problems. Boundaries, as contextual structures, govern behavior and beliefs and may function at the conscious or subconscious level. When you have difficulty acting upon your conscious beliefs or desires, it is because some subconscious boundary (or context) is governing your behavior. Most often your conscious thoughts, wishes and beliefs become mere content that is controlled by some subconscious or semiconscious boundary.

Look at an example of how a boundary, or context, governs thinking, feeling and behavior. Remember Barbara's context about herself was that she was always bad and wrong. Any of her wishes, her desires, her thoughts were governed by that context. If she had a wish or desire that was in disagreement with anyone else, especially her mother, her perception was that these thoughts of hers were somehow wrong. The desires and thoughts became the content governed by her context of wrongness.

In addition, Barbara held many subcontexts within the major context. I explained to her that things can become fairly complicated because it was possible for her to have many simultaneous boundaries or concentric boundaries within boundaries or a combination of both. When Barbara went to see the evangelist and heard him talk about adultery, she related to everything he said from her context of *I'm Bad*. What he said about adultery and sin easily fit into her *I'm Bad* context. When her mother told her that their religion did not believe in public confession, Barbara had to place herself in the context of her religion, even though she had very little idea about what her religion was. Because of the nature of our consciousness and our ability to create varying contextual structures, it is possible for some people to see themselves within the context of their religion while others see their religion within the context of themselves. This means that a person either sees himself as a part of a larger group, a religion, or he sees his religion as part of him. (See Figure 8.2.)

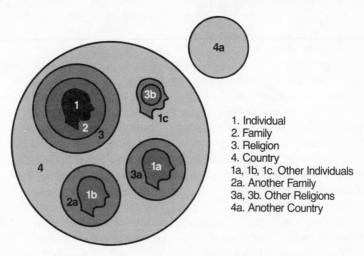

1. Individual
2. Family
3. Religion
4. Country
1a, 1b, 1c. Other Individuals
2a. Another Family
3a, 3b. Other Religions
4a. Another Country

Figure 8.2. Boundaries

Here is another example of the difference between context and content. Let us say that you are a first-born child. You have been an only child for six years. Your father is very angry and controlling with you. Your mother, who is moderately functional and caring, is pregnant and due to bring home a new baby any day now. You believe that the new baby will be a new friend for you, perhaps a new plaything.

When Mother brings the baby home, nothing is the way you imagined it would be. In fact, things are awful. The attention that you used to have for yourself you must now share with this screaming thing that you cannot play with. Your mother is all wrapped up in the new baby. Although she tells you that she loves you, you do not believe that she really loves you anymore. Because your father has been so judgmental with you, you have already started to judge the things that you do as bad. With the new belief that Mother doesn't love you anymore, you decide that *you must be a bad person* for Mother not to love you anymore. The decision becomes subconscious and *contextual.* It now governs all your interactions with your mother. No matter what she does (which will be the content in your life together), from this point on, your subconscious will twist it to fit your new context: Mother does not love you anymore, and you are a bad person.

No matter what Mother does, your context will twist it. If she spends time with the baby, it proves that she loves him. If she tries to get you to spend time with her and the baby, you will see it as a desire to do something for the baby and not a desire to make you feel a part of the family. If she takes you on a trip alone, you may see it as an attempt on her part to buy you off. Anything that she does, which is now the content, will be twisted to fit your new context.

Then add to all of that the fact that you cannot admit to yourself that she does not love you because you need her for your survival. Children need to believe they will be taken care of, and their need to survive does not allow them to see anything negative about the parent that might threaten that survival. Instead you will perceive yourself as bad in order to avoid any possibility of admitting that your parent might not love you and might abandon you. If she does not love you, there is a high risk that she will abandon you. Unwilling to admit this possibility, you would instead tell yourself that she acts this way because you are bad, so you must try harder to be good.

You will, therefore, go through life thinking you believe your mother loves you, when you really believe she doesn't love you. This may sound confusing because it is. What I am demonstrating is the capacity we humans have for many layers of thoughts and beliefs and self-deception. A great deal of confusion occurs when you cannot distinguish between the contextual beliefs and the beliefs that they govern, which become the content.

Personal, Intra-Familial And Familial-Cultural Boundaries

On the physical level we are born with wonderful talents and abilities and an enormous capacity to live and experience life. We are also born with the mind's ability to set limits and define ourselves, and one of the ways we do that is by setting boundaries.

When we define what we might call our personal "I" boundary, we are declaring to ourselves and the world that this is "me" and that is "not me." (Remember that this "me" is not the me of the Self, but the "me" of the mind.) We are distinguishing for ourselves and others what we consider acceptable boundaries for . . .

1. who, what and how we are in the world
2. what, how and with whom we may experience and communicate our thoughts or our emotions
3. how and with whom we will be physical or sexual or familiar and intimate
4. and what our values will be.

Since most of our boundaries were not created by conscious direct thought processes, what we realize when we question their appearance is that they were formed in the larger context of our family system. As physical beings we exist in an environmental field, which includes *both* the environment and us. We interact with the environment. And the nature of the relationship between the environment and us will determine how we behave. This is not a simple cause-and-effect situation. Our environmental field (remember, it includes us as an integral part of it) is a system governed by the previously mentioned systems' principles: The whole is greater than the sum of the parts. Any change in any part of the system affects the system as a whole, as well as each and every part of the system. All systems attempt to maintain their original structure and balance. This means we would be affected not only by other individuals in our surroundings, but also by such things as the attitudinal or atmospheric environment of the surroundings themselves (see Figure 8.3a).

Let's look at Barbara and her family. Barbara perceived the who, what and how of herself in the world as a fat, bad, stupid person who couldn't do anything right. She did not believe that anything she felt or thought was acceptable, so she rarely communicated what was really going on inside her. She believed that her body was not her own, that she had very little say over who she was physical or sexual with. The reason she stopped Jim's sexual advances was her sincere belief that she was sinning. This belief set the sexual activities in a new context for her, which enabled her to remove it from the "Jim gets whatever Jim wants" context. She had developed her contextual structures growing up first, in the dysfunctional, physically violent, and emotionally and verbally abusive

natural father's family environment, second, in the emotionally and verbally abusive home of her mother, and third, the sexually, physically,
emotionally and verbally abusive household of her stepfather.

Imagine, then, that you are looking at Barbara within her family (see
Figure 8.3b). You see a circle within a larger circle. The larger circle also
has other smaller circles in it which are the other family members.

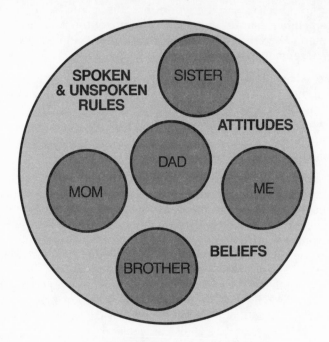

Figure 8.3a. Healthy Family System

When you look at her interaction with her immediate field, you must
include not only the individuals of her family but the family as a field with
which Barbara had to interact. This field with which she interacted included spoken and unspoken values, attitudes and rules and, of course,
alcoholism.

When Barbara contacted her environment, she began forming herself
into a Gestalt, an experiential whole. As with most of us, Barbara's initial
environmental interactions were with her parents and the environmental
field which they created called family. Therefore, it is at the point of
contact with them and their family system where she began to define
what a human being is and what she was, specifically. Unfortunately, the
environment she made contact with was alcoholic and diseased, so with-

drawing into herself for closure meant that Barbara had to deal with trying to integrate disease into her system. Since her parents' conception of what a human is and does presented a narrow distorted image, that is what she interacted with to define herself, to define her boundaries within the family and to define her family within the larger cultural structure. Using her parents' concepts then became a trap. Since Barbara was dependent on her parents for her survival, she would have had to make them and, therefore, their boundaries right. Once she had done this, she then made their boundaries her boundaries. She then became trapped within those structures. This accounts for the difficulties that Barbara, like most Adult Children, had — first, in being able to see how the boundaries are formed and, second, in attempting to change them.

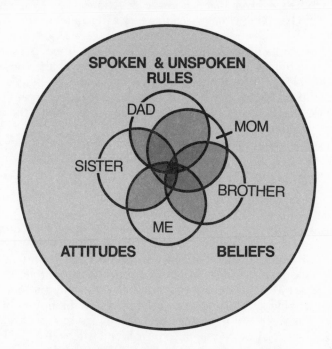

Figure 8.3b. Dysfunctional Family System

For a greater understanding of Barbara as an individual within the context of the family, we need to at least touch on intra-familial and familial-cultural boundaries. A discussion of boundaries would be incomplete if we did not deal with those two other psychological and social boundaries.

Barbara existed as an individual within the family system unit. Also existing within her family unit were sub-units, some of which she belonged to and some of which she did not. The intra-familial sub-units are defined by generational (the adults versus the children) or gender (male versus female) differences and depending on how they are perceived and defined, they strongly influence in a healthy or dysfunctional way the roles we take within the family. The generational boundaries in Barbara's home were in total confusion. She was cross-generationally bonded to Jim as a lover and had been moved inappropriately into other adult roles, such as the household cleaning.

As in many alcoholic homes, the gender roles were set up in a rigid yet confusing way. Jim was in charge of the family. Maureen deferred to him even when he knew very little about things in general. Shawn had helped with the household chores until Jim no longer considered him a little boy. Then he was given male chores to do, chores which Jim never did. Barbara was given the woman's chores very early in her childhood.

Because the family system also exists within several larger environmental fields, such as neighborhoods, cultures and in some cases the sub-culture, the family must interact with these larger fields. The way the family interacts will be determined by whether the family is either an open or closed system in relationship to the immediate larger field. The point of contact between the family and the larger field is the familial-cultural boundary.

For a better understanding of these interactions between the individual, the family, and the environment, it would help if we looked at an explanation of boundary states and boundary disorders.

Boundary States: Flexible, Rigid, Blurred

Boundaries operate as states of existence (see Figure 8.4). For a boundary to be healthy, it must be a flexible state. Because we must be able to interact with a continually changing environment, it is important that we remain responsive to the environmental processes around us. When we make contact with our human environment, our family and our society, we must be able to find a point of balance where the outside does not impinge too much on us, and we do not impinge too much on it. We must be able to say no to helping a dear friend when we are exhausted, and we must be able to recognize when our own need to avoid embarrassment stops us from taking charity to provide some pleasure for our children. If you are healthy, you are in charge of your boundaries and you are the one who decides how open or closed the boundaries will be.

What makes a boundary flexible is that it can be moved in or out, can be completely opened for short periods of time or totally closed for short periods of time or it can be partially opened, acting as a filtering device. When our boundaries are flexible, we are able to remain responsive to our present environment.

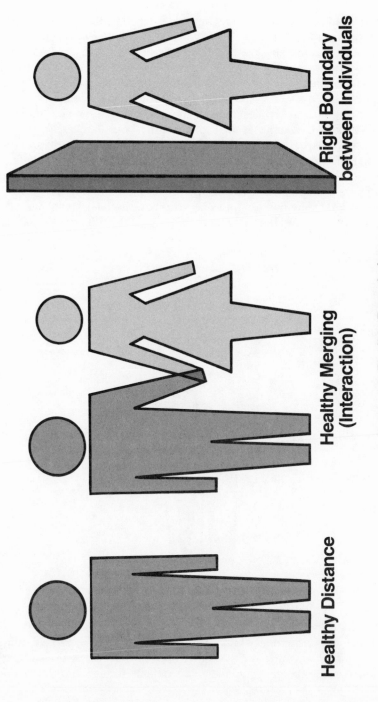

Rigid Boundary between Individuals

Healthy Merging (Interaction)

Healthy Distance

Figure 8.4. Flexible Boundaries

If our boundaries are too movable and weak, they become blurred. We then cannot tell what to let in and what to keep out. We confuse ourself with our environment. We cannot withdraw into ourselves, because we have no sense of self. We do not know where we end and where someone else begins. Blurred boundaries make us extremely vulnerable (see Figure 8.5). We are constantly exposed, constantly invaded.

In dysfunctional families many of the various personal boundaries are blurred, and the family is said to be enmeshed. Barbara's family was enmeshed. Barbara had no identity of her own. She was expected to think, feel, believe and do what Maureen and Jim thought, felt, believed and did. Barbara had no body boundary, no sexual boundary, no space boundary she could call her own. Before she came into therapy, she did not know that she had a right to have boundaries. Her family had taken her rights away, and because she did not know she was entitled to them, she let them.

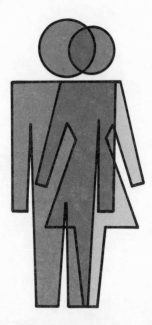

Figure 8.5. Blurred Boundaries

Rigidity is the last boundary state (see Figure 8.6). Rigid boundaries are like steel walls around us. No one and nothing can get in, and we cannot let ourself or anything out. While it appears safe to us to have rigid boundaries, we can get very lonely. It is difficult for us to remain isolated behind rigid boundaries, so we often flip-flop between the supposed safety of the rigid boundary and the enmeshment of the blurred boundary.

It is possible for an individual to experience both rigid and blurred boundaries simultaneously or serially. A person may, for example, have a very rigid idea about the chores she performs as a mother but a very blurred boundary around herself emotionally so that she takes on the emotions of everyone in the family.

Barbara's childhood gave us several examples of both rigid and blurred boundaries. While Barbara was totally enmeshed at home, she was unable to trust or be close to anyone at school. So she ended up leading a lonely isolated adolescence.

Boundaries exist, not only for individuals, but also for entire systems. Since a family is a system, the family as a unit may also create flexible, rigid or blurred boundaries, both at the intra-familial and familial-cultural boundaries. The family with flexible boundaries is a healthy family. The unhealthy family is a closed system with rigid boundaries surrounding it and isolating it from the outside and with blurred boundaries with severely enmeshed individuals inside.

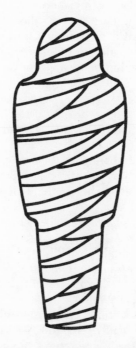

Figure 8.6. Rigid Boundary

Closed Systems

In a closed system the outside boundary to the environment and to other systems is rigid and closed. It allows very little real interchange to take place across the boundary. Within the closed system, relationships, roles, structures and the rules that govern these may be rigid, while at the same time, the boundaries between individuals are often blurred and enmeshed so that the persons within the family have lost their ability to identify their individuality. The Dysfunctional Family is an example of the closed system at work.

Boundary Disorders

A boundary disorder is a dysfunction in the *"What We Do"* operations that occur at the contact boundary. There are four basic disorders which pertain to the way we incorporate or reject material into our individual personalities. These disorders can usually be detected by the misuse of personal pronouns.

Confluence

When I blur my boundary with someone else's so that the other person overlaps into my boundary that is called *confluence.* Blurring my boundary means that I will constantly take in emotions, beliefs and values which are not really me but belong to someone else. In essence I cannot make the distinction between "me" and "not me." I will tend to use the pronoun "we" instead of the pronoun "I." For instance, if I'm *confluent* with my husband and I'm angry with my daughter-in-law, instead of saying, "I am angry with my daughter-in-law," I might say, "We're angry with our daughter-in-law," assuming that my husband and I are the same person.

When Maureen told Barbara that their religion did not use public confession, her boundary was so blurred with Barbara's that she assumed Barbara's belief in her religion when Barbara did not even know anything about the religion.

Most parents in dysfunctional families suffer to some degree from confluence. I often say to ACoAs in my practice that their parents saw them as extensions of their right arm. It is this perception by their parents that leads to a demand for total agreement and the black-and-white type of thinking that insists that "If you are not with me, you are not me, therefore you must be against me."

Maureen's boundaries were so confluent and blurred with Barbara's that Barbara had great difficulty separating herself from her mother and finding out who Barbara really was. From a very early age, Barbara was so engulfed by Maureen's thoughts, beliefs, needs and values that there was very little room inside of Barbara for the real Barbara to show up. The space inside Barbara's boundaries was taken up by Maureen.

Introjection

Introjection is the name of the mechanism used when I swallow into my system *unintegrated* foreign matter. As a human I must be able to take from the environment whatever I need that will serve me and assimilate it into a healthy integrated whole. That is what I do with food and physical sustenance.

The same process is necessary with psychological events. When I take into an already existing system ("me") foreign matter such as beliefs, values, limits, ways-of-being-in-the-world, I must assimilate the matter in some healthy integrated way into the already existing system. If this foreign psychological matter is indigestible, as a thumbtack is physically indigestible, I must find a way to expel it or I will develop severe problems.

With lumps of unintegrated psychological and emotional matter in my system, I cannot develop an integrated positive self-image, and if those undigested lumps are incompatible, as they often are, I will find that I am constantly struggling to reconcile the warring pieces. Since they cannot be reconciled without taking them apart and digesting them and eliminating the remains, and since I have not learned this process of integration from my dysfunctional family which also does not know the process, I will eventually suffer some form of personality disintegration.

If I look at *introjection* in terms of my boundary, what I will see is that I have expanded my boundary too far. I have brought in so much foreign material, I am stuffed with it. I make myself responsible for what really is part of my environment and not actually me. One of the language clues to watch for is the use of the word "I" when the real owner of the material is "you or they."

Whenever Barbara believed the negative judgments that were heaped on her, she was introjecting evaluations about herself that had nothing to do with who Barbara really was as a person. Each time that Maureen told Barbara that she shouldn't feel the way she felt and Barbara believed her, Barbara was rejecting herself and taking on, introjecting, Maureen's beliefs about how Barbara should feel. A rule of thumb that I taught Barbara was: Whenever you find yourself taking on *shoulds,* you are introjecting. Whenever you hear yourself saying "I should" ask yourself, "Where did I get that should?" This will show you who you introjected.

Projection

Projection occurs when I deny aspects of myself that I have somehow decided are wrong and therefore too painful to own. This denial of myself usually happens when I have introjected beliefs that are in conflict with who I am or what I need.

Let's look at the example of making mistakes. All human beings make mistakes; mistakes are a way to grow and learn. If I have grown up with either critical or perfectionistic parents who saw making mistakes as bad, I will probably believe that I am bad if I make mistakes. I may then try to avoid being bad by disowning any mistakes that I make and projecting them onto those around me. I may totally disavow any mistakes that I have made, or I may admit to a mistake but try to make someone else responsible for it.

To discover if *projection* is being used, look again for language clues. The projector will tend to use the pronouns you, they and it, when "I" is actually the responsible party. Unwilling to own responsibility, the projector attempts to make others outside of himself responsible for his beliefs, values, emotion, desires or needs. The projector may even disown a portion of his own body and then project responsibility onto that body part as if it were another human being. Working with children makes this particular form of projection especially evident.

I was working with a little girl who had hit her little brother and hurt him. When I asked her what had happened, she told me, "It hit him." I asked her what it she was talking about, and she pointed to her hand and said, "That." Unwilling to own what she had done, she projected the event onto her hand and disowned her hand.

In incest and abuse cases, survivors often disown their bodies or parts of their bodies. They will talk about the body or parts of the body as if it is a separate entity. They cannot accept what happened to their bodies, nor can they accept what the bodies have done so they refuse ownership. When this happens, partial or total numbing of the body may take place, spatial disorientation or partial disassociation may occur. In extreme cases almost total disassociation, multiple personalities or psychotic breaks occur.

Projection is one of the major boundary disorders of the addict. It represents total denial of the responsibility for personal issues, problems and activities. Everyone else is the reason the addict/projector's life does not work. Because addicts project so much, they are apt to demonstrate paranoia.

Paranoia is an extreme form of projection. The paranoid person is an extremely aggressive person who does not want to take responsibility for rage-based desires and thoughts, so projects them out on the environment.

One of my clients complained frequently of not being able to sleep for fear that someone was going to come in and kill her. In our process work, we found that as a very small child she had wanted to kill her mother with a knife. Given permission, through her work, to experience the feelings and desires she could not previously admit to, she decided to play-act out the murder by stabbing a pillow. She was able to release the rage without hurting anyone, and the fear of being killed in bed ceased.

Retroflection

The last boundary disorder is *Retroflection*. The retroflector turns back on himself the behavior he wanted to put out on someone else. The disorder can be spotted by the misuse of the reflexive pronoun "myself." The retroflector, who believes that he should eat carrots even when he hates them, might say something like, "I have to force myself to eat carrots." The "I" and myself are seen as separate. The part that does not want to eat the carrots is then forced by the "I" part.

Fritz Perls summed up the activity of the four boundary disorders succinctly:

> "The introjector does as others would like him to do, the projector does unto others what he accuses them of doing to him, the man with pathological confluence doesn't know who is doing what to whom, and the retroflector does to himself what he would like to do to others."[1]

I have found that a large number of my co-dependent clients are retroflectors. Co-dependent retroflectors are the people who are angry with someone else and take that anger out on themselves. They implode rather than explode. If you are "accident" prone, you are probably a retroflector. When you begin dealing with your anger and learn to feel it and communicate it, you may discover that your accidents begin to disappear. The same thing is true of many types of stress, tension and illness. Rather than expressing the feelings outward, you may retroflect them inward.

Dysfunctional Families

Dysfunctional Families are Closed Systems. They have rigid external boundaries and rigid rules governing the interactions with the world outside the family. Inside the family system, the boundaries may be both rigid and blurred. Some things, such as rules or certain types of relationships within the family will be inflexible, while other things, such as personal boundaries, may be frequently blurred. Often individuals within the system are expected to think, feel, believe and operate the same as everyone else within the family. Because differences are frowned upon, the individual has difficulty defining his individuality within the closed system of the dysfunctional family.

Barbara has a wonderful example of this covert demand in the dysfunctional family for each family member to be the same. According to Barbara, her parents often talked to Barbara about growing up and learning to think for herself. While this communication sounded healthy, it was actually a sham, as Barbara was to find out.

One day when Barbara came home from college with some new ideas that were very different from those of her parents, she was told that she should think for herself and not be swayed so much by her friends. Her parents were threatened by Barbara's growing independence and difference. What they had really meant in telling Barbara to think for herself and not be swayed by her friends was, "If you are not thinking like us, you are not us and you are, therefore, wrong."

Those differences represented a serious threat to Barbara's dysfunctional family because the dysfunctional family is a closed system. The family builds rigid walls around itself to keep itself closed in and safe. To do this the family has had to make itself right and others wrong. This is a survival mechanism perpetuated by dysfunctional families. It occurs because the dysfunctional family lacks the ability to create flexible boundaries, lacking the tools for integrating new material into the system in a healthy way.

The dysfunctional family, like any family, is a system. Like all systems it tends to maintain a state of balance or homeostasis. Maintaining rigid boundaries on the outside to keep out intrusion, the dysfunctional family frequently suffers from internal boundary disorders. Members in dysfunctional families lack the ability to create flexible healthy boundaries. Instead the members are frequently enmeshed in an undifferentiated mass. Members often do not know whose ideas, beliefs, values or even thoughts belong to whom. Family members in dysfunctional families have poor communication skills, lack healthy emotional skills, tend toward secrecy and distrust.

Gender And Generational Boundaries

In addition to the other problem areas that manifest, dysfunctional families also suffer from gender and generational boundary issues. Interestingly, I have found that dysfunctional families are often rigid in their beliefs about gender-appropriate behaviors and blurred in their generational-appropriate behaviors.

Many dysfunctional families, like Barbara's, assume that there is something inherent in the male or female organism that would dictate roles like housecleaning, dishwashing, carwashing, lawn work and carpentry. Therefore, they limit family members to tasks that they believe are acceptable but may have nothing to do with the family members' talents or desires. The family members' growth and self-actualization are severely limited by these beliefs about gender-appropriate tasks. In Barbara's family, the situation was made worse. Barbara was expected to clean up after all the family members and do all the "woman's work" in the household, while Shawn had pool duty and other so-called "man's work."

In addition to the unhealthy approach to gender issues, the dysfunctional family also has difficulty with generational and age appropriateness.

Dysfunctional families may expect children to take on age-inappropriate tasks that are beyond the child's stage of development or are beyond the child's physical stamina and capacities. Sometimes the parents may claim that children are too young and prevent them from participating in things that they are capable of doing.

In unhealthy homes, the child is often put into a role-reversal situation and expected to take care of the parents' emotional, psychological, physical or sexual needs as if the child were either the parent or the spouse. It is not unusual in alcoholic and incest families like Barbara's to see children expected to go to school, come home and do their homework, prepare meals and keep house, while the nonworking alcoholic goes drinking and the co-dependent comes home from work and follows the alcoholic around to the bars, leaving the children at home to do the adult's homemaking tasks.

One classic example that shows up in many alcoholic homes is the case of the preteen or early teen driver. In alcoholic families, children are often supported to do illegal age-inappropriate things that support the alcoholic disease process (like driving a car before reaching the legal age to take the drunken parent home), but are punished for doing other age-inappropriate things because the parents don't need the children to do those things.

In situations where children are expected to perform age-inappropriate tasks, they will suffer from chronic depression and shame. Taking on activities beyond the appropriate developmental stage or beyond their physical capacities causes children to experience terror, abandonment and loss of self-esteem. These children lose their childhood and develop pseudo-adult images.

To outsiders, Barbara frequently appeared as a little adult. The neighbor, who had taken Barbara to a revival meeting, had probably seen Barbara's appearance as a little woman.

Rules In Dysfunctional Families

One of the things that all families, functional or dysfunctional, have in common is rules. Family rules are a type of family boundary. Rules define how, when, where, what and with whom our activities and our thinking and feeling is to take place. Rules may be spoken or implied and may be behavioral or attitudinal. The family rules set up the acceptable limits of our behavior and beliefs. These rules govern the various roles or personal boundaries that people can have, the way the boundaries between individuals are set up and the way communications are handled.

In the dysfunctional family the rules are usually rigid, absolute, unrealistic and not open for discussion. They are frequently unspoken, and they block honest, direct, clear communications both within the family and outside of family. Frequently the unhealthy family's rules are outdated and have been handed down for generations without question.[2]

The unhealthy family has rules that drive members into the Drama Triangle because the rules are inhuman and impossible in terms of expectations, and because they deny the need for the expression of emotion. Rules such as, "Be strong, be perfect, protect your parents, and don't feel," will push a family member immediately into the Drama Triangle. Rules such as, "Don't talk about anything important, especially if it pertains to feelings or the silent inflexible family rules," are the foundations for the dysfunction in unhealthy families.

Some Dysfunctional Family Rules

Here are some of the rules you will find in a dysfunctional family. If you have even a few of these in your family, it is dysfunctional.

1. Do not have any emotions, and if you happen by chance to have one, don't express it. (I can't handle emotions, so you are bad and wrong to have them.)
2. Be perfect.
3. Do not make mistakes.
4. Parents are always right and perfect and do not make mistakes.
5. Be nice, be mannerly, do not be rude.
6. Protect your parents at all costs.
7. Do not make your parents uncomfortable.
8. Do not make your parents look bad in public.
9. Protect the family secrets. Do not hang your dirty wash out in the open.
10. You should love your parents.
11. You should not hate your parents.
12. It is your duty to obey your parents.
13. Do not talk about the real problems inside or outside the family.
14. Do not cry.
15. Do not get angry with your parents.
16. Do not talk back to (or sass) your parents.
17. Always respect your parents.
18. Never disagree with your parents, even when they contradict themselves.
19. Do not discuss any of the family rules, especially the unspoken ones.
20. Deny everything that does not fit the rules, the disturbed thinking that results from the rules, or the family image.
21. Do not trust your own experience.
22. Be in control.
23. Children should be seen and not heard.
24. Never talk about being neglected; pretend that it is a sign of liberal parents.

Family Roles

Whether healthy or dysfunctional, all family members have roles. In healthy families roles are flexible, frequently discussed and tend to nurture. In dysfunctional families the roles are rarely discussed, are often fixed and confining. Children tend to take on their roles to keep the family balance and fill in for the unmet family needs.

For example, in one home where the parents need dependency, the youngest child who may be an older teenager is treated as a baby, while in another home, where the parents fail to provide for the children's needs, one of the young children takes on the parenting role.[7]

Often the oldest child, or sometimes the oldest girl takes on the role of the *little parent.* This is the child who takes care of the younger children, getting them ready for school, feeding them, protecting them and often providing for their emotional needs as well. This child has been called the *responsible child, the do-er, the hero, the helper,* and is often the child who attempts to boost the pride and image of the family in the community. This child, who takes on both the parental and spousal chores in the family, is often the one earmarked for incest, although all of the girls and sometimes even the boys may be molested if the parent is a sexual addict.

The family *scapegoat,* or the *acting out child* is fairly easy to spot. This is the child who is blamed for the problems of the family and is seen as the reason the family doesn't work. On the outside, this is the child who may act out the family pain by getting in trouble at school or with the law.

Both Frank and Barbara were family scapegoats. At first Frank's acting out was more obvious than Barbara's, so he was more visible in the early part of his adolescence. As the family scapegoating got worse, and Barbara's problems became more serious, her problems with low grades and truancy increased.

Almost everyone has the need for some laughter or lightness in life. This is provided by the family *pet,* or *mascot.* This child tries to humor the family and usually can be seen in school as the *class clown.* While this child is often very talented, his humor is frequently overdone and unfortunately often inappropriate.

The role of the *peacemaker* or *placater* is taken up by the child most desirous of avoiding conflicts and smoothing things over. This is the *advice-giver.* This role may also be combined with either the *pet* or the *responsible child.*

The *loner* or *lost child* is the child who disappears into the woodwork, out into the neighborhood or into the loneliness of insanity. This child is detached from the family and often from himself. Sometimes this child becomes an *adjuster* because adapting to whatever circumstances show up is the best way to disappear.

Frequently children in dysfunctional homes may find themselves taking on different roles serially or even simultaneously. Barbara was the child responsible for the housework but she was also the family scapegoat. After Barbara had removed herself from the family, her brother told her years later that he experienced himself as the scapegoat.

Pitfalls

The following is a list of symptoms or issues of a dysfunctional family:

1. Denial
2. Control
3. Perfectionism
4. Double binds/double messages
5. High tolerance levels
6. Compulsivity in family rituals, cleaning, work, religion, eating, etc.
7. Enmeshment
8. All-or-nothing thinking
9. Blame
10. The Drama Triangle
11. Trust issues
12. Intimacy problems
13. Chronic physical illness.

If you were raised in a dysfunctional family, your boundaries of acceptability of life are narrow and confining. Their rigidity has been cemented in place with fear of punishment and retribution or manipulative controlling niceness. You were raised with your parents' boundaries of acceptability, their beliefs, their fears, their rigidity. Their boundaries did more than confine you to believing absurdities, like there is only one right way to wash the dishes, but often they forced you to deny your emotions as well as your natural wants and needs in life. Because you grew up enmeshed with your family, you may find as you begin to heal yourself that it is necessary to break away from your family, at least for a time, in order to get some distance from them. Give yourself permission, as Barbara did, to get out from under the oppression of the family unit.

The Incest Family

Incest crosses all social, economic, cultural, national and religious borders, and the common thread is the existence of the Dysfunctional Family. By its very nature, the Dysfunctional Family is a spawning ground for the emotional, psychological, physical and sexual abuse of its children. Until we are able to face this fact, we are in danger of creating a severely dysfunctional world which allows for the physical, sexual and emotional abuse of its young in the name of familial, cultural or religious rights.

In 1955 Dr. S. Kirson Weinberg published a study claiming that the incidence of incest was 1.2 offenders per million. In 1978 Sandra Butler noted in *Conspiracy of Silence* that the problem was much larger than the figures given in Dr. Weinberg's study. According to Butler, in 1977 in Santa Clara County alone with a population of one million, 600 families received help for incest.[3] Susan Forward has said, ". . . it is a fact of life that has involved at least one out of every twenty Americans."[4] After spending nine years in private practice therapy and eight years as a high school teacher, I would say from personal experience that even those figures are low. It is no wonder that the figures have been so inaccurate when one of the key symptoms in the addictive process is denial or minimization of the problems.

One of the most important rules in the dysfunctional family is the *Keep the Secrets* rule, which isolates the family from the outside world and is usually in place, as with Barbara's family, long before the incest ever takes place. This rule prevents us from ever knowing what the actual incest figures are or, for that matter, what the actual child abuse figures are.

Repression of the incest trauma is another reason why our numbers are so inaccurate. If the child does not speak of the incest at the time that it actually occurs, the child may bury the memories of the incest and may not rediscover them until years later when the adult symptoms force the survivor into extensive therapy and recovery. By that time, the reports rarely find their way to any central fact-finding bureau.

Adele Meyer, in her incest treatment manual, notes eight major reasons for inadequate reporting and fact-finding, ranging from inadequate training of the police who are handling the cases, avoidance and denial by therapists (especially Freudians who claim the reports are mere Oedipal fantasies) and inadequate reporting and classification laws. What is most evident from what Meyer says is that we, as a society, have not wanted to face how serious the problem of incest is in our country because we would also have to face how serious the problems of family dysfunction are in this country.[5]

Many therapists today recognize the incest family as one variation on the severely dysfunctional family. Like all dysfunctional families, the incest family suffers from poor communications within the family, poor links to the external environment, rigid rules and low self-esteem of family members. Both parents suffer from unmet dependency needs, and both expect the child to be an adult and somehow fulfill the role of a parent.

Characteristics Of The Offender

In addition to the low self-esteem and unmet childhood dependency needs, the parent offender usually suffers from several other emotional and psychological dysfunctions. Since most perpetrating parents are male,

I am going to refer to the offender as masculine. This does not mean that there are no female offenders. There are. Their numbers are fewer and they frequently suffer from the most severe forms of psychological disorders, such as schizophrenia.

Because the perpetrator is often arrested developmentally, he will suffer from emotional and sexual immaturity, low tolerance for frustration, poor impulse control and the need for immediate gratification. Frequently these problems are coupled with some form of substance abuse which exacerbates the dysfunctions even more. The offender lacks the ability to deal with and be responsible for his own emotions and actions, tends to deny or rationalize the incest and has no remorse for what he has done.

The offender often focuses his sexual attention on the children within the family because they are accessible physically, dependent emotionally on him and pose no threat to his already minimal ego strength. Bolstered by Alice Miller's "poisonous pedagogy," the perpetrator often believes that he owns the child and therefore has the right to do whatever he wants with the child's body.

Most offenders have themselves been either sexually or physically abused and in some way have bonded and identified with their own abusers. Barbara believes that Jim was not only a physically abused Adult Child of an Alcoholic but in all likelihood was also sexually abused.

The Offender's Partner

Whether the spouse of the perpetrator is directly aware of the incest or not, there are certain characteristics that show up in either case. He/she is usually operating from chronic co-dependency, especially in the areas of control, denial, rigidity, gullibility, fear of abandonment, inability to deal with emotions, blurred boundaries, black-and-white thinking, people-pleasing and overconcern with how he/she and the family appears to others.

When the spouse is unaware of the incest, he/she is dysfunctional in a very different way than the aware spouse. The unaware spouse is out of touch with what is going on in the family or into denial about it. Barbara's mother appeared to have been completely unaware of the incest up to the time of the Jim and Frank episode. The fact that she so quickly accepted Barbara's denial of any problem points to her desperate need of and bonding to Jim. Whether she was aware of the incest or not, she certainly was neglecting her parenting role when she turned over to Jim the job of telling Barbara about sex. This avoidance of sexual issues is a form of sexual neglect and transmits an unhealthy air around sex by the very omission of sexual information. Many women today suffer because of their mother's embarrassed fumbling communications about sex.

The Child-Victim

The child-victim of incest may suffer from similar symptoms of children raised with physical and emotional violence. In addition to that, they may also suffer from symptoms very specific to their sexual victimization. The symptoms that they have in common with children of violence are denial and minimization of the severity of the problem, ownership of blame for the parent's behavior, shame, inability to trust others, somatized emotions, isolation, chronic depression, thought disorders, intimacy problems, inability to feel and communicate emotions, hypervigilance, eating disorders, under- or over-reaction to external stimuli, perception of self as a perpetual victim, lack of boundaries, perfectionistic and people-pleasing.

Additionally children of sexual abuse may also demonstrate sexualization of relationships, intergenerational confusion and role reversal, seductive behavior, anxiety attacks, gag responses, suffocation experiences, bedwetting, severe disassociation, confused sexual boundaries, acute startle responses, physical shaking when under extreme stress and delinquency.

Frequently children of sexual abuse become prostitutes and hard-core drug users. According to Sandra Butler, a New York City drug program reported 44% of all female addicts in their center had been incested, and in a Minneapolis study 75% of the women working as prostitutes were incested as children.[6] Although I have had women who demonstrated many of the above symptoms, especially anxiety attacks and acute startle responses, in relation to violent family life, sexual violence appears to bring out these symptoms in a more consistent manner.

Overt And Covert Sexual Abuse

Denial is such a potent psychological defense mechanism that incested Adult Children must often deal with it even in families where the incest was overt. I have had several women whose mothers either totally deny the incest or refuse to see it as damaging. One mother, clinging to any thread of denial, refused to address the issue of incest because no intercourse had taken place.

There are many forms of overt incest, ranging from sexually abusive language, voyeurism and exhibitionism and refusal of a child's privacy rights through fondling of and from the child, to genital contact and rape. While the traumas involved in overt sexual abuse are horrendous, I would be remiss in not mentioning the problems of covert sexual abuse.

Covert sexual abuse is the sexualization of the relationship between parent and child without any actual sexual activity. The child takes the emotional place of the spouse. While overt sexual abuse is usually perpetrated by the male parent, frequently covert sexual abuse is perpetrated on children of either sex by the female parent who is starving for love and affection from an emotionally absent spouse.

Alcoholic Families And Incest

If you have been raised in an alcoholic family, the probability of sexual abuse is very high. There is a very high correlation between alcoholism and incest, as my friend's ACoA meeting so poignantly pointed out. Since alcohol lowers already low impulse control and frustration levels, alcoholics find it more difficult to contain their sexual thinking and activities. In addition, co-alcoholic spouses are already bonded and enmeshed with their alcoholic spouses, ensuring denial and minimization of the signs.

PART III

Road To Recovery

9

Same Story, Different Day

In the fall of 1965 I entered college. My low grade-point average from high school made acceptance at a university impossible. I was terrified that even our local community college would reject me but I applied anyway because I thought I had to go to college. I didn't want anyone to think that I was a stupid failure. I was admitted on probation, which meant that I had to maintain at least a C grade average or they would drop me.

Tossing and turning the night before the first semester's classes began, I wondered if I would or could succeed. After almost failing high school, college seemed doubly hard. What if I didn't have whatever it took to succeed? I needed to make Mother and Jim proud of me. I vowed to try very hard.

During the first few weeks I was the model student, arriving on time for each class ready to take extensive notes, studying for hours each night. Even so, a voice in my head warned of impending doom and failure. Whenever the voice got especially loud, I ate.

In high school, other than my friend, Samantha, I had few casual friends. After a few weeks of college I made friends with a rag-tag group of long-haired guys and waifish looking girls who happened to be sitting at the same table I was one day in the outside lunch area. After that I sought them out every day until I was included as part of the group. My new friends scoffed at the "Soshes," their term to describe those more in the social mainstream. Inside I was envious of the Soshes, but to ensure acceptance, I echoed the snide comments and put-downs.

At home nothing had changed. Jim was drinking more than ever, stopping at the bar almost every night. I was expected to assume the same array of chores and responsibilities and not use my extra study load as an excuse to neglect housework.

I worked part-time at a local fast-food restaurant. The meager amount of money I earned was reduced by ten dollars each week, rent for the privilege of being allowed to continue living at home.

About a month into the semester I met Daryl, a tall lanky bespectacled young man, who was a friend of one of the other fellows in the group. Daryl's father had died several years before, and he was very attached to his mother. His main love was his Volkswagen which he spent countless hours washing and waxing, yelling at anyone who dared put so much as a fingerprint on it. He talked mainly about the rallies he wanted to organize for a VW club he had formed with the support of a local car dealership.

Daryl was attracted to me the first time we met, although I couldn't understand why. I believed I was fat and unattractive, and wondered what was wrong with him that he liked me. But hungry for attention, I jumped at the chance when he asked me for a date. With no dates since my sophomore year in high school, I mistook the warm and giddy feeling he gave me for love.

Within a few weeks I was fantasizing and talking about marriage. Being engaged would make me look better and enhance my chances for social acceptability. After manipulative prodding on my part, Daryl asked me to marry him and I eagerly accepted. Then I badgered him to buy me a ring as proof to everyone else that we were engaged. Daryl worked part-time and couldn't afford a real diamond. Instead he bought me a white sapphire ring. I told everyone it was a diamond.

As the weeks went by and the demands to study increased, Daryl seemed to have less time to spend with me. I didn't believe that studying was the real reason. I thought he had grown tired of me. I became obsessed with being with him, spending countless hours contriving ways to keep his attention on me. I called him at all hours of the day and night, stopping only when he told me that my frequent and repetitive late-night calls were upsetting his mother. Eventually in order to keep track of him, I stopped going to most of my classes and gave up studying all together. Consequently out of four classes I received one "D," the rest were "Fs." A letter from the Dean's office informed me that I would not be invited to return for the next term.

The night the letter came, Jim became enraged. With a can of beer in one hand and a cigarette in the other, he stood in the hallway outside my room and told me that I had always been a disappointment, a good-for-nothing who would never amount to anything. Even though I was ashamed of the failure, I didn't let on. In a rare display of defiance, I began to shout at Jim. Mother stared at me in wide-eyed shock and disbelief.

"Just leave me alone!" I shouted.

"I will not leave you alone! And don't you raise your voice to me!" he yelled.

"Right!" I hissed. "You can dish it out but you can't take it!"

"I can't stand to look at you!" Jim bellowed, his face an angry sneer.

"What else is new?" I screamed at him. I glared at him, trying to put all the hatred I had ever felt into my expression. I wanted to pay him back for the times he had bullied me, shamed me or forced me to surrender. Underneath my carefully manufactured facade, I was shaking like a leaf. A red flag went up in my mind warning me that I should stop. I couldn't.

"I want you to move out of this house!" he yelled, breaking the silence.

"I'd move right now, but I don't have any money," I shouted bravely, hiding the shock I felt at the prospect of being thrust out on my own. It was a consequence I hadn't considered.

"How much money do you need?" he raged, reaching for his wallet.

"One hundred dollars," I hissed, knowing that he never kept that much money on him.

"Will you take a check?" he said sarcastically. I considered his offer for a moment. I wasn't going to let him win, not when I had gone this far.

"Write it!" I hissed, my voice filled with venomous hatred.

He glared at me, his face turning bright red. I reveled in the sudden realization that for once he didn't know what to do to make me submit, that he was as surprised as I was at my refusal to back down. Slowly he turned to Mother and said, "Get the goddamn checkbook."

"Jim," she started to protest, tears forming in her eyes. "Barbara, please . . . !"

"Now!" he interrupted, silencing her objection. "Get it now! By God, she's not going to sleep one more night in this house!"

Without another word I walked into my room and slammed the door as hard as I could, knowing the action would infuriate him. "You son of a bitch!" I muttered under my breath, flinging the closet open. I grabbed clothes, hangers and all, and threw them on the bed.

Minutes later, Jim opened my door and threw the check at me. "Tonight!" he snarled. "I want you out of here tonight!"

I sat down on the bed, took a deep breath, then slowly looked around the room that had been mine for the last six-and-one-half years. The familiar furniture, stuffed animals, accumulated paraphernalia of eighteen-and-a-half years of life stood silently staring at me, as if telling me that this time I had gone too far. I swallowed hard to keep from crying, but it was too late to back down.

I wasn't sure where I could go or who to call for help. Walking the streets with my clothes was out of the question. I had no furniture, dishes or appliances, not even a car, ill-equipped to be starting out on my own. I had been fired from the restaurant two days before for talking back to the manager, so I didn't even have a job. I decided to call Samantha, my friend from high school.

As I passed by Mother's room, I heard her weeping behind the closed door. I closed my eyes for a moment and took a deep breath. I refused to cry or give them the satisfaction of knowing how frightened I was. Jim was sitting in his chair in the living room, drinking a beer, a scowl on his face.

Samantha said I could stay with her family for a week or two until other arrangements could be made. My next call was to Daryl, who said he would drive me to Samantha's. He arrived in less than an hour, bringing cartons for my belongings.

As Daryl carried my things to his car, Jim badgered him drunkenly from his chair, "So you think you're man enough to handle her, huh? Well, I wish you luck, my friend, because you're going to need it!"

Daryl kept on moving until we finished, trying to ignore Jim's tirade. After so many years of verbal abuse and harassment, I still wasn't used to it, and was embarrassed to have Daryl hear. What if he agreed?

We stuffed Daryl's Volkswagen with as much as it would carry and were were about to drive away when I asked him to wait a moment while I looked at the house one last time. The tears I had held back all evening finally began to fall. Nearly seven painful hideous years of my life had been in this house, and even though the nightmare was over, a sadness from somewhere deep inside erupted from my lips in choking sobs. I had never been able to succeed in making them love me. And now it seemed I never would.

Suddenly, the front door flew open and Mother ran out. Maybe she wanted to say they were sorry and wanted me to stay.

"Barbara, please don't do this," she begged, tears streaming down her face. Clutching my shoulders, she cried, "All you have to do is tell him you're sorry and everything will be okay. Please, honey, do it for me!"

For a split second I considered giving in. But I couldn't swallow my pride one more time, no matter how much Mother needed it. With tears in my eyes, I hugged her and whispered, "I can't, Mom, I'm sorry. I love you but I can't do it anymore."

"Please, Barbara, I'm begging you. You're breaking my heart," she sobbed, her body convulsing in my arms.

I wanted so much to make her feel better, to make all of the hurt go away. After so many years of acquiescence I'm not sure what inner reserve I called on to give me the strength to do what I did next. With tears streaming down my face, I pushed her away from me. "Goodbye, Mom," I cried and sat down in the car seat.

We drove away leaving her weeping at the curb.

A month later I moved into an apartment with an acquaintance from high school. After a short stint working as a waitress, I was hired as a nurse's aide at a local hospital. Several weeks later Daryl broke up with me. He said his mother told him that he was too young to be making such a commitment. I didn't believe that was the real reason, convinced that once he'd really got to know me, he didn't like me anymore. I wept for two days, refusing to talk to anyone. I was sure they were laughing at me anyway.

Mother and Jim sold the house, and with Shawn moved to another state. A week before they moved Mother phoned me and asked me to help her clean the house, wash walls, scour bathrooms and kitchens, wash and wax the floors and wash the windows for the new owners. I didn't want to go back into that house or spend time with her, in case she tried to talk me into living with her and Jim again. I was afraid she would be mad if I said no, so I said yes, and when the day came, I called and told her that I had to work, which was a lie. She was very disappointed and I felt guilty. After all, helping her was the "right" thing to do.

The next few years were lonely painful ones. Cast adrift from my family, believing that no one really cared about me, fearing that I was unworthy of love, I floated from one casual relationship to another, usually ending up in bed with men I hardly knew. Few of them ever called again. Even though I saw myself as cheap, I couldn't seem to stop myself from giving in to their inevitable advances. I needed their acceptance. Same story, different day.

Paul, a man I met through one of Jim's relatives, actually tried to tell me what I was doing. Our first date ended up in his apartment where we listened to music and talked. He put his arm around my shoulder and leaned over to kiss me. I opened my mouth and gave him a deep passionate kiss. I thought that I could make him like me by arousing him. Within seconds I was unbuttoning his shirt, and in a short time we were both naked. In the end I practically raped him. When the frenzy was over, he tried to talk to me.

"Bobbi," he said, "why did you do that?"

"What do you mean?" I asked, feeling alarmed.

"I just wanted to kiss you. You didn't have to do that," he answered. "I liked you and thought we could be friends."

I was stunned. He had said "liked," past tense. He was going to reject me like all the others. I tried to hang on.

"We can still be friends," I said tentatively, "can't we?"

He looked so sad as he shook his head and said, "You're moving way too fast for me. I don't think I can keep up with you. It's too bad. I thought you were really special. Maybe you should think about slowing down."

I was devastated. Instead of liking me, he didn't want to see me again. I tried to tell myself that he was a clod, like all the other men I'd dated. But he wasn't and inside I knew it. I had wanted to look good to him and here I was looking very bad.

I had to get out of there before I broke down and cried. I begged a headache and asked him to take me home. He never called me again and a week later began dating my roommate. Bubble baths, trashy novels and food helped ease the pain. After a few weeks the memory withdrew into a private room in the back of my mind. Whenever he came to family dinners, I would recall the humiliation of that night.

The Pattern Continues

When Barbara entered junior college, she had decided to go for all the "wrong reasons." Having no desire at that time to learn anything in particular, Barbara resolved to go to college with the hope of proving to herself and her parents that she was not stupid nor a failure. Concerned as ever over her mother's and Jim's approval, Barbara faced college the same way she had faced the rest of her life — with a tremendous need to succeed and an equally large belief that she would fail.

The truth was it was inevitable that she would fail, not because she was stupid, but because she *believed* that she was stupid and that she would therefore fail. This belief set up the contextual structure for her failure. It did not allow her to seek help to see if she needed to know how to study or plan her time. It did not allow her to see that her family's demands were still unreasonable and not supportive of her education. It did not allow her to see that her family's and her own disease process were at the root of her disastrous end to high school. It also did not allow her to see that her profound need for attention and approval would turn into an addiction and become dangerously active in undermining the manageability of her life.

When Barbara told me some of her history in the early stages of therapy, I was surprised to find out that she had not finished college. She was bright, articulate and read voraciously. She was far from stupid. In fact many times during her therapy, I pointed out how intelligent she had to have been to manage to maintain the level she had in school for as long as she had.

Barbara could not have realized at the time that it was her pressing need for approval that was eating away at her ability to focus on school. We know that up to the end of high school, Barbara was constantly trying to gain some pittance of approval from her parents, especially Maureen. College became the place where Barbara made her switch from seeking most of her approval at home to seeking approval outside the home.

Although joining her new group of friends in mocking the "Soshes," assured her place with her new friends, it also assured her of a further slide into active co-dependence with people outside the family and marked the onset of the next phase of what Barbara calls being an "attention junkie."

Her relationship with Daryl marked the second major attempt in her life to manipulate and control a boy in a romantic situation. Frank had been the first. Her attention addiction took off quickly when she began dating Daryl and escalated into fantasies of marriage almost immediately. Persisting until she got the much-needed marriage proposal and lying about her white sapphire engagement ring, Barbara would do whatever she thought she needed to do to fit in and be accepted. When I questioned her later, I found, as I had guessed, that the "Soshes" were the ones she was really hoping to impress with the ring. Barbara told me that her mother had been the one to suggest the white sapphire because she also wanted Barbara to have some sort of ring to look good and white sapphires were not only inexpensive, but looked like diamonds.

When Daryl became more involved in his studies, Barbara felt rejected. Although it is very probable that Daryl had not wanted to get engaged in the first place, it is equally as probable that his school load *had* increased and that he felt that this was a good excuse to take some breathing room from Barbara. Driven by her addiction, she became obsessed with being with him, and as with any addiction, her life soon became unmanageable. Focused on keeping an eye on him, she needed her schedule to be free to spend whatever time he had available for her, Barbara stopped her efforts at school and slid into, what Robin Norwood would have called, chronic relationship addiction.[1]

When Daryl broke off the engagement, Barbara used it against herself. Although she had never actually loved Daryl, she had needed the engagement as a sign of her acceptability. Without the engagement or college, Barbara had no external signs of approval and very little attention.

The fight with Jim, one of her rare moments of defiance, was in all likelihood aided by Barbara's having already switched most of her approval-seeking to Daryl and her friends. Unfortunately, even her defiance had been framed by Barbara's negative "I am a failure" context. She saw her departure as a result of her inadequacy, her inability to be "good enough to make them love her."

When I mentioned to Barbara in therapy that had she not had Daryl at the time, she would probably have backed down when her mother approached the car in tears and gone in and apologized to Jim, Barbara agreed that knowing Daryl was there had helped. Daryl had served her. Her jump did not take her from the frying pan into the fire, but simply another frying pan. Nothing that Barbara ever had to live through from that point on, with the exception of the brief period at home when she was in nursing school, would ever be as awful as the emotional, psychological, physical and sexual abuse Barbara had already suffered while growing up in her family.

Since love had only been given in Barbara's home conditionally and rarely, Barbara did not understand until therapy that she could not make people love her. Having been raised in a dysfunctional family, Barbara had no way of knowing that she was lovable and that her family's inability to love had nothing to do with her. Because of her upbringing she simply assumed once more that she was inherently unlovable and damaged.

The next few years after her break up with Daryl, Barbara demonstrated a typical pattern of relationship addiction and promiscuity. Her bed-hopping was a result of her need for attention and a desire to be accepted. Never really enjoying sex, she gave sex in the hope of receiving some attention and acceptance. Even when the men vanished after the first or second date and she felt cheap, she was powerless to stop the activity.

When Barbara met Paul, she was left with a memory that would haunt her until years later when she could process it in therapy, release the pain of the humiliation and come to understand the nature of her addiction to acceptance, her distorted picture of relationships and her violated sexual boundaries.

As is the case with many incest survivors, Barbara had a tendency to view male-female relationships in sexualized terms as a result of the incest. Although sex had been a frightening and disgusting experience to the child Barbara, it was also the only way she knew to relate to men. For Barbara sex was given in the hopes of receiving attention and caring.

Getting acceptance is not the only reason incest survivors are promiscuous. Sometimes sex is viewed as a way to control men who had been in control before. Taking control of the sex also insures that there will be no surprises. In addition incest survivors frequently perceive themselves as dirty loathsome creatures who deserve to be degraded. Sex, then, becomes a way to act out and make that perception right. Driven by shame, they push themselves further into what they believe are shameful situations, the only situations they believe that they deserve. Then they deny that judgment and pretend the situation is right. This is frequently what happens with prostitutes.

The System In Operation

Watching the "leaving home" drama, you can see that Maureen was playing the role of pathetic Victim. Deeply enmeshed with her daughter and still clinging to the subconscious hope that her pretense of the perfect family could continue to live on, she begged Barbara to apologize to Jim, pretending that if he would accept the apology, everything would be fine. She still could not see Jim's abusive behavior nor could she realize that what she really wanted was to continue her illusion, especially to the outside world. As usual all she could see was her own pain. She had no perception of Barbara's pain or Barbara's basic need to be treated with respect.

Making her mother right again, Barbara left her mother and her home, believing that it was her inability to swallow her pride that kept her from apologizing. Neither she nor Maureen recognized that although Barbara was bolstered by the fact that she now had Daryl in her life, it was a supreme act of courage that allowed Barbara to take a few steps outside of her dysfunctional family. Even though Barbara believed that it was still her duty to take care of her mother's pain and problems, Barbara intuitively knew that she could not easily stay out of the dysfunctional family if she got too close or spent time with her mother. Still operating without any sense of power, Barbara's instincts about avoiding helping with the cleaning were basically healthy, even if the way she handled it was not.

There are two factors to remember when looking at their parting scene. First, Maureen and Barbara were confluent and enmeshed with each other. Maureen truly did not know where she ended and Barbara began. Second, Barbara's leaving meant a huge upheaval in the family system, something that is intolerable in a closed dysfunctional system such as Barbara's family. The system fights to maintain itself and regain balance. Barbara and Maureen were a part of that system, and the system was putting pressure on Maureen to maintain the original balance.

As Barbara worked on her mother in therapy, she went through the confusing process of learning to be angry with her mother and stop protecting her while at the same time learning not to blame her mother or see her as a bad person. This concept was foreign to Barbara because she, like most Adult Children, had been raised in blame, shame, guilt and "make wrong." She had been taught black-and-white, all-or-nothing thinking. She had no way to relate to confronting what someone had done and being angry about it without blaming the person or seeing that person as bad. So I taught Barbara to start her process work from where she was, not where she wanted to be. This meant that each time she did a process on her mother, she would start by "dumping" on her. She would yell at her, blame her, call her names, tell Maureen that she was bad and wrong. By doing this dumping, Barbara was unloading all the blame and "make wrong" that was *already there.* I told Barbara to start with the dumping because that was already stored in her, and if she were to pretend that it wasn't there, she could not complete the energy of it and release it. After she had dumped sufficiently, and banged on the futons or twisted a bath towel, I would ask her to see if she could get to the fear, hurt and anger and express them without blame. If she could, she would begin the next part of her process. If she could not, she would go back and dump some more until she felt clear enough to go on.

I taught Barbara to use the dumping process whenever she was angry and needed to communicate her anger to someone. I showed her how the energy of the dumping would dissipate, and she would then be able to find a clean form of anger that she would be able to communicate clearly and honestly with whomever she was angry.

Once she had moved out of a dumping process with her mother, I would have her switch chairs and see if she could be Maureen, not just on the superficial level. I would ask her to reach inside and find her experience of what was truly happening in Maureen. This would allow Barbara to sense what she felt were the unspoken communications and what Maureen had been trying to hide. This would also allow Barbara to externalize anything that was actually Maureen, and separate it from Barbara. She would then be able to create a healthy integrated whole Barbara.

When Barbara had advanced further in her process, she was able to recognize that she had moved from seeing her mother as a saint, to seeing her as a bad person, to seeing her as she really was, a profoundly pained, frightened, angry woman deeply mired in her co-dependence and the Drama Triangle with no tools to relieve her of her emotional burden or take her out of her dysfunction.

Very early in her process, Barbara had brought up a topic of concern that is often raised by Adult Children in therapy. Barbara had asked me if it was possible that she had no happy memories of her family from childhood, other than those of Jim's entry into the family, which had taken on a tainted aspect in light of Jim's betrayal. I told Barbara that it was possible but not probable, but she would have to wait and see. Frequently, positive or enjoyable memories are buried along with the pain. In suppressing the painful memories of the past, the Adult Child also suppresses the more positive ones. To allow any memories of that time is to risk the surfacing of the painful ones.

The point at which Barbara was able to face the pain of her relationship with her mother as well as having confronted her worst fears and most horrid traumas, a few precious moments of childhood surfaced. Barbara remembered a tea party when she was small and a dance recital in which her mother beamed love and joy to her. She also remembered a shopping day early in adolescence when she and her mother went shopping for a dress for Barbara for her induction into Job's Daughters. Over the years, Barbara has told me that although the pleasant memories of childhood were few and very far between, at least she had had a few. Those few memories also helped her to gain perspective on her mother's disease process as well.

Frequently I have found myself working with or facing the parents of the Adult Children with whom I have worked. On one occasion, one of my Battered Adult Children brought her mother in for a session. The mother had battered her daughter with everything from coat hangers to wooden spoons and had frequently thrown her daughter down the stairs. Seeing the mother huddled terrified in the chair facing me, it was hard for me to even remember the years of therapy I had done with her daughter concerning the abuse by this woman. What I saw in the chair was the mother's pain. Softly, I asked her, "Who beat you?" She looked up, obviously surprised, and burst into sobs. More generational pain handed down from mother to daughter. Hopefully we were breaking the cycle.

. . . Try, Try Again!

Six months after my disaster with Paul, I met Jake, my first husband, who had recently moved to California from the East Coast and was a student at a local university and a member of a fraternity. I liked being a small part of the academic and party atmosphere again, even if it was only vicariously through Jake.

After dating him for a few months, I thought that I should go back to college. My supervisor at the hospital, who thought I would be a natural at nursing, encouraged me to enter nursing school. I was popular with the patients on our ward who asked for me by name for back rubs, trips out into the sun or just to chat. I liked feeling special and wanted to please my supervisor. I also wanted to be accepted by Jake and his friends.

In order to go to college I needed financial support. When I shared my plans with Mother, she became very excited and volunteered to get information about a college that was forty miles from her. I could live with her and Jim, and work at the local hospital on weekends. The tuition was reasonable and Mom would help.

Strong misgivings surfaced about living with Mother and Jim. Giving up independence and being forced to clean up after other people again plus the possibility of having to fight off Jim were serious considerations. But eclipsing that was the fear of disappointing everyone. Mother seemed to be so pleased with the fact that I was even thinking about college, so I decided to go for it. I foolishly convinced myself that maybe it wouldn't be so bad, that after two years things had changed.

Mother obtained the college applications and arranged for high school transcripts to be sent. I gave notice at my job and cried when several of my co-workers gave me a going away party. I hoped I would be able to live up to their expectations.

This second college attempt started out like the first. I attended every class and studied hard. My friends were long-haired, philosophical types, high on dreams, low on action. The good intentions lasted until one rainy night in the middle of the term.

It was late fall and my room in the attic was not heated, so I was sleeping downstairs on the sofa until the cold snap passed. Jim stumbled drunkenly into the house at eleven-thirty, waking me as he tripped over a corner of the bed on his way to the bathroom. My body was stiff and taut. He was drunk and there was no way to tell what he would do.

Several minutes later the bathroom door opened. After a trip to the kitchen for a can of beer, he sat in his favorite chair and turned on the television. The raucous sounds of a western movie made going back to sleep impossible. Instead of asking him to turn down the sound, I lay unmoving, not wanting him to know I was awake.

Suddenly the bed moved and I felt his hand caress my shoulder.

"Barbara," he whispered, "are you awake?"

Wanting him to think I was angry because he woke me, I let out an annoyed moan. What had I done to make him think I wanted this? I was devastated, dreading what was coming next.

"Come on, Sweetheart, wake up, I want to talk to you," he said as he slipped his hand under the blankets and grabbed my breast.

"Leave me alone!" I cried. "I have to get up in five hours, leave me alone."

"Aw, come on," he protested.

"Go to bed, Dad, you're drunk," I said trying to sound as disgusted as I could, so maybe he would be angry and leave me alone.

"Bitch!" he muttered angrily as he got up to leave. A few moments later I heard him in the bedroom angrily throwing his shoes down on the floor, and muttering under his breath.

At a party during the following weekend, I drank glass after glass of cheap wine until I was too drunk to stand. I don't remember the rest of the party.

I awoke the next morning, horrified to find myself in bed with a man I barely recognized as someone who had been at the party. I stared at him for several moments, trying to remember his name, wishing the nightmare that had become my life would stop. I hated myself for ending up this way. I craved approval and they wanted sex. Sex had become a means of exchange for fleeting moments of acceptance. I didn't realize that I was as addicted to approval as I was to food, and that no amount would satisfy my insatiable appetite. I was caught in a nightmarish maze, and not only didn't I know how to find the way out, I didn't realize I was in one.

After the party the rest of the semester passed by in a daze. Even though I went to the campus every day, I stopped attending classes, spending hours in the student lounge, eating, chatting with friends who stopped by between classes. After a futile attempt to pass December finals week, I passed one class and failed all the others. Same story, different day.

On New Year's Day I boarded a bus back to Southern California, my existence once again reduced to several cardboard boxes. I took everything except for an electric typewriter, a birthday gift from Mother the previous summer. In a moment of anger, she had taken it back as I was packing to leave, saying she had given it to me for college and since I had failed, she would keep it.

Trying To Leave The Pattern Behind

For Barbara the need for attention went beyond the bounds of relationship addiction. Her attention and approval-seeking activity was not only directed toward men who couldn't be there for her, it was directed toward anyone who would come into her life, male or female. What we see is the continuation of the original pattern that had been established in the framework of her dysfunctional family. Raised by her family to look outside herself for what was "right," she transferred her approval-seeking process now to the outside world. Although Barbara had left her family, she did not know that she could not simply leave the dysfunction behind. Her people-pleasing and need for acceptance and attention was fed by her nurse's-aide job. Barbara's supervisor praised Barbara as a natural for nursing, never realizing what we know today, that nursing is one of the occupations frequently entered by nonrecovering co-dependents. In therapy, Barbara told me that she had misgivings about going back to school and into nursing, but she had so desperately needed the attention she was getting and had got everyone so caught up in the excitement, she could not stop the process.

When Barbara returned home to go to nursing school, she could not have realized that she was living out a cycle that was to continue throughout her life until she could confront it first in therapy and then later by herself. Barbara was to find herself bouncing between being serially addicted (going from one form of addiction to another) to multiple addicted (having two or more addictions operating together). Jim's advances that evening reactivated every negative tape and self-shaming activity that Barbara had. Although Barbara had been dating Jake steadily before nursing school and had been writing frequently, she suddenly found herself back in her attention-getting and sexual addictions that marked the beginning of another failure spiral that would be interrupted for a short while when she returned to Southern California.

"Happily Ever After"

Back in Southern California after living for a short time with Jake's parents, I was hired at another hospital, moved into a bachelor apartment and lived alone for the first time. I spent most evenings eating a solitary dinner in front of the television. For several months I rarely slept through the night, waking at even the slightest noise. Even though I often begged Jake to spend the night, he always went home, unwilling to face his parents who disapproved of premarital sex.

As with Daryl, I began badgering Jake into marrying me. His parents were against the marriage for many reasons, not the least of which was the difference in our religions. They were Jewish. That was no problem for me. After months of tutoring from a local rabbi, I converted to Judaism, embracing a faith that was vastly different from my childhood beginnings. Years later my first therapist told me that in order to survive formative years I had become an "adaptive child," who like a chameleon, modified behavior to fit the ever-changing requirements of her parents. Throughout my life I had adopted any image that fit what I thought other people wanted. The habit was so ingrained as to no longer be a conscious thought process. I reacted to my environment quickly and automatically.

One month after my twenty-first birthday, Jake and I were married. Standing in front of the mirror on our wedding day, perfecting makeup and hair, I looked into suddenly terrified eyes as a voice from deep inside asked me if I knew what I was doing. For a split second I let myself hear the truth and feel the terror that I was marrying a man I didn't love. I was settling for security. In the past year I had witnessed the marriage of several friends, weddings filled with expressions of love and joy. I was marrying to be married and to not be alone. Speaking to my reflection, I said out loud, "What are you doing?"

A sob caught in my throat and tears threatened to ruin my facade. I turned away without answering, blinking back the tears. I was getting married and that was, as they say, that. Besides if I didn't marry Jake, maybe no one else would ask.

A year and a half after the wedding I gave birth to our son, Jason, followed sixteen months later by the birth of our daughter, Andrea. We bought a house and, on the outside at least, looked like an average young couple building a life in the suburbs. Jake's job provided enough income to make it possible for me to be a full-time mother and housewife. Underneath the facade of a good life was a vague uneasiness that I couldn't shake. How could I have everything that was important, and yet still believe that something was missing? Maybe there really was something wrong with me.

Jake and I were both nonrecovering Adult Children of Alcoholics. Even so, our priorities and escape mechanisms were vastly different. I wanted someone to talk to, to lean on, to care about me. Jake wanted to make lots of money so people would respect and admire him. When Jake refused to defend me after his mother began finding fault with everything I did, I assumed he agreed with her. Unable to communicate my unhappiness to him, I tried to please him. When my efforts didn't work, I gave up.

My life took on a colorless, predictable routine. Typical weekday mornings found me still in bed when Jake left for work at seven, unless one of the children had wakened me earlier or I had made plans to see a friend, which was rare. I never seemed to get enough rest. Only when the children began to stir would I drag myself out of bed to take care of them, silently resenting their intrusion into my sleep. After they were changed and fed and settled into morning play, I took my first cup of coffee and the morning newspaper into the living room to watch television, which was one of my "drugs" of choice. First food, second television and third sleep.

Unannounced visits from my mother-in-law, who rarely had anything positive or nice to say about me, interrupted some mornings. She found fault with my housekeeping, care of "her grandchildren." After she left I would cry and eat. Early afternoons were time for more television and usually a nap.

At about three o'clock, realizing that Jake would be off work in two hours and would expect a clean house and dinner on the table when he came home, I would drag myself off the couch and make myself get moving. The next two hours were filled with picking up toys, making the bed, putting clean clothes on the children, doing loads of wash, vacuuming, dusting, preparing dinner and then getting myself dressed.

Day after day, the routine rarely varied. Unless I made social plans for us, Jake was content to stay at home and putter around the garage, working on some project or another. Looking at the marriages of other couples we knew, I saw men who seemed to care for their wives. Other husbands were attentive, caring, thoughtful and helped out around the house. Jake seemed to barely notice that I was there except when dinner wasn't ready on time or on the very rare occasion that he wanted sex. We talked but we didn't communicate. I didn't know how and Jake didn't want to.

Inside a nagging voice told me that the reason I was unhappy was because I needed to be thinner, more attractive, smarter, a better housekeeper or a more stimulating companion. The eating disorder that began to surface when I was ten years old had progressed throughout the years and by the time I was twenty-three my overeating was out of control. Never able to stay on a diet long enough to reach a goal weight, I was on an up-down-up cycle. After gaining twenty pounds, I would panic, go on a diet and lose fifteen pounds, slowly go off the diet until my eating reached binge proportions, gain back the fifteen and another five; then find another fad diet. For a while I experimented with binge-purge cycles. Finally, I gave up.

Had it not been for my sister-in-law, Loretta, I probably wouldn't have started a new one. In the few years I had been married, Loretta and I had developed a fairly close relationship. She was single, several years older, independent and everything I thought I should be.

She had been going to a 12-Step group for overweight and seemed be succeeding. She invited me to join and after some reluctance, I agreed.

On the drive to the meeting I silently prayed that I wouldn't be the fattest person there, forgetting about Loretta, who was much heavier than me. What if everyone laughed at me? Had Loretta told them anything about me? Were they expecting me? What if they wanted to weigh me in front of everyone? What if they thought I was beyond help?

When we arrived, I got out of the car, took a deep breath, pasted a smile on my face, sucked in my stomach and walked into the meeting room, all the time wishing I was invisible. Not wanting to draw attention to myself, I sat in a chair near the back and within a few minutes the meeting began.

A middle-aged man with thinning grey hair and a slight paunch led the meeting. He started things off by asking everyone to join hands and recite a prayer. After several people shared about their weight loss, as well as the problems in their lives and what they were doing to get better, Betty, a slender, well-dressed woman about my age, began to speak. She shared her weight loss to the loud approval of the audience. Then, speaking in a soft voice, she began to tell her story, relating portions of her life that she considered either traumatic or representative of why she had become overweight. As she talked about her childhood, speaking as if it were a common everyday experience, she said, "When I was five years old, one of my stepfathers molested me."

The room stood still. I stopped breathing. What had she said? I felt slightly faint and my whole body felt numb. I couldn't believe that I had heard her correctly. I must have misunderstood. Her next words pierced through my protective veil of secrecy and denial as quick and sure as a sword could pierce my skin.

"He took me into the garage one afternoon and forced me to perform oral sex with him several times. After that two different stepfathers also molested me."

Instantly the room and the people dropped away from my awareness. I could see and hear Betty alone. Riveted to my seat, I focused my attention on each word she spoke. My mind began to whirl as I absorbed this new information: I was not alone.

I had never told anyone about Jim and me. I came from a nice middle-class home. Things like that didn't happen in nice middle-class homes. It had happened to me, I believed, because I was defective. Before that moment, I had truly believed that I was the only one.

Yet here was Betty, an attractive young woman, who looked and sounded bright and healthy, standing in front of a room full of people and exposing a secret like the one I had spent over twelve years concealing. In the vast ocean of life in which I had felt cast adrift, I had found a life preserver. I couldn't speak for fear I would burst into tears. I could barely breathe. I wasn't alone.

I wanted to talk to Betty, to hear more details, to find out how she could even talk about her experience, but with so many years of silence and denial I would need many months before I could tear down enough of my defensive barriers and share my experience with her. However, that night, for the first time in my life, I did tell a portion of my story to Loretta. As we rode home I told her that I had been raped by my stepfather but I did not tell her that the experience had gone on for more than five years. I thought that she might blame me for not having told someone. Being raped once made me "look better" than admitting that the incest had continued. But the door had finally opened.

She didn't judge me. Instead she gently patted my hand then hugged me. "I wondered what was causing you so much pain," she said softly. "This only helps me understand you more, you poor thing."

The next step in my recovery process evolved just as I was considering having an affair with Tom, the husband of one of my friends. After losing thirty pounds, my life still wasn't very happy. Reading books on personal improvement, becoming actively involved in the 12-Step program, motherhood, becoming an active hostess at couples' parties, nothing seemed to give me any lasting sense of worth.

The morning of the day I was scheduled to meet Tom in a local motel I looked in the mirror and saw a twenty-five-year-old woman who felt more like twelve, with dark circles under the eyes aging an otherwise youthful face. I glanced at my opened closet, wondering what one wears to an affair. I started to cry and fumbled in the pocket of my robe for a tissue.

Instead of a tissue I pulled out a business card I had put there a few days before. I read the inscription. "Aaron Miller, Family and Child Counselor," a therapist some of my women friends were seeing. "I need help," I said out loud to an empty room. I believed I was slowly going insane.

I stared at the telephone for several seconds. Before I could change my mind, I dialed Aaron's number. The secretary told me that he had an opening that very afternoon — at three o'clock. I made the appointment, hung up and called Tom. I told him what I had done and that I wouldn't be meeting him. To my chagrin he sounded relieved. I hung up the phone feeling a strange combination of rejection, relief, fear and hope. Maybe this would be the magic solution, the answer to all my problems. Maybe now I could be happy.

I arrived at Aaron's office fifteen minutes early and sat in the reception area, nervously thumbing through a magazine without really reading anything. Promptly at three o'clock a door opened and out stepped Aaron Miller, a middle-aged slightly overweight, balding man with a warm smile and a kind face.

"Hello," he said, extending his hand. I stood up and accepted his handshake with a smile on my face, trying hard to act like I didn't really need to be in a therapist's office.

We went into his office and my first experience of therapy began. In that first session I told him about the incest, that I had considered having an affair and that I wanted to be happy.

I saw Aaron once a week for about a month, then he suggested that I join a group session that contained three of my friends. I was nervous about that. The wife of the man I had almost gone to that motel with was in the group and Aaron knew that. I really wanted to continue the private sessions, but I was afraid that if I said no, he would be angry with me.

Being in a group with my friends was difficult. What I didn't consciously realize at the time was how much I wanted to please everyone around me. In the private sessions with Aaron I had begun to talk about some of the deeper pain and sadness. Thrust into a group situation I did what I did in groups. I put on an act. When I needed attention, I would just come in with some problem, either with my husband or perhaps after a telephone conversation with my mother. I would cry, receive the attention I wanted, and feel like maybe I was getting somewhere. I experienced some relief in the "talking about it." Some of the things that Aaron said seemed to make some sense or at least to take some of the pressure off me.

One night he said that he thought that my mother had precipitated the incest through an unconscious desire for me to have a better relationship with my father than she had had with hers. I asked him what he meant by "precipitated." He explained that when a person has an unconscious unful-filled need, like Mother needing to have a better relationship with her father, the person could actually set the stage for the need to be fulfilled vicariously through their child.

Even though that didn't fit my experience of my mother, what I heard was a way I could blame someone else. After so many years of blaming and hating myself, this explanation provided me with the excuse to blame her, bringing with it a welcome, though temporary, relief from the self-inflicted pain I had experienced for years.

An interesting and obvious void was evident in my therapy with Aaron. Not once did we deal with the fact that Jim was an alcoholic. I knew he drank too much, but I believed that the incest had caused the drinking and that, therefore, I was partly to blame.

I did begin to loosen the lid on many previously suppressed emotions. As a result I began to vent some of the rage I had stuffed during my childhood, and Jake was often the recipient. The more I exploded, the more Jake withdrew. Soon he was in the garage every night after dinner and most of the weekends as well, only coming in for meals, to sleep and on the rare occasion that we joined friends for dinner or some other social occasion.

When Jake couldn't stand my increasing attacks, he accused me of over-reacting, inferring that I might be a little crazy. Even though I hated being out of control, I couldn't seem to stop the explosions. I never knew what would set me off. Sometimes it was as if a part of me was standing to one side, yelling at me to take it easy, but once I was triggered I couldn't seem to stop.

In the spring of 1973, before our fifth wedding anniversary, after years of trying to keep up the facade of being a model wife and happy homemaker, my energies were exhausted and I was at a breaking point.

I desperately needed to succeed at something, so I decided to find a job, reasoning that Jake and I could use the money for savings and a few extras. My decision launched the beginning of the end of my marriage. Not long after I started working, I began spending time with John, a fellow employee. We started out eating lunch together in the company lounge area, then extended those talks into the parking lot after work. We had marvelous conversations. John seemed to be interested in my points of views, thought I was pretty, bright and smart, and I was deeply flattered. When I realized that the attraction I felt for him was mutual, I became very confused. On the one hand I loved the attention, on the other more serious hand, I was still married.

Our relationship made a sudden turn that summer when John gave me a funny sentimental card for my birthday. I felt warm and special and gave him a kiss in thanks. What started as a peck on the cheek turned into a passionate embrace, leaving us both breathless and stunned. I left work even more confused than before.

That night Jake's birthday gift was a vacuum cleaner with a power drive to make housekeeping easier for me. The following month he forgot our wedding anniversary. It wasn't long after that that I realized that I was falling in love with John. I had a difficult decision to make.

I tried to get support, or more accurately, permission from Aaron to ask Jake for a trial separation. Aaron's professional opinion was that I wasn't ready or capable yet of making such a life-changing decision, and he advised me to try to make my marriage work. I knew I was risking disapproval from every corner of my life, my parents, Jake's parents and quite possibly my friends. In the end as difficult and painful as the decision was, I made it.

One month after our fifth wedding anniversary, I asked Jake for a separation. As certain as I had been that I was taking the right step, when I watched Jake put a few things into his car, and then drive down the street that Friday morning, I had a massive attack of the "What Ifs." What if this was the wrong decision? What if I was wrong about Jake? What if the whole problem was me? At least Jake had taken care of me, what if no one else would? What if I couldn't support myself? What would happen if one of the children got sick?

Several weeks later, in a moment of deep sadness, I knew that I had to get away not only from Jake, but from the responsibilities of being a mother. Resentment for having to take care of them when no one had ever taken care of me was growing to the point that sometimes I had to force myself not to hurt them. Knowing that Jake could provide for the children's needs, I asked him to move back into the house and to take custody. Telling Mother was the next hardest job I had to do. She had never left Shawn and me, and I was certain she would disapprove. I was right. In her opinion, since Jake was a good provider who "came home every night," I should hold on to him. When I told her that I had found someone else, her final words shocked me. Advising me not to give up security, she said, "Stay married to Jake and have affairs if you need to."

I hung up on her.

Resistant at first, Jake finally agreed to the divorce and the actual proceedings were civil and uncontested. I left the marriage with precious little to show for five years of my life — my clothes, a few linens, some pots and pans I had purchased when I was single and a stereo. Jake kept all the furniture, the house and both cars. I wondered if the future would be better. I didn't think it could be worse.

I moved from the house into an apartment with John, and a year later we were married. In the next four years, John started his own business and we bought a house. On the outside, once again, I had everything I had ever wanted and yet the uneasiness that had always plagued my life was still there. Nothing I did seemed to change what I thought about myself for any length of time.

By December of 1979 I had spent over eight years searching for answers and yet the elusive satisfaction seemed always out of my grasp. There had to be an "it," a right answer out there somewhere that would change my life, making everything fine. I didn't know that the road to emotional health would be long, at times painful and that I would need to confront the dragons and nightmares of my past in order to heal.

After a second stint in therapy with a woman who was not licensed to practice, and who had been a friend and confidant, I could list many of the reasons I was dysfunctional, why I reacted the way I did, but I hadn't stopped reacting. I still believed that no one would really like me if they really got to know me. By the time an argument with my therapist/friend resulted in her terminating our relationship and recommending that I call Marsha Utain, I had almost given up hope.

As I drove to Marsha's office, I tried to imagine what she would be like as a therapist based on past experiences. Aaron, who was basically a talk-therapist, had given me an understanding of some aspects of my problems. My friend and second therapist had practiced what, in retrospect, I have termed "therapy du jour," experimenting with any new mode of therapy she heard or read about.

I wanted to start on the right foot, to make Marsha like me, to impress her with how "together" I was. Maybe then I could believe it.

The first session didn't resemble any other experience I ever had. I began by giving her important facts about my life, trying to impress her with all the insights I had into why I acted the way I did. Near the middle of my discourse, she interrupted and asked if I was willing to try an experiment with her. Even though I said I was, I was embarrassed, worrying that I had said something wrong. Marsha wasn't giving me any clues. Perhaps she had seen underneath my carefully manufactured facade and knew that I didn't have a handle on anything. I wondered if my ex-friend had said anything to her. Swallowing hard I checked the tears that threatened to melt my mask. I didn't know where I would go if Marsha rejected me, too.

She asked me to close my eyes and then gently guided me into a process where in that very first session I confronted my scariest nightmare, the night Jim raped me. Somewhere in the middle of the process, I screamed, something I had never done before. For the second time, I had lived through that hideous scene, only this time I had been given a voice. At the end I felt some relief, although I didn't know why. I was still crying when I left, makeup in streaks down my face and onto my blouse, nose running and eyes swollen and red. So much for looking good and appearing together!

Overwhelmed with shame for having made such a spectacle of myself, I was sure Marsha thought me too far gone to help, even after her reassurance that what I had done in the session was necessary. At one point during the following week I considered canceling the next appointment. Terrified at the prospect of facing Marsha's rejection, a part of me knew I had to go on with what I had started. I had heard about "spiritual awakening." I wanted one. Maybe with Marsha I would find the key, the answer, the "ah-ha!" that would make my life work.

More Patterns

Returning to Southern California did not alleviate Barbara's problems. Because she had no tools to deal with her emotions, she became driven by the terror of loneliness. Loneliness, the fear and sadness associated with being alone, is an important driving force for Adult Children. Having little self-worth outside of someone else's approval and no tools to deal with the pain, Adult Children will often do almost anything not to be alone. Barbara was no exception. So she pushed for marriage with a man she did not love. Even then she was aware of her justifications for marrying. "He was a good provider. He didn't drink. He wasn't overtly abusive."

According to Barbara, Jake was also an Adult Child of an Alcoholic. This meant that he would have fit Barbara's family model for relationships. Without realizing it, Barbara was recreating her family system all over again.

Observing one of Barbara's typical "day-in-the-life" routines, we see Barbara once again as she had been in her parents' home, suffering from chronic depression, unable to get herself going all day long and finally frantically rushing around doing household chores the last two hours before Jake returned home. Her excessive need for sleep and her inability to get up in the morning and do her work in the home was a symptom of the chronic depression that followed her from childhood. Her days were a quiet misery with the children and her evenings a quiet misery while Jake puttered around in the garage. Although Jake was sober and doing something useful, Barbara felt that he was just as distant as the members of her family had been, but she had more difficulty understanding her problems in the marriage because Jake was a good wage earner and came home each night.

During one particular session early in therapy, when Barbara was doing a process to complete some anger with Jake, she began telling him how angry she had been with him for never giving her any warmth, and for always working, trying to control her, ignoring her needs and putting her down for her upsets. I was listening to her process, when she suddenly paused for some air. I decided to interrupt and ask her who Jake reminded her of. Barbara looked at me, looked at the empty chair where she had originally imagined Jake, blinked, and then laughed. "My mother just sat down in that chair."

Although Jake was very much like Maureen, using work to avoid intimacy or his emotions and calling Barbara over-reactive rather than trying to find out what was bothering her, it was not until that moment of insight that Barbara realized that she had brought her dysfunctional family system with her. Even without her parents, Barbara found herself with a husband and mother-in-law who helped her recreate and reinforce the old pattern.

Moreover, Barbara was also repeating her mother's pattern. Totally unprepared for motherhood, terrified of not knowing what to do with the children, Barbara used this situation to further blame herself for her inadequacy. Although she had actually entered therapy, her therapist had not helped her to confront her addictions, her chronic depression, the fact that she had been raised by an alcoholic, her severely dysfunctional family system, her poor preparation for motherhood nor especially her negative false-self. In her first therapy, Barbara had talked about the incest and even learned phrases like the "adaptive child" but everything was informational, and she even used phrases like the "adaptive child" to blame herself and make herself wrong. None of the group talk sessions ever brought her any closer to breaking up the negative false-self or to nurturing the wounded child inside who was struggling to stay alive.

When Barbara approached her therapist with the idea of a separation from Jake, she was told to try to make her marriage work. Her therapist did not work with Barbara and Jake on the dysfunctional marriage. Instead, Barbara told me that he saw Jake for a few sessions because Jake wanted to know what was wrong with Barbara. Given no tools to look at the marriage together, Barbara decided not only to leave Jake but also to leave her therapist.

Taking some courageous steps, Barbara turned her children over to their father. While it appeared that Barbara had no other options, she certainly could have listened to her mother's dysfunctional advice to stay married and have affairs. Had Barbara done that, she probably would have slipped quickly into alcohol, prescription drugs and sexual addiction. Barbara did not realize it at the time but her intention to heal was already at work.

Her intention took her one step further in her quest for what was missing in life. She left Jake and married John, a gentle loving man. Although once again she had all the trappings of middle-class contentment, Barbara continued to feel the gnawing in her guts that told her that something was missing and the happiness she had sought was still eluding her. She continued to believe that it was because she was inherently defective.

Recognizing the obvious weight problem and the enormous terror in Barbara's eyes when she came in for her first session, I guessed that Barbara was a survivor of serious traumas. I realized during that first session that for a while, until she could develop her own self-support, I would be doing a balancing act between giving her the support she needed to do her healing and watching out for her attention addiction and her obsession with people-pleasing.

At that time there was no popular literature on Adult Children of Alcoholics, no ACoA groups and no talk of second stage recovery from addictions so Barbara came in without any language or ideas about dysfunctional families. Coming to me had not been directed by any ideas of what to look for in a therapist, but rather by the fact that she had met me and her friend had recommended me. Later in therapy, I told Barbara that it was her intention to heal that brought her to a therapist who did more than just talk about her problems.

Barbara needed new tools and a lot of support to go back and feel her emotions once again, to grieve over her lost childhood, to complete the traumatic experiences of her past, to confront her underlying addictive process and her negative critical false-self, to find and nurture the wounded child within and to discover the spirituality that had been put away during the years of abuse. In short, Barbara needed to find Who she was and to make contact with her Higher Power. I told Barbara that it was my job not just to support her in feeling her emotions and completing her past, but to give her the tools with which to face and complete any new obstacles or traumas in her life and to help her to find her spirituality.

10

There Is Life
After Therapy!

Over the years since the formal therapy ended, I have had my measure of
ups and downs. In 1983 John's business experienced a severe downturn with
debts severely out of proportion to projected income. For several months I
shared with him in the process of making payment arrangements with
creditors, closing the office we had occupied for five years and moving it to
our home to reduce overhead expenses.

There were times during that long and difficult process that fear loomed
large in front of me, paralyzing forward movement. Trusting in myself and the
process was especially difficult not knowing how everything was going to
work out. There were moments when I indulged in self-pity and self-blame,
wondering what I had done "wrong" to bring about the problems we were
having. The tools learned in therapy: experiencing feelings, taking responsibility, telling the truth and good friends, who supported and encouraged me,
were ultimately what got me through the process.

For the first ten years John and I were married, my two children lived with
their father, visiting us on weekends and holidays. We had made a decision that
our marriage would not include bearing more children, and were content with
being "weekend parents." Jake married and divorced once more, and then
married again. His third wife had children of her own. They moved to a larger

237

house in a nearby community, enabling us to see the children more often. Unfortunately, with the entrance of a new wife and for the first time, stepchildren, problems began to surface in Jake's relationship with his own children.

Near the end of summer in 1984, we received a tearful call from my daughter, Andrea, who had just turned thirteen. Having run away from home, she begged me to pick her up and let her live with us. Over the years Andrea had shared with me many of the difficulties she had in her relationship with her father. The sound of her voice told me that this argument had been the final straw.

As we drove the thirty mile distance, John and I reached out to each other, our hands clinging tightly. Did we have what it took to be good parents? Did we even want to be full-time parents? Was Andrea using us to avoid working things out with her father? Were we doing the right thing to bring her into our home when our financial affairs were on such shaky ground? After so many years of being weekend parents, suddenly our life as a childless married couple was about to change and we had only forty-five minutes to prepare.

Two years later in the middle of a party in celebration of Andrea's fifteenth birthday, I received a call from my son, Jason. Jason had visited us often after Andrea came to live with us, and had recently earned his driver's license. He and his father had had an argument about Jason's car which ended in a heated physical exchange. Jake demanded that Jason move out and Jason was calling us to ask if he could move in with us.

With two years experience as full-time parents, this transition had some familiar ground. Nevertheless, John and I were both scared. Expanding our relationship and our home to include another person who had been exposed to our way of life only on a weekend basis was a change that carried with it many of the same fears. Could we do it? Did we have what it took to support, financially and emotionally, a son as well as a daughter? My Higher Power doesn't always give me much time to prepare before opening up new processes. Again we had forty-five minutes.

Being a full-time parent has been interesting to say the least. In my need to "look good" and be a "good mother" I have made many mistakes. The tools Marsha taught me have been and are utilized often.

Recently, Andrea asked to speak with me about something in our relationship that was troubling her. With tears in her eyes, she started, "Mom, I love you. What I need to say is difficult for me."

"I got it, honey," I said quietly. "What is it?"

"Well, you know how you like to make comments about the clothes I wear, how much makeup I'm wearing or the way I comb my hair?" she asked. "Well I want you to know it hurts when you do that."

I gulped. I hadn't meant to hurt her. I thought I was helping to guide her. At least that was the justification I had used.

"How I look doesn't have anything to do with you, Mom," she went on. "And I want you to make an agreement with me to stop bugging me about how to look."

Internally I wrestled with making myself and her wrong. I felt awful and wanted to lash out at her and tell her that if she would just dress "right," I wouldn't have to "bug" her. Then I realized how scared I felt. I knew that what she was saying was valid, so I thanked the voices for sharing and invited my negative tapes to shut up!

Looking up at Andrea, I could see, perhaps for the first time, that she had already grown into a beautiful young woman. Even though she is "only seventeen," Andrea is past the point that she needs me to teach her about clothes, hair or makeup. Taking a deep breath, I realized with sadness that I had seen her as an extension of me. I was afraid that people would judge me a bad mother if she didn't "look good." My breath caught as I understood that I was up against letting go of Andrea, the child, as well as Barbara the "good mother." She was accurate, how she looked had nothing to do with me.

With tears in my eyes, I began to tell her the truth about what was going on. She listened intently and when I told her I was willing to make the agreement she had asked for, she put her arms around me and said, "Thanks, Mom."

Jason was already sixteen when he moved in, and his self-worth was at an all-time low. He hadn't done well in school for several years and had essentially given up on himself academically. When we enrolled him in our local high school, we knew he would need lots of support to find his own niche.

There were many painful times when we watched and listened to Jason verbally abuse himself. If he were playing a computer video game and wasn't scoring high, he would yell at himself, calling himself stupid and dumb, calling the computer an idiot. I knew with painful certainty that the words he was using were not coming from Who Jason is, but rather a mirror of the lies that he had absorbed from a critical parent or stepparent. I saw in Jason what I had done to myself as a result of believing the negative messages I had received as a child. My heart went out to him.

The truth is that Jason was and is very bright and learns very quickly. With our support Jason began to see a therapist where he had the opportunity to get in touch with those negative tapes and messages and begin the process of separating from them. We encouraged him to take courses in subjects he was interested in and to stop trying to please everyone but himself. As a result he found he has an aptitude for physics, and has developed some high political aspirations as well. In 1988 he graduated from high school and entered a university. To date he is doing very well. He still struggles with those old tapes, but their effect has diminished considerably.

An important and still ongoing process of my recovery was confronting co-dependence. Marsha had already supported me in dealing with many of the issues associated with co-dependence, even though the wealth of material available today wasn't there when we first started to work. I thought my worth depended on how well I took care of everyone, a difficult belief to let go.

My Higher Power was at work once again, supporting my process one cold rainy Thursday morning. It was about eight o'clock and John was in the bedroom, preparing to leave for work. I was in our attached garage doing a load of Jason's dirty clothes, feeling angry since Jason had an agreement to do his own laundry. I was feeling a little sorry for myself that, "I always had to do things for everyone else." I was sorting jeans from underwear when the phone rang. Without stopping to think, I dropped the clothes, turned and rushed to the door, flung it open and started madly through the doorway to answer the phone before whoever was calling hung up.

Just as I put my right foot on the carpeted floor, the big toe of my left foot caught on the threshold, causing me to trip. I landed face down on the floor. Grabbing my foot, I screamed in agony. I had broken my toe. I looked up to see John running towards me.

"What happened?" he exclaimed.

"The phone . . . I tripped . . . my toe!" I answered cryptically.

"I answered the phone," he said. "It was a wrong number."

John drove me to the doctor's office, and while I was waiting in the examining room for the results of the X rays, I decided to take the time to process my toe. I have learned to use everything in my reality as a mirror. I knew by this time that there were no real "accidents" in my life, that each supposed mishap was actually an attempt by the Self to get in contact with some resistant part of my personality. There was a lesson in this broken toe.

The first thing I did was close my eyes to shut out external distractions. The "make-wrong" tapes surfaced first.

"You're really stupid," I said out loud to myself. "Look at what you did. You can't do anything right. What will everyone else think? I'll tell you what! They will think you're stupid. If your toe is broken, everyone else will have to take care of the things you're supposed to do."

Childhood scenes of Mother letting me know how much I had inconvenienced her when I was sick by making her do the dishes or some other of my chores, played like a slide show in my head. I remembered the time she had bullied me into going to school with the flu and a fever in order to present a joint project with a friend so the friend wouldn't be bothered by having to do it on a different day.

I let myself verbalize the tapes until they began to lose their charge. Then I switched and became Barbara again.

"I am not stupid," I said firmly. "Get off my back!" I repeated that phrase several times. Then taking several deep breaths I took myself deeper into my experience and focused my attention on the bruised tissue and broken bone.

"I'm Barbara's toe," I said out loud. "I wouldn't be hurt if other people would take care of themselves. Barbara always has to do everything. Do the laundry, answer the phone, do the shopping, clean the house, cook the meals — everything!"

As Marsha had taught me, when I start using words like "everything" and "always," along with other words like "never," "everyone," and "no one," there is usually a lie at work, and I would need to find it if I was going to get the lesson of this process.

"What's the truth?" I heard myself say out loud. "Do I really have to take care of everything and everyone?"

"No," I answered. "John answered the phone. Jason has an agreement to do his own laundry and he's not keeping the agreement. I haven't confronted him because good mothers do everything for their children."

Suddenly, I started to laugh at myself. When the bell rang, like Pavlov's dog, I had responded automatically. That John would answer the phone, that Jason was not keeping his agreements had not even been a consideration. I was being a martyr. Several days of verbal and written processing resulted in the dawning of the experiential awareness of my co-dependence. Much of my sense of worth had been measured by how much I did for other people and how much I could make them need me. When I could confront the fear and the lie that I would be no one if no one needed me, a lifetime of lies began to disintegrate, leaving me to integrate the truth, that my true worth comes from inside, not from outside.

Recovery Is A Process

When Barbara left therapy, I reminded her that the recovery process was not over, but was simply moving into another phase. What we had worked on over the years was breaking up the negative false-self as well as making sure that Barbara had all the tools she had lacked from growing up in a dysfunctional background. She knew when she finished therapy that she was not done with the problems of life; they would always be there. She also knew that the tools she had were not merely content tools, that is Barbara's tools would give her the ability to do more than simply change the superficial information or beliefs that she held. The tools that she had when she left were tools that would help her to find and change the contextual structures that had run or would run her life in the future.

Barbara had learned how to feel her emotions and complete them, to find any remnants of her false-self that were still operating and stop its control over her and to deal with, to confront her addictive processes and to get support when she slipped.

During the time Barbara had been in therapy with me, we had spent several sessions working on her guilt over leaving the children with their father. We had never really had to face the daily issues of living with children because at the time the children were not staying with Barbara. Barbara had been a weekend mother. When Andrea moved in with her mother, Barbara had to face the day-to-day experience of living with an adolescent daughter. Barbara found herself confronting her own co-dependence issues with her daughter. Having only her mother's blurred boundaries and unhealthy mother-daughter relationship model, Barbara had slipped into seeing Andrea as a part of her, or at the very least, a reflection on her as a mother.

Barbara's internal dialogue, as she went through the conversation with her daughter about her hair and dress, is a clear indication of Barbara's process. Realizing that she had hurt her daughter when she hadn't meant to, bouncing between making herself and then Andrea wrong, and finally recognizing the scare that was triggering the negative tapes and the co-dependent reaction, Barbara was able to step back and tell the negative voices to be quiet.

This is what recovery is about, the ability to catch the negative-self in action and call a halt to it. When Barbara left therapy with me, she was not "done" with her process. She had, in a sense, really just begun, on her own. She had all the tools; she had dis-integrated enough of the false-self to have room for the real Barbara to come through, and she knew that recovery did not mean that she would never get caught by her tapes. It meant that she had the tools and the awareness to work her way through to clarity.

By the time Barbara's "toe incident" occurred, Barbara had been out of therapy almost five years, and she and I had been doing our radio show for several months. Barbara called me during her writing phase to let me know that she had broken her toe and what she had got so far in process. She was already beginning to laugh at her co-dependence and told me that she wanted to talk about it on the show. I agreed.

The "toe process" demonstrated exactly what I had taught Barbara during her years of therapy, that she could use her body and the events in her life as a mirror to reflect back to her the context in which she was operating at any given moment in her life. As Barbara found out with the toe incident, co-dependency issues are some of the sneakiest issues of all, and as she had found out from her daughter's confrontation with her, life must go on after therapy. I knew it was important to remind people that the process never ends. It may change form, but it never ends. We decided to do a show on co-dependence that would include Barbara's "toe process."

Confronting The Disease

In mid-1987 Jim's drinking was at an all-time high. After an almost two-year period of self-induced sobriety without the benefit of a 12-Step group or therapeutic support, he had recently started drinking again. It didn't take long before his habit had reached and surpassed previous highs.

As his drinking escalated again, so did Mother's anxiety level. Most of our phone conversations included reference to his drinking sprees which were almost nonstop. Each time I tried to support her to begin to take a look at the issue of co-dependence, co-addiction and to go to Al-Anon or to find a therapist, she resisted by immediately diminishing the problem, saying it was her fault or by denying that there really was a problem.

"I'm just having a bad day," she would say. "I shouldn't be burdening you with my problems." Or she would tell me that just because I had gone to a therapist to work out my problems didn't mean that was the only way. Then she would change the subject.

After several weeks of this, I realized that I was getting hooked into a Triangle with Mother. Each time she complained, I tried to rescue her by trying to convince her to get some help. Then she would turn around and make me wrong. I remembered the "escape hatch." The next time I talked with her I stopped playing.

"Mother," I started, as soon as she mentioned Jim's drinking. "I need to talk with you about something."

"What?" she asked warily.

"Each time you bring up the subject of Dad's drinking, I try to support you to get some help for yourself and to take a look at the fact that Dad's an alcoholic."

"I know he's an alcoholic," she said defensively.

"Good. Anyway, what I want you to know is that I've noticed that when I support you, you resist by diminishing the problem, changing the subject or telling me that it's your fault. What seems to be evident is that you don't want support, you want agreement of how bad everything is. I am willing to support you. I am not willing to commiserate with you. It's okay with me if you don't want to get help. And as long as that's so, I will not discuss Dad's drinking with you or how bad you feel. Nor will I have a relationship with him."

"Oh!" she said quietly. I knew she was hurt. "I'm sorry I was burdening you," she said quickly, then changed the subject.

We didn't speak of it again until one evening shortly before Christmas when she called and asked for help. I could hear that the pressures of thirty years of marriage to an alcoholic had taken a tremendous toll on her — emotionally, physically, and spiritually. A heart attack several years before had left her with the reality of facing her own mortality.

"I don't want to live the rest of my life with a drunk," she cried. "I want out. Maybe I should just pack my bags and leave."

"Sounds like you're really scared," I said. I knew from past experience that she would resist any suggestions about Al-Anon or therapy. Since she hadn't really told me what she wanted, I decided to wait and see.

She went on to tell me that she was hurt because he couldn't stop drinking for her and how frustrated she felt that nothing she did seemed to make a difference. I told her that she would need to get support, gently prodding her to realize that her way of "handling" Jim wasn't working.

Even though it looked like something might be shifting and that Mother might be willing to confront the problem, I reminded myself not to build up any expectations. Over the years since I had begun my recovery process that first evening in Marsha's office, I had wrestled with my fantasy of having a perfect family. Eventually I released the fantasy, not a sudden event but rather the gradual prying loose of a tight-fisted grip on a myth.

Several years before near the end of therapy, I made a decision to tell Mother about the incest. It was solely my decision and Marsha did not counsel me to do it or not to do it. Before I could decide, I first I had to be willing to face the possibility that she would reject me.

A point had been reached where the secret over-shadowed every communication. Phone calls, writing letters, reading her letters, visits, the simple act of picking out appropriate greeting cards were all clouded with the fear that if she knew the truth, she would reject me. Even reminiscing about childhood memories was difficult because her memories included only happy times. A relationship could work for me only if it was based on the truth, all of the truth.

Several months before, I had revealed the secret to Shawn for the first time during a holiday visit. He told me that it helped him to understand what he hadn't been able to before. I told Shawn that I wanted to tell Mother. He said that he would support my decision and that he would be there for Mom when the time came. I loved him for that.

I spent several sessions in Marsha's office dealing with all my fears. Marsha supported me to begin writing a letter to Mom that would eventually result in the one I would send. Countless pages were filled with years of pain and rage. I reached a deeper level than before of anger that Mother had not been there for me. Sometimes while writing, I would weep out years of sadness and isolation. Other times, I would wad each finished page into a ball and throw it on the floor while shouting my anger at an empty chair.

I spent two final days writing the letter I actually mailed. I brought it with me to a session and read it to Marsha:

"Dear Mom,
    "I love you.

"I am writing this letter to tell you something that has been part of my life for over 24 years. Something I have never shared with you."

I told the "secret" and ended by telling her again that I loved her, and that I would be waiting. Over the weeks Marsha had supported me to confront my fears about the possible consequences of what I was about to do, and in this last session we went over them one last time.

Mother could reject me. After a lifetime of wanting her approval, I became willing to let go of the hope. Jim might deny that it had ever happened, leaving her to think I was lying. Through the years in my attempts to please Mother and manipulate what she thought about me, I had lied. Having arrived at a period of my life where truth was important to me, I risked not being believed.

The shock of finding out could cause her to have another heart attack and die. Although I had cognitive information that told me that probably wouldn't happen, I had to confront the fear. In all probability, she was going to be deeply hurt and very angry. That was the hardest part, being willing for her to be in pain.

The session ended and I sealed the envelope planning to stop by the post office on the way home. As I walked out a postman walked up to Marsha's door. I smiled, knowing my Higher Power was on the job. I took a deep breath and handed him the envelope.

The morning the letter was to arrive, I awoke before dawn, dressed quietly so as not to awaken John. Sitting at the dining table I wrote in my journal.

"March 13, 1982. Well, today's the day. I feel scared. No, I feel terrified. I can barely breathe. The terror is centered in my chest. It's huge, filling my heart, my lungs, my rib cage."

I closed my eyes, allowing myself to experience the fear that she might have a heart attack. As the fear passed through, it was followed by a deep sadness, not only because I might lose all hope of ever having her in my life, but also for all the years that had passed by without me really knowing my mother's love. I wept tears of grief.

Later that afternoon, filled with nervous energy, I decided to clean out my closet and bureau drawers, an interesting choice, since as a child I had resisted Mother's need for me to do that very thing. After filling several bags with clothes for a local charity, I decided to call Mother. I had to know. Shawn answered the phone and confirmed that Mother had read the letter.

At first she thought that I had made the whole thing up. Even though I had prepared myself for that possibility, the reality of it stabbed my heart. Then she had confronted Jim. At first he had denied it, but then he said that it had only happened once, when I was sixteen, that he was drunk and that I had seduced him. She believed him. Shawn told me that Mother didn't want to talk to me and advised me to give her a few days.

When I hung up John wrapped me in his strong arms, holding me tightly while I wept. It seemed that the worst fears had come to pass. Mother was abandoning me. I was overwhelmed with a sense of grief, my whole body shaking with choking sobs.

The next several days were spent in a partial daze, much like that of someone who experiences the death of a loved one. I went through the motions of living: cooking dinner, working, attending a lecture. But the rest of the time was spent staring blankly into space, thinking of nothing else but Mother. I couldn't get away from the fear that I had lost her.

On March 15th I called Mother again. As I dialed the phone I wondered if she'd hang up on me. She didn't, but she had a great deal of difficulty talking to me. She told me Dad was at their mountain cabin drinking and if it had been my intention to break up their marriage, I had been successful. When she said that she didn't want to say anything else that might cause me to "go over the deep end," I told her she didn't have that power. "Thanks a lot," she responded, sounding rather disappointed.

She asked me why I hadn't told her way back when it happened. I explained to her that all the reactions she was having now were all the things that I had always been afraid of . . . she would hate me, blame me, make me wrong and ultimately that she would never want to see me again. She said she didn't hate me but that if I had wanted to ruin her life, I had. Then she hung up on me. I stared at the phone for several minutes, shaking my head at the irony of it all. Jim had raped and molested me but she was blaming me, typically giving no thought at all to what I had been through.

Realizing that if I didn't process what I was feeling, I could get hooked into a Drama Triangle with Mother, I sat down, closed my eyes and imagined her in the chair in front of me. I started by telling "her" what I was feeling.

"I feel sad and scared. I want to be reassured that we'll get through this. I want to know that we have a chance. And I know that you can't tell me that."

Then I switched chairs and became Mom.

"I feel betrayed and hurt. I want to wake up and find this is all just a bad dream and not the truth. I don't want to believe the truth. I'm scared. I want to hurt you so you'll say this is a lie."

Suddenly I could sense what she might be feeling, how terrified, hurt and angry she must be. She would have to wrestle with her dragons as I had had to wrestle with mine. I knew that I had to give her and the process time. I reminded myself that I wanted a relationship based on the truth. I had dropped a bomb in her lap and she would need time to be with it. Tearfully, I took several deep breaths and made a decision to let her go, to give her time.

Almost a year passed before she could speak to me and another five would pass before she called for help. By that time I had already realized that I no longer needed Jim to stop drinking nor to acknowledge or apologize for the incest in order for me to be whole. My life was working well without Mother's approval. For the first time in my life, I was free from that old bondage. I had let go of any attachment I had about the way they lived their life.

By the winter of 1987 Marsha and I had interviewed several people from various chemical dependency treatment disciplines in Southern California on our radio program, *Mental Health Magazine.* I contacted one and found out about a free program near Mother that was designed to inform families of alcoholics about the disease, talk about intervention and to let them know the treatment options available in their area.

A week before Christmas Mother and Shawn entered that program, a series of four weekly meetings. Early in January Mother called me to tell me that she decided to do an intervention and asked me to be a part of it. The intervention would take place on February 3rd, and my brother and stepsister, Carol, would join us.

John drove me to the airport on February 2nd, a cold rainy Tuesday morning. I clung tightly to his big strong hand. Over the years this wonderful man had given me so much room to go through all the pain, sadness, terror and confusion, quietly encouraging me to keep going. I thought about the irony of this point in my process.

"For so many years," I said, "I hoped that something like this would happen. Isn't it wonderful how all of this works! When I could let go of needing this, I can have it."

With tears in my eyes, I hugged John one last time at the gate and boarded the plane. As the pilot waited on the runway for clearance to take off, anxiety began to overwhelm me.

I closed my eyes for a moment and took a few deep breaths, allowing myself to feel the scare. The little child within me was frightened about going alone back into "their" space. I reassured her that I had the right to leave anytime the situation became toxic, and that taking care of myself would be my first priority.

By the time the plane landed I was feeling much more centered, willing to take care of myself and to let go of expectations. Mother was waiting for me at the gate. I marveled at the courage it had taken, after all these years, to be willing to open the rusted and creaking door of denial and confront the reality of being married to a fourth-stage alcoholic.

Wednesday, February 3, 1988, dawned with dark foreboding overcast skies. A light drizzle was dampening the roads. As I was drinking a cup of coffee, the phone rang. It was Mother telling us that all the electricity had gone out on the highway where they lived and that the house was very dark. She had contacted the power company and they didn't know when the lights would come back on. If this wasn't a mirror of how scary it is to shine the light on the truth, I didn't know what was. I told Mother we'd bring candles.

Shawn, his wife and our stepsister met the interventionist and another recovering alcoholic who would support the process at a local restaurant.

Carol was sitting on one side of me and Shawn on the other. Before we left I grabbed both their hands and said, "I want us all to remember that no matter what happens, no matter what Dad says or does today, that we have already won. We cannot really fail when we tell the truth. I'm proud of all of us." We held hands for a second as a last symbol of the unity we had finally achieved. Then we drove the distance to Mom's house.

The intervention went better than any of us had hoped. Jim agreed to enter a treatment program that same day.

I called Marsha later that afternoon, as well as a few other friends who had supported me. I was delighted to find out that several people who knew where I was had called John to find out what had happened. I am surrounded by a loving support group. Hearing their concern and receiving their good wishes was an added blessing.

The next day, Thursday, I spent most of the morning alone while Mother went to her office to take care of some business. I spoke with Karen who was beginning to read a book I had given Shawn on Adult Children of Alcoholics. As his wife of several years, she could identify many of the characteristics described in the book as part of Shawn's personality. She was concerned because she wanted him to talk about it and he kept stonewalling her, saying that, "All of that is in the past. There's no need to bring it up now." I was concerned, knowing that recovery requires honest confrontation with our past.

One of the important lessons I learned as a recovering ACoA and incest survivor is that healing doesn't mean never having to deal with painful childhood issues again. In my experience each time I make new strides forward, many times a lot of the old issues surface again. I was back in the middle of my co-dependent family and I would have to stay very conscious not to hook back into rescuing or fixing them. I had to remember to let them have their process and not to confuse theirs with mine.

Mother came home at noon to take me out to lunch. On the way to the restaurant I attempted twice to voice my concerns about Shawn. Both times she listened for a few seconds then abruptly changed the subject, an old control pattern designed to deflect me. Even though I knew what she was doing, I hooked, making myself wrong for making her uncomfortable. Then I got angry with her for not wanting to face the pain of what was going on. By the time lunch was over I had withdrawn into resentful silence.

Afterwards I dropped her off at her office, then went to a nearby park where I sat on a bench and closed my eyes, allowing my feelings to surface until I could get what had happened.

Later that afternoon on the way to visit Jim, I attempted to bring up the subject again. Within seconds Mother interrupted me again. But this time instead of withdrawing, I confronted her.

"Mom, I need to talk to you about something that's bothering me. I've noticed that each time I try to talk about something that might be painful, you change the subject."

"I don't do that!" she protested. "But if I do . . . well . . . I'm sorry for being rude."

"I'm not accusing you of being rude, Mom. This isn't about making you wrong. I want to support you in taking a look at this. It seems to me that one of the ways you avoid facing painful things is to change the subject. If we're going to have a relationship that works, we have to confront things that don't work."

She had tears in her eyes. My heart went out to her. I knew from personal experience how difficult it is to hear the truth we have been avoiding. Marsha had confronted me over and over again with my own dysfunctional behaviors. It had never been easy to hear, especially in the beginning when all I could do was make myself wrong.

I reached over and held her hand. "You're not wrong, Mom. You're just scared. It's okay to be scared. If you keep on avoiding your feelings, healing will be difficult at best and probably impossible. I want to support you in getting help, too. This isn't just Dad's disease, you know that, it's all of us."

Pulling her hand from mine she said, "I'm not a public person, Barbara. I can't just change everything now. I'm not dramatic like you are."

That did it! She had manipulated my feelings all my life with that judgmental accusation. I exploded with anger. Doubling my hand into a fist, I raised my arm and pounded the dashboard.

"Goddammit, Mother!" I shouted. "You have always made me wrong for the intensity of my emotions. I am not wrong for the way I show my feelings, Mother. I'm not telling you that you have to be like me. But stop making me wrong for doing what works for me. I'm not doing anything to you!" By this time I was crying, too.

"I'm sorry, Barbara," she said softly. "I didn't mean that as a put-down."

"Mom, just have your own feelings and stop worrying about the way I do mine. What are you feeling right now?"

"Embarrassed, for one thing," she said, tears spilling down her face.

"What else?" I asked.

"Scared," she said, "really scared."

"It's okay to be scared," I said, reaching for her hand.

We drove the rest of the way in silence, each of us lost in our own thoughts. After we spent a short visit with Jim, we stopped at a lovely restaurant overlooking the river. Seated in a quiet out-of-the-way corner near the back, we ordered dinner, then began to talk. The conversation found its way to my childhood and the incest. Mother held my hand while I told her for the first time about the night Jim raped me. When I finished, we were both crying.

The next day Mother went to her office and came back about noontime with sandwiches. While we were eating, we talked about Dad and how Mother was feeling. I was in the middle of supporting her to go to an Al-Anon meeting when she abruptly changed the subject.

"Mother, you're doing it again," I said gently.

"What?" she said, defensively.

"You changed the subject again . . ."

I was about to ask her to look inside and see if she could identify what she was feeling, when she stood up and started shouting.

"I can't do anything right, I guess! You're so perfect, you have all the answers. I guess I'm just stupid!" With that she walked out of the room into the kitchen. I knew this was important and that we had to complete it. I followed her.

"Mother," I said. "I'm not making you wrong. You did change the subject again. What happened?"

"Why does everything I do always have to mean something else? Why can't it be that I just wanted to talk about something else? Why do you keep pushing me? I'm not like you. I can't do it your way. Why does everything have to be so painful? Aren't you ever happy? Is it not okay to be happy in your life?"

I was hooked and angry. Why did she always resist me? Why couldn't she — what? Listen? Hear me? I started making myself wrong for upsetting her. Maybe I was expecting too much. Confused I realized that I needed some time to process my feelings, to think, to get support from someone not involved in the moment.

"Mother," I said with tears in my eyes, "I need some space so I'm going for a walk."

I walked a half mile to a little neighborhood market and gas station and called John from the phone booth. As I told him what had happened, I started to sob. There I was standing on the side of a busy interstate highway, trucks and cars whizzing by, customers buying fuel twenty feet from where I stood, sobbing hysterically, tears and makeup dripping down my face. In that moment I was in so much pain I didn't care about looking good.

John supported me to both have my feelings and to take care of myself. If Mother and I had reached a point where we could no longer communicate, it was okay for me to come home early. I didn't have to stay in a toxic situation and tough it out. About that time Karen, my sister-in-law, drove up. Apparently Mother had called her when I walked out of the door. Karen wanted to help. She drove me to a wooded area near the river and we sat for a while and talked. Or rather I talked and she listened.

Later that evening Karen drove me back to Mother's house. I had made a decision that if Mother still needed to make me wrong, I would need to leave, not to punish her but to take care of myself. Mother's eyes were red and puffy from crying. I knew that she was in a great deal of pain.

"Can't we talk?" she asked.

"Mother, we've been talking," I said sadly, "I'm not sure you want to listen."

With tears in her eyes, she said, "I'm willing to listen." It had taken a great deal of courage for her to say that.

I hugged her and said, "Okay, Mom, let's talk."

Mother made coffee while I changed into something more comfortable, then we both sat facing each other on the living room floor. Over the next several hours we shared and cried and began to build a bridge after so many years of being emotionally estranged.

"I grew up without a mother," I said at one point, tears streaming down my face. "You were so busy working, being with your clubs and taking care of Dad, that you had no time for me. I was so lonely."

Reaching out to grab my hand, she said, "I wish I could go back and change everything."

"You can't, Mom. I used to wish you could, too. But neither of us can. What we can do is start from here, telling the truth, taking responsibility and healing our own pain."

Later she told me how frightened she had been as a young mother. I had always been very emotional and Mother had no idea how to handle it. When I was very young, one of Mother's friends, who babysat occasionally, told Mother that she should do something about my outbursts. Mother had felt embarrassed. She had never had support to believe in herself, so she thought that her friend must be right and tried to stop the flow of my emotions by shaming me, thinking that's what she had to do to be a good mother.

We didn't stop talking until the wee hours of the morning, both of us drained emotionally and physically. At the end I was able to honestly say something to her that nine years before when I first began therapy with Marsha I would not have believed possible.

"Mother," I said holding her in my arms in a warm embrace, "I know that you never did anything to me with the intention of hurting me." That didn't mean that she wouldn't have to confront the damage that she had done and the pain she had caused. We cannot heal without taking responsibility for our dysfunctional past. Mother had barely scratched the surface. She had a lot more work to do.

"Thank you, Barbara," she answered. "That means a lot. I want you to know that I'm proud of you. I know I could never have done this without your support. I love you so much."

"I love you, too, Mom."

My life had come full circle. The last several days had happened, I knew, because of my intention. The willingness to tell the truth, to experience feelings, to process and complete old scenes, to seek out and let go of dysfunctional behaviors, old beliefs, tapes and ideas, had created the space for me to know that I am whole, complete and at last Who I am.

More than a year has passed. Jim is still sober. When I let them know that I had chosen to be public with the old secret, there was quite a stir within the family. At first Mother and Jim both made me wrong, saying that I only wanted to hurt them. Since then, Jim has come partially around and has begun for the first time in my life to listen to the pain that I went through as a result of his actions. He still denies the extent of the incest, but admits that even a few times would hurt. As I said earlier, he has given me his blessing to go forward in the direction I have chosen.

Mother has not. She is hurt and angry and blames me, as she always has, for making her look bad. There is a difference in me. I know that I am not the cause of her pain. The cause of her distress is her unwillingness to confront the truth, her continuing need to hide, to look good, to manage what others think of her. When I reached a point of reconciliation with my past, it no longer mattered who knew. What people think of me no longer counts. Telling the truth was my doorway to recovery, a door I stepped through a long time ago.

That same doorway is available to you. It stands before you now. Reach out and open it. The rest of your life is waiting.

A New Context

Although it is not absolutely necessary to confront your violators in order to heal, Barbara had decided that it was something that she wanted to do. Over the years I had pointed out to Barbara that if confronting was absolutely necessary for completing, there would be a lot of people who could never complete their past because their parents were dead. Barbara knew that I have supported numerous people in completing their relationships with their dead parents so it became obvious to her that a direct confrontation was not necessary for the completion process. Since completion is something that we do for ourselves, in order to let go of the energies that bind us to our past, the only elements necessary are the intention to heal and complete and the tools to do it.

Of course, there was an obvious difference between Barbara's desire to complete with her mother and someone who needed to complete with a dead parent. Barbara wanted to attempt to have a real relationship with her mother, if there was even the smallest chance, and she would not be able to do that when there was such a huge lie between them. Barbara had realized over the years of therapy that she really did not have a relationship with her mother. Her mother's dysfunction was so extensive that there had never been any room for the real Barbara nor for any honest communication, without which there could be no relationship.

Barbara knew that Adult Survivors frequently had to cut off communications between themselves and their abusers (both the perpetrators and the enablers) if the toxicity of childhood continued and the enabler was still bonded to and protecting, defending, justifying the perpetrator. At the point at which her formal therapy was drawing to an end, Barbara realized that withholding the truth from her mother was taking too much of her energy.

Telling the truth and feeling whatever emotions were connected to it would help free Barbara from using the various defense mechanisms that she needed to stop the feelings. Each time Barbara spoke to her mother, the conflict between Barbara's real memories and Maureen's delusions would surface. At one point, toward the end of the therapy, Barbara came in and told me that she wanted to tell Maureen the secret. Although there really wasn't a problem with Barbara's desire to tell her mother, I knew that for Barbara to be powerful and approach the task from a clear place, she had to be aware of her motives for telling her mother the truth, the consequences which she might incur and, most of all, her own emotional response to however her mother reacted.

Instead of discussing these issues, which would have given Barbara some cognitive insights, I asked Barbara to process them instead. This would allow Barbara not only to understand what might happen, but to allow her to begin dealing with the process and the results on an emotional level. She could begin to release her emotions before she actually approached her mother. Using the familiar two-chair technique, I asked Barbara to put her mother in the other chair. Barbara looked at the chair, took a deep breath, closed her eyes and imagined her mother sitting opposite her. Before she could say a word, she started to cry.

"I'm so scared, Mom, scared you won't love me anymore." She paused a moment, barely breathing.

"Can you keep going, Barbara?" I asked.

"I'm scared you won't believe me, that you'll think I'm lying," she cried.

"How do you feel when she doesn't believe you?"

"It hurts, Mom," she sobbed. "It really hurts." Barbara continued sobbing for a few minutes.

"What else are you afraid of, Barbara?"

"I'm afraid you'll make me wrong. I'm afraid you'll reject me."

By this time Barbara was beginning to cough a little, a small remnant of her earlier choking spells. Barbara blindly reached her hand out for support. I took her hand and held it.

"Barbara, are you ready to tell her the secret?"

She sat quietly for several moments. Later she told me that the words stuck in her throat because although she knew she was in a "safe place" and Maureen was not really in the room, Barbara found that just practicing telling her mother the truth was almost impossible. She recognized that she wasn't prepared to "just go and tell Mother the truth."

Barbara spent many weeks processing telling her mother the truth. At times I played Maureen using Barbara's worst possible case and best case and many variations in between. I suggested to Barbara that she begin writing letters to Maureen to allow Barbara to continue her process at home. After several weeks of hard work, Barbara came in one day and announced that she was ready to tell her mother, but wasn't sure how she wanted to do it. She told me that Shawn had wanted her to fly up there and tell Maureen.

Barbara needed to make this decision herself. I put out several chairs, one for Shawn, one for the part of Barbara that wanted to please him, one for the part of Barbara who wanted to tell Maureen in person, one who wanted to write a letter. As Barbara went from chair to chair, talking from each part and having the others answer back, she began to deal with her fear and her needs and to crystallize what she really wanted to do. When she finished, she said she was going to write a letter, not go up and tell her in person. Barbara wasn't ready to deal with her own emotional process and her mother's at the same time. Given Maureen's reaction, which was to be expected, Barbara's decision to write the letter instead of going in person was the best choice.

Shortly after informing her mother, Barbara completed her formal therapy. She kept up her processing and writing and letting go of her mother. Barbara was growing stronger and clearer as she used the tools she had received in therapy. Her relationship with her mother had taken an upturn when Jim had stopped drinking for that short period of time, but she knew not to get her hopes up since neither Jim nor her mother were in any form of recovery. Jim was dry, but that was about all he was, and Maureen was still operating from chronic co-dependence. When Jim returned to drinking, Barbara was disappointed, but went through the process well. She knew that alcoholism was progressive and that Jim would soon be drinking at the levels he had stopped at earlier. She also had had enough experience with her mother to realize that any suggestion to get help was met with Maureen's standard, "Your way isn't the only way." While that was true, it was also true that Maureen's way of chronic co-dependence wouldn't work at all.

By the time Barbara had taken a stand with her mother in 1987, we had begun our radio show and were in touch with a number of alcohol rehabilitation facilities and had access to an interventionist. Although the intervention was painful, it was not the most painful part of the trip for Barbara. When I spoke with her, Barbara said that the most difficult part of the process was realizing how easily she fell back into the pattern of rescuing her mother from discomfort.

One of the best parts of the process, however, was the point at which she had given herself permission to be angry with her mother and had slammed her fist down on the dashboard. Smiling as she told me the story, she said, "That was the first time in my life that I actually got angry and yelled directly at my mother. I finally did it."

When Barbara relayed to me what her mother had said about being stupid and Barbara being so perfect, it reminded me of all the times I had to point out to Barbara that looking at the addictive behaviors did not mean that she was bad or stupid. It was also a strong indication of Maureen's black-and-white, either/or thinking as well as her continuing need to avoid pain.

Barbara had realized, on her own that if her mother was not ready to feel the pain and face the truth, the development of a real relationship with her mother would have to wait until her mother had some time in recovery. Once Barbara had let go and given herself permission to go home, she was willing to let her mother be wherever she was in her process. As I frequently pointed out to Barbara, letting go shifts the energy around an issue and frees people to move to another place emotionally. Maureen opened up to Barbara, and Barbara finally was able to discuss, at times, some of the family issues.

This is not an "and they all lived happily ever after" story. Barbara and Maureen and Jim and Shawn are live human beings with ongoing issues and pain. When Barbara decided to go public on a national show, once again she had to deal with her mother's chronic need to look good and hide the truth. The pain was the same. Only this time Barbara chose to take care of herself, rather than protect her mother and the family secret. The difference for Barbara in dealing with the pain and problems in her life is that she is now operating in a different context than before. The pain and problems Barbara experiences are no longer the context of Barbara's life. Instead, the problems she faces in life are the content, while Barbara's context is that her life works, and she has the tools to live and enjoy it. This shift was only possible because of the years of work Barbara had done on herself which allowed her to begin to heal the wounded child within, disintegrate the negative false-self and reintegrate with the magical child.

I made a new friend today.
He doesn't say mean things
he won't ever Hit me.
He listens to me and
        holds me when I am sad.

I MADE A NEW FRIEND today.

by Patrick

Resources For Recovery

Before we give you some suggestions for beginning and continuing your recovery, we would like to share with you a gift from our dear friend, Patrick. Patrick is a gifted artist who often expresses the steps and process of his recovery in delightfully creative ways. A while ago Patrick created a "friend" for the inner child. Because many of us did not feel safe as children, felt abandoned by family and didn't trust our friends, we longed for someone who wouldn't hurt or abandon us. Patrick's "friend" began as an old sweatsuit which he stuffed with mismatched socks and rags. Adding the head of an old teddy bear, Patrick put the finishing touch on a new, huggable, trustworthy, nonjudgmental, accepting "friend." Patrick shared his friend with us in the form of a drawing and poem. We wanted to share him with you.

Suggested Steps

When in doubt, join a 12-Step program. If you are wondering about how to go about your healing process and have never done any work on yourself, joining a 12-Step program or programs will give you support for confronting your dysfunctional processes, moving out of your isolation and recovering the spirituality that is both your heritage and your birthright.

Once you make the decision to start a program, don't be afraid to shop around either for different 12-Step programs that fit your particular process or for different meetings within a particular 12-Step program. If you find yourself angry in meetings, stay with the meetings for a while. Anger in this case frequently indicates that your defense mechanisms are at work. If you are not angry and the steps are meaningful to you, but you find only a few of the issues dealt with in a particular program fit your problems, you may want to look for an additional 12-Step program to fit your needs. You may find that although you are an ACoA, Co-dependents Anonymous (CODA) meetings seem more appropriate to your particular situation. If you can go to both, do so. If not, pick the one best suited to your needs at the moment.

If there isn't a 12-Step meeting in your area, find one close enough so that you can go to at least one meeting. Get their literature, ask for the central office address and phone number, get an "old-timer" to come and help you set up your meeting. Put an advertisement in your local paper and you'll be on your way before you know it.

Remember, it is difficult to do this work alone. You will continually bump up against your own defenses, and it helps to have loving, supportive people around to help you deal with the dysfunctional processes.

There are a number of 12-Step programs in existence. The following are only a few that are available:

Alcoholics Anonymous
P.O. Box 459 Grand Central Station
New York, NY 10163

Al-Anon
P.O. Box 862 Midtown Station
New York, NY 10018

Adult Children of Alcoholics
P.O. Box 35623
Los Angeles, CA 90035

Cocaine Anonymous
World Service Office
(213) 559-5833

Coc-Anon
World Service Office
(818) 377-4317

Co-dependents Anonymous
P.O. Box 5508
Glendale, AZ 85312-5508
(602) 944-0141

Debtors Anonymous
General Service Board
P.O. Box 20322
New York, NY 10025-9992

Families Anonymous
P.O. Box 344
Torrance, CA 90501

Gamanon
P.O. Box 967
Radio City Station
New York, NY 10019

Gamblers Anonymous
P.O. Box 17173
Los Angeles, CA 90017

Incest Survivors Anonymous
P.O. Box 5613
Long Beach, CA 90805

Narcotics Anonymous
P.O. Box 9999
Van Nuys, CA 91409

Nar-Anon Family Groups
350 5th St., Ste. 207
San Pedro, CA 90731

National Association for Children of Alcoholics
31706 Pacific Coast Hwy.
South Laguna Beach, CA 92677

Overeaters Anonymous
4025 Spencer St., Ste. 203
Torrance, CA 90503

Sexaholics Anonymous
General Services Office
P.O. Box 300
Simi Valley, CA 93062
(805) 851-3343

S-Anon
P.O. Box 5117
Sherman Oaks, CA 91413

Survivors Network
18653 Ventura Blvd., #141
Tarzana, CA 91356

Publications

The following publications are only a few of the resources available:

CHANGES for Adult Children
3201 S.W. 15th Street
Deerfield Beach, FL 33442

COA Review, The Newsletter
About Children of Alcoholics
P.O. Box 190
Rutherford, NJ 07070

FOCUS
3201 S.W. 15th Street
Deerfield Beach, FL 33442

Read

Set yourself a reading program. We suggest that you read *Bradshaw On: The Family* and *When Society Becomes an Addict* as basic material in your reading program because these books cover the range of addictive processes and can act as primary source books for understanding all addictive processes.

In addition, see if you can read at least one book in each area of dysfunction, such as ACoA, relationship addictions, incest, sexual addiction and co-dependence. Since many addicts tend to be either serially or multiple addicted, it helps to know what signs to watch for in other addictions. You will find that the various addictive areas abound with books. Don't be discouraged. While most of the books have similar information, each book holds its own "gems" of wisdom. In addition, you may need to read about addictive processes in many different ways before you have a clear idea about how the process affects you.

Watch out for becoming addicted to reading this literature and using the information to avoid your feelings. Reading books is not a substitute for process. Use the workbooks we have suggested. The exercises may help you to begin processing. If you are not a reader, many of the authors in this field have audio and video tapes available. Check with their publishers.

Seminars And Workshops

Most of the authors in the field of addiction offer workshops around the country. Look for process-oriented workshops. Ask questions. "Do they lecture only in your workshop? Do they give exercises or processes to take you back to your original pain and grief work? What type of processes are they, small group, individual, pairs or a combination? Do they have support people in the workshop? Do they expect you to do a lot of crying in the workshops?"

Be aware of getting addicted to workshops. Adult Children are notorious seminar junkies!

Find A Therapist

Therapy is not for crazy people. It is for survivors. If you are a survivor, you deserve to heal; you deserve therapy. You may also have a tendency to believe that you should be able to do this yourself. That is a dysfunctional belief that comes from being raised in dysfunctional families.

Finding a therapist can be a difficult process. In some states, such as California, stringent laws govern the licensing of psychologists, Marriage, Family, Child Counselors, Licensed Clinical Social Workers and Certified Alcohol Counselors. In other states, a person may call himself a counselor or therapist or psychologist without any training and minimal or no credentials.

What makes things more difficult for the searching Adult Child is the issue of co-dependency in the helping professions. Many therapists, no matter what their credentials, are nonrecovering co-dependents who will block your healing process because they have not dealt with their own pain or their own co-dependency. You will want to ask the therapist what he or she knows about co-dependency, alcoholism, incest or Adult Children problems. A good therapist will not be offended by your questioning. You have a right to know.

When working with a therapist, there are several things to look for:

1. Do you feel safe and supported? Do you have a desire to go on with the therapy even if it is painful? If you do not have this experience within the first two months, find another therapist. If you find yourself leaving therapist after therapist, stop for a while and attend a 12-Step program. You may be resisting and not ready yet to do the work.

2. Does your therapist shame you, or does your therapist help you to deal with your shame? This is a difficult thing to evaluate sometimes because shame-based people often feel shame when they are confronted with the truth, even in a nonshaming environment. However, if you feel shamed often with your therapist and even after talking it out with your therapist have no reprieve, change therapists.

3. Does your therapist do feeling work? If your therapist only sits and talks with you, or only sits and listens, and you don't know what the word process means except from this book, you are not doing feeling process work. Go back through chapter seven of this book and read chapters six through twelve in John Bradshaw's *Healing The Shame That Binds You.* This material will give you some idea of what to look for in a therapist.

4. Are you getting tools that you can use on your own?

5. Do you sense a change in yourself that you can't put your finger on? Or are you in a group where you see others changing dysfunctional behaviors and beginning to heal? Then chances are you have a good therapist.

6. You may have a question about whether to do individual or group therapy. There is no set answer. Since Adult Children have a tendency to isolate and believe that they are different and odd, it is important to have feedback from others like yourself. However, if you are just beginning your healing process and have had severe trauma, you may not want to join a group unless it is a group of survivors of severe traumas.

7. If you sense that you are being invalidated or you are hurt or angry by what happens between you and your therapist in a session, talk to the therapist about this. If the therapist's response is defensive, or the therapist minimizes your experience, find another therapist. Even if the therapist is good, you don't have to stay with someone you don't feel comfortable with.

8. If your therapist even suggests a sexual relationship with you, walk out of the door and report them to the authorities.

Remember, therapy isn't fun. While your therapist may be able to teach you how to enjoy yourself more, don't expect your sessions to be fun or even comfortable.

When you are healing the addictive process, you will also be rediscovering your spirituality. While you do not need to be practicing the same religion as your therapist, or for that matter any religion, you will want a therapist who recognizes and supports the spiritual aspect of the healing process.

Chapter Notes

Chapter One

1. Virginia Satir, conjoint family therapy, a guide to theory and technique (Palo Alto: Science and Behavior Books, Inc., revised edition, 1967).
2. J. Polster and M. Polster, Gestalt Therapy Integrated: Contours of Theory and Practice (New York: Brunner/Mazel Publishers, 1973).

Chapter Two

1. Virginia Ward, Father-Daughter Rape (New York: Grove Press, Inc., 1985), p. 78.
2. John Bradshaw, Bradshaw On: The Family (Pompano Beach, Health Communications, Inc., 1988), p. 116.

Chapter Three

1. Wayne Kritsberg, The Adult Children Of Alcoholics Syndrome: From Discovery to Recovery, (Pompano Beach, Health Communications, Inc., 1985), p. 45.
2. Alice Miller, For Your Own Good: Hidden Cruelty in Childrearing and the Roots of Violence. (New York: Farrar, Strauss, Giroux, 1983).

Chapter Five

1. Jael Greenleaf, Co-Alcoholic Para-Alcoholic, Who's Who and What's the Difference, (Paper presented at the National Council on Alcoholism, 1981 Annual Alcoholism Forum, New Orleans, 1981).

2. Riane Eisler, **The Chalice and The Blade** (San Francisco: Harper & Row Publishers, 1988), p. xvi.

3. Bradshaw, p. 17.

4. Eisler.

5. Adele Meyer, **Incest: A Treatment Manual For Therapy With Victims, Spouses and Offenders**, (Holmes Beach: Learning Publications, Inc., 1983).

6. Bradshaw.

7. Patrick Carnes, **Out of the Shadows: Understanding Sexual Addiction**, (Minneapolis, CompCare Publications, 1983), p. 19.

Chapter Seven

1. Stephen B. Karpman, "Fairy Tales And Script Drama Analysis", (Carmel, *Transactional Analysis Bulletin*, April 1968). p. 40.

2. Virginia Satir, **peoplemaking**, (Palo Alto, Science And Behavior Books, Inc., 1972).

Chapter Eight

1. Fritz Perls, **The Gestalt Approach and Eyewitness to Therapy**, (New York, Bantam Books, 1976), p. 407.

2. For more information on family rules see **peoplemaking**, by Virginia Satir (Behavior Books, 1972); **Bradshaw On: The Family**, by John Bradshaw (Health Communications, Inc., 1988); and **It Will Never Happen To Me**, by Claudia Black (Ballantine Books, 1981).

3. Butler, Sandra. **Conspiracy of Silence, The Trauma of Incest.** (San Francisco: Volcano Press, 1978).

4. Forward, Susan and Buck, Craig, **Betrayal of Innocence, Incest and Its Devastation.** (New York: Penguin Books, 1979), p. 3.

5. Adele Meyer, Incest: **A Treatment Manual For Therapy With Victims, Spouses and Offenders**, (Holmes Beach: Learning Publications, Inc., 1983).

6. Butler, Sandra. **Conspiracy of Silence, The Trauma of Incest.** (San Francisco: Volcano Press, 1978).

Chapter Nine

1. Robin Norwood, **Women Who Love Too Much, When You Keep Wishing and Hoping He'll Change,** (Los Angeles, Jeremy P. Tarcher, Inc., 1985).

Bibliography

Axline, Virginia M. **Play Therapy.** New York: Ballantine Books. 1969.

Bass, Ellen and Davis, Laura. **The Courage to Heal. A Guide for Women Survivors of Child Sexual Abuse.** New York: Harper & Row, 1988.

Beattie, Melody. **Co-dependent No More: How to Stop Controlling Others and Start Caring For Yourself.** San Francisco: Harper/Hazelden. 1987.

Black, Claudia. **It Will Never Happen To Me.** Denver: M.A.C. 1982.

_____ **Repeat After Me.** M.A.C. 1985.

Bradshaw, John. **Bradshaw On: The Family.** Pompano Beach, Florida: Health Communications. 1988.

_____ **Bradshaw On: Healing the Shame that Binds You.** Deerfield Beach, Florida: Health Communications, 1988.

Butler, Sandra. **Conspiracy of Silence. The Trauma of Incest.** San Francisco: Volcano Press. 1978.

Carnes, Patrick. **Out Of The Shadows. Understanding Sexual Addiction.** Minneapolis: CompCare. 1983.

Crawford, Christina. **Mommie Dearest.** New York: William Morrow. 1978.

_____ **Survivor.** New York: Donald I Fine. 1988.

Diagnostic and Statistical Manual of Mental Disorders (III) Third Edition (Washington, D.C.: American Psychiatric Association, 1980).

Eisler, Riane. **The Chalice and The Blade.** San Francisco: Harper & Row. 1988.

Forward, Susan and Buck, Craig. **Betrayal Of Innocence. Incest and Its Devastation.** New York: Penguin Books. 1979.

Friel, John and Friel, Linda. **Adult Children, The Secrets of Dysfunctional Families.** Deerfield Beach: Health Communications. 1988.

Friends In Recovery. **The 12 Steps, For Adult Children.** San Diego: Recovery Publications. 1987.

_____ **The 12 Steps, A Way Out. A Working Guide for Adult Children of Alcoholics and Other Dysfunctional Families.** San Diego: Recovery Publications. 1987.

Gil, Eliana. **Outgrowing the Pain: A Book For and About Adults Abused as Children.** Walnut Creek, California: Launch Press. 2nd Ed. 1984.

Gravitz, Herbert L. and Bowden, Julie D. **Guide to Recovery. A Book For Adult Children of Alcoholics.** Holmes Beach: Learning Publications, Inc. 1985.

Greenleaf, Jael. **Co-Alcoholic Para-Alcoholic, Who's Who and What's the Difference.** Los Angeles: Jael Greenleaf. 1981.

Herbruck, Christine Comstock. **Breaking the Cycle of Child Abuse.** Minneapolis: Winston Press, Inc. 1979.

Karpman, Stephen B., "Fairy Tales and Script Drama Analysis" in _Transactional Analysis Bulletin._ April 1968, Carmel. Vol. 7, No. 26, pp. 39-40.

Kritsberg, Wayne, **The Adult Children Of Alcoholics Syndrome, From Discovery to Recovery.** Pompano Beach, Florida, Health Communications. 1985.

Meyer, Adele. **Incest: A Treatment Manual for Therapy with Victims, Spouses and Offenders.** Holmes Beach, Florida: Learning Publications. 1983.

Middelton-Moz, Jane and Dwinell, Lorie. **After the Tears, Reclaiming the Personal Losses of Childhood.** Pompano Beach: Health Communications, Inc. 1986.

Miller, Alice. **The Drama of The Gifted Child, The Search For The True Self.** New York: Basic Books Publishers. 1981.

_____ **For Your Own Good: Hidden Cruelty in Childrearing and the Roots of Violence.** New York: Farrar, Strauss, Giroux. 1983.

Norwood, Robin. **Women Who Love Too Much, When You Keep Wishing and Hoping He'll Change.** Los Angeles: Jeremy P. Tarcher. 1985.

Perls, F. S. **The Gestalt Approach and Eyewitness to Therapy.** New York: Bantam Books. 1976.

Polster, J. and Polster, M., **Gestalt Therapy Integrated: Contours of Theory and Practice.** New York: Brunner/Mazel Publishers. 1973.

Ryerson, Eric. **When Your Parent Drinks Too Much.** New York: Facts On File Publications. 1985.

Satir, Virginia. **conjoint family therapy, a guide to theory and technique.** Palo Alto: Science and Behavior Books, Inc., revised edition. 1967.

_____ **peoplemaking.** Palo Alto: Science And Behavior Books, Inc. 1972.

Schaef, Anne Wilson. **Co-Dependence. Misunderstood-Mistreated.** Minneapolis: Winston Press. 1986.

_____ **When Society Becomes an Addict.** San Francisco: Harper and Row. 1987.

Schneider, Jennifer P. **Back From Betrayal, Recovering From His Affairs.** San Francisco: Harper/Hazelden. 1988.

Seixas, Judith S. and Youcha, Geraldine. **Children of Alcoholism. A Survivor's Manual.** New York: Harper & Row. 1978.

Utain, Marsha B. **Using Gestalt: A Manual for Elementary and Secondary School Counselors** (Unpublished Masters Thesis). Long Beach. 1979.

Ward, Virginia, **Father-Daughter Rape.** New York: Grove Press. 1985.

Woititz, Janet G. **Struggle For Intimacy.** Pompano Beach: Health Communications. 1985.

_____ **Adult Children of Alcoholics.** Pompano Beach: Health Communications. 1983.

Books from . . .
Health Communications

AFTER THE TEARS: Reclaiming The Personal Losses of Childhood
Jane Middelton-Moz and Lorie Dwinnel
Your lost childhood must be grieved in order for you to recapture your
self-worth and enjoyment of life. This book will show you how.
ISBN 0-932194-36-2 $7.95

HEALING YOUR SEXUAL SELF
Janet Woititz
How can you break through the aftermath of sexual abuse and enter into
healthy relationships? Survivors are shown how to recognize the problem
and deal effectively with it.
ISBN 1-55874-018-X $7.95

RECOVERY FROM RESCUING
Jacqueline Castine
Effective psychological and spiritual principles teach you when to take
charge, when to let go, and how to break the cycle of guilt and fear that
keeps you in the responsibility trap. Mind-altering ideas and exercises will
guide you to a more carefree life.
ISBN 1-55874-016-3 $7.95

ADDICTIVE RELATIONSHIPS: Reclaiming Your Boundaries
Joy Miller
We have given ourselves away to spouse, lover, children, friends or
parents. By examining where we are, where we want to go and how to get
there, we can reclaim our personal boundaries and the true love of
ourselves.
ISBN 1-55874-003-1 $7.95

RECOVERY FROM CO-DEPENDENCY:
It's Never Too Late To Reclaim Your Childhood
Laurie Weiss, Jonathan B. Weiss
Having been brought up with life-repressing decisions, the adult child
recognizes something isn't working. This book shows how to change
decisions and live differently and fully.
ISBN 0-932194-85-0 $9.95

SHIPPING/HANDLING: All orders shipped UPS unless weight exceeds 200 lbs., special routing is requested, or
delivery territory is outside continental U.S. Orders outside United States shipped either Air Parcel Post or Surface
Parcel Post. Shipping and handling charges apply to all orders shipped whether UPS, Book Rate, Library Rate, Air
or Surface Parcel Post or Common Carrier and will be charged as follows. Orders less than $25.00 in value add
$2.00 minimum. Orders from $25.00 to $50.00 in value (after discount) add $2.50 minimum. Orders greater than
$50.00 in value (after discount) add 6% of value. Orders greater than $25.00 outside United States add 15% of
value. We are not responsible for loss or damage unless material is shipped UPS. Allow 3-5 weeks after receipt of
order for delivery. Prices are subject to change without prior notice.

Enterprise Center, 3201 S.W. 15th Street,
Deerfield Beach, FL 33442
1-800-851-9100

Daily Affirmation Books from . . .
Health Communications

GENTLE REMINDERS FOR CO-DEPENDENTS: Daily Affirmations
Mitzi Chandler
With insight and humor, Mitzi Chandler takes the co-dependent and the adult child through the year. Gentle Reminders is for those in recovery who seek to enjoy the miracle each day brings.
ISBN 1-55874-020-1 $6.95

TIME FOR JOY: Daily Affirmations
Ruth Fishel
With quotations, thoughts and healing energizing affirmations these daily messages address the fears and imperfections of being human, guiding us through self-acceptance to a tangible peace and the place within where there is *time for joy.*
ISBN 0-932194-82-6 $6.95

CRY HOPE: Positive Affirmations For Healthy Living
Jan Veltman
This book gives positive daily affirmations for seekers and those in recovery. Everyday is a new adventure, and change is a challenge.
ISBN 0-932194-74-5 $6.95

SAY YES TO LIFE: Daily Affirmations For Recovery
Father Leo Booth
These meditations take you through the year day by day with Father Leo Booth, looking for answers and sometimes discovering that there are none. Father Leo tells us, "For the recovering compulsive person God is too important to miss — may you find Him now."
IBN 0-932194-46-X $6.95

DAILY AFFIRMATIONS: For Adult Children of Alcoholics
Rokelle Lerner
Affirmations are a way to discover personal awareness, growth and spiritual potential, and self-regard. Reading this book gives us an opportunity to nurture ourselves, learn who we are and what we want to become.
ISBN 0-932194-47-3
(Little Red Book) $6.95
(New Cover Edition) $6.95

Enterprise Center, 3201 S.W. 15th Street,
Deerfield Beach, FL 33442
1-800-851-9100

Health
Communications, Inc.

Other Books By . . .
Health Communications

New Books . . .
from Health Communications

HEALING THE SHAME THAT BINDS YOU
John Bradshaw
Toxic shame is the core problem in our compulsions, co-dependencies and addictions. The author offers healing techniques to help release the shame that binds us.
ISBN 0-932194-86-9 $9.95

THE MIRACLE OF RECOVERY:
Healing For Addicts, Adult Children and Co-dependents
Sharon Wegscheider-Cruse
Beginning with recognizing oneself as a survivor, it is possible to move through risk and change to personal transformation.
ISBN 1-55874-024-4 $9.95

CHILDREN OF TRAUMA: Rediscovering Your Discarded Self
Jane Middelton-Moz
This beautiful book shows how to discover the source of past traumas and grieve them to grow into whole and complete adults.
ISBN 1-55874-014-7 $9.95

New Books on Spiritual Recovery . . .

LEARNING TO LIVE IN THE NOW: 6-Week Personal Plan To Recovery
Ruth Fishel
The author gently introduces you step by step to the valuable healing tools of meditation, positive creative visualization and affirmations.
ISBN 0-932194-62-1 $7.95

CYCLES OF POWER: A User's Guide To The Seven Seasons of Life
Pamela Levin
This innovative book unveils the process of life as a cyclic pattern, providing strategies to use the seven seasons to regain power over your life.
ISBN 0-932194-75-3 $9.95

MESSAGES FROM ANNA: Lessons in Living (Santa Claus, God and Love)
Zoe Rankin
This is a quest for the meaning of "love." In a small Texas Gulf Coast town a wise 90-year-old woman named Anna shares her life messages.
ISBN 1-55874-013-9 $7.95

THE FLYING BOY: Healing The Wounded Man
John Lee
A man's journey to find his "true masculinity" and his way out of co-dependent and addictive relationships, this book is about feelings — losing them, finding them, expressing them.
ISBN 1-55874-006-6 $7.95

Enterprise Center, 3201 S.W. 15th Street,
Deerfield Beach, FL 33442
1-800-851-9100

Health
Communications, Inc.

Helpful 12-Step Books from . . .
Health Communications

HEALING A BROKEN HEART:
12 Steps of Recovery for Adult Children
Kathleen W.
This useful 12-Step book is presently the number one resource for all
Adult Children support groups.
ISBN 0-932194-65-6   **$7.95**

12 STEPS TO SELF-PARENTING For Adult Children
Philip Oliver-Diaz and Patricia A. O'Gorman
This gentle 12-Step guide takes the reader from pain to healing and self-
parenting, from anger to forgiveness, and from fear and despair to
recovery.
ISBN 0-932194-68-0   **$7.95**

THE 12-STEP STORY BOOKLETS
Mary M. McKee
Each beautifully illustrated booklet deals with a step, using a story from
nature in parable form. The 12 booklets (one for each step) lead us to a
better understanding of ourselves and our recovery.
ISBN 1-55874-002-3   **$8.95**

WITH GENTLENESS, HUMOR AND LOVE:
A 12-Step Guide for Adult Children in Recovery
Kathleen W. and Jewell E.
Focusing on adult child issues such as reparenting the inner child, self-
esteem, intimacy and feelings, this well-organized workbook teaches
techniques and tools for the 12-step recovery programs.
ISBN 0-932194-77-X   **$7.95**

GIFTS FOR PERSONAL GROWTH & RECOVERY
Wayne Kritsberg
A goldmine of positive techniques for recovery (affirmations, journal
writing, visualizations, guided meditations, etc.), this book is indispens-
able for those seeking personal growth.
ISBN 0-932194-60-5   **$6.95**

Enterprise Center, 3201 S.W. 15th Street,
Deerfield Beach, FL 33442
1-800-851-9100

Health Communications, Inc.